P9-DUE-615

THE BEDFORD SERIES IN HISTORY AND CULTURE

The Cherokee Removal

A Brief History with Documents

THE BEDFORD SERIES IN HISTORY AND CULTURE

The Cherokee Removal

A Brief History with Documents

THIRD EDITION

Theda Perdue

University of North Carolina at Chapel Hill

Michael D. Green

Late of University of North Carolina at Chapel Hill

bedford/st.martin's
Macmillan Learning
Boston | New York

For Bedford/St. Martin's

Vice President, Editorial, Macmillan Learning Humanities: Edwin Hill
Publisher for History: Michael Rosenberg
Senior Executive Editor for History: William J. Lombardo
Director of Development for History: Jane Knetzger
Developmental Editor: Alexandra DeConti
Executive Marketing Manager: Sandra McGuire
Production Editor: Lidia MacDonald-Carr
Production Coordinator: Carolyn Quimby
Director of Rights and Permissions: Hilary Newman
Permissions Assistant: Michael McCarty
Permissions Manager: Kalina Ingham
Cover Design: William Boardman
Cover Art: Courtesy John Guthrie
Project Management: Books By Design, Inc.
Cartographer: Mapping Specialists, Ltd.
Composition: Achorn International, Inc.
Printing and Binding: RR Donnelley and Sons

Copyright © 2016, 2005, 1995 by Bedford/St. Martin's.

All rights reserved. No part of this book may be reproduced, stored in a retrieval system, or transmitted in any form or by any means, electronic, mechanical, photocopying, recording, or otherwise, except as may be expressly permitted by the applicable copyright statutes or in writing by the Publisher.

Manufactured in the United States of America.

1   0   9   8   7   6
f   e   d   c   b   a

For information, write: Bedford/St. Martin's, 75 Arlington Street, Boston, MA 02116
   (617-399-4000)

ISBN 978-1-319-04902-7

Acknowledgments

Acknowledgments and copyrights appear on the same pages as the text and art selections they cover; these acknowledgments and copyrights constitute an extension of the copyright page. It is a violation of the law to reproduce these selections by any means whatsoever without the written permission of the copyright holder.

Foreword

The Bedford Series in History and Culture is designed so that readers can study the past as historians do.

The historian's first task is finding the evidence. Documents, letters, memoirs, interviews, pictures, movies, novels, or poems can provide facts and clues. Then the historian questions and compares the sources. There is more to do than in a courtroom, for hearsay evidence is welcome, and the historian is usually looking for answers beyond act and motive. Different views of an event may be as important as a single verdict. How a story is told may yield as much information as what it says.

Along the way the historian seeks help from other historians and perhaps from specialists in other disciplines. Finally, it is time to write, to decide on an interpretation and how to arrange the evidence for readers.

Each book in this series contains an important historical document or group of documents, each document a witness from the past and open to interpretation in different ways. The documents are combined with some element of historical narrative — an introduction or a biographical essay, for example — that provides students with an analysis of the primary source material and important background information about the world in which it was produced.

Each book in the series focuses on a specific topic within a specific historical period. Each provides a basis for lively thought and discussion about several aspects of the topic and the historian's role. Each is short enough (and inexpensive enough) to be a reasonable one-week assignment in a college course. Whether as classroom or personal reading, each book in the series provides firsthand experience of the challenge — and fun — of discovering, recreating, and interpreting the past.

Lynn Hunt
David W. Blight
Bonnie G. Smith

Preface

In December 1828, a young Cherokee student attending a mission school in her homeland polled her playmates on the issue of Indian removal. Andrew Jackson, an advocate of removal, had just been elected president of the United States, and the possibility of being forced west of the Mississippi dominated the children's thoughts. "If the white people want more land, let them go back to the country they came from," one child told the informal pollster, while another demanded, "They have got more land than they can use, what do they want to get ours for?" For these children, the issue was a simple one, both practically and morally. For us today, Indian removal may well retain its moral simplicity, but the issue as it unfolded was exceedingly complex. Not all white Americans supported Cherokee removal; not all Cherokees opposed it; and the drama itself took place against a complicated backdrop of ideology, self-interest, party politics, altruism, and ambition.

The purpose of this book is to help students and other serious readers of history understand the complexity of Cherokee removal. The editors' headnotes and the original documents tell the story, but the volume's value does not end there. We have used these documents and the historical event of removal to introduce readers to the methodology of ethnohistory, which focuses on culture and the ways in which culture changes. Ethnohistorical research is on Native peoples rather than on Indian-white relations. Consequently, this volume begins and ends with the Cherokees, and it never loses sight of the fact that they were principal players in the drama. Nevertheless, the Cherokees would not have migrated to the West if the U.S. government had not forced them to do so. The Indian policies of the United States are, therefore, necessary parts of the historical picture. These selections also introduce readers to the broad array of primary documents—those contemporaneous with the event—for the writing of Indian history. Many people assume that Indians left no records, but, where removal is concerned, that assumption could not be further from the truth.

The response to the first two editions of *The Cherokee Removal* was very gratifying. We were pleased that so many teachers and students have found it useful. Since the publication of the second edition, my co-author and husband, Michael D. Green, has died. I alone undertook this revision, and it reflects my current interest in the construction of race and the ways in which we remember the past. Part One, the introduction, has been revised and updated, and it continues to offer students context for the documents they will encounter in this volume. In Part Two, the documents, I have added sections on reading race in portraits, conflicting newspaper accounts, oral history, public history, and commemorating removal. With brevity in mind, I ruthlessly edited some of the longer documents. In the book's appendixes, an updated chronology of the Cherokee removal and new questions for consideration and selected bibliography serve to facilitate the use of this volume in the classroom.

Any kind of historical research depends on a careful reading of primary sources and secondary works, and the questions that emerge from this reading shape the finished product. The organization of this book reflects the belief that sources, previous insights, and new questions are inseparable and that they should not be segregated in bibliographies and appendixes. Therefore, the headnotes usually include information about the complete documents from which selections are taken, citations of important secondary works, and questions to ponder while reading the selections. The intent is to inspire readers to think more deeply about the issue of removal and to embark on further study of the sources cited.

A NOTE ON THE DOCUMENTS

Historical documents sometimes go through many changes as people copy, recopy, and edit them. Rather than impose another round of changes in an effort to modernize spelling or achieve consistency, the previously published documents in this collection have been reprinted essentially as they appear in the source from which they have been taken. Manuscript documents—that is, handwritten documents never before published—have been edited as noted in our headnotes.

ACKNOWLEDGMENTS

Graduate students have enriched my personal and professional life in many ways. I would like to thank George Frizzell, Susan Hult, Bryan McKown, George Ellenberg, Craig Friend, Matt Schoenbachler, Jamey Carson, Tim Garrison, Rowena McClinton, Dave Nichols, Izumi Ishii, Greg O'Brien, Andrea Ramage, Lorri Glover, Randolph Hollingsworth, Joe Anoatubby, Karl Davis, Cary Miller, Rose Stremlau, Malinda Maynor Lowery, Meg Devlin O'Sullivan, John Hall, Christina Snyder, Julie Reed, Courtney Lewis, Mikaëla Adams, Katy Smith, Jonathan Hancock, Warren Milteer, Brooke Bauer, Liz Ellis, and the late Victor Blue. I would like to express special appreciation to Dave Nichols, who helped me update my bibliography for this edition. At Bedford/St. Martin's, thanks are due to Publisher Michael Rosenberg, Senior Executive Editor Bill Lombardo, Director of Development Jane Knetzger, Executive Marketing Manager Sandi McGuire, Developmental Editor Lexi DeConti, Production Editor Lidia MacDonald-Carr, Cover Designer William Boardman, and Production Coordinator Nancy Benjamin of Books By Design.

Theda Perdue

Contents

Map and Illustrations

THE BEDFORD SERIES IN HISTORY AND CULTURE

The Cherokee Removal

A Brief History with Documents

PART ONE

Introduction:
The Cherokees and
U.S. Indian Policy

THE CHEROKEE PEOPLE

The Cherokees lived in the valleys of rivers that drained the southern Appalachians. The United States did not exist when the Cherokees first inhabited this land, but today we might describe their homeland as extending from North Carolina into South Carolina, Georgia, Tennessee, and eventually Alabama. There they built their towns, cleared their fields, planted their crops, and buried their dead. The Cherokees also laid claim to a larger domain extending into Kentucky and Virginia, where they hunted deer and gathered raw materials essential to their way of life. Modern archaeologists believe that the Cherokees had lived on this land for hundreds, perhaps even thousands, of years; the Cherokees believed that they had always been there.

According to the Cherokees, the little water beetle created this land out of an endless sea by diving to the bottom and bringing up mud. The great buzzard shaped the mountains and valleys when his wings touched the soft earth. The first man and woman, Kana'ti and Selu, lived on that land. Their son and the unnatural Wild Boy, who had sprung from blood that Selu washed off dead game, unwittingly forged the Cherokee way of life when they spied on Kana'ti and Selu. The boys discovered that Kana'ti obtained the family's meat from a cave he kept covered with a large rock. When they pushed away the rock and accidentally released

1

the animals, they condemned all future generations of Cherokee men to have to hunt for game. Then they found that Selu produced corn and beans by rubbing her stomach and armpits. They decided that she was a witch and that they must kill her. Realizing what her son and Wild Boy intended to do, Selu instructed them to clear a circle and drag her body over the cleared ground seven times. Where her blood dropped, corn grew. The boys tired of their task, however, and they cleared seven little spots instead of a circle and dragged Selu's body over them only two times. Therefore, corn grows in only a few places, and Indian women must hoe their corn twice.

For many generations after Kana'ti and Selu, Cherokee women farmed and men hunted. Although the Cherokees divided tasks rather rigidly on the basis of gender, men helped clear fields and plant the crops and women helped dress and tan deerskins. Nevertheless, the Cherokees associated farming with women and hunting with men, and young women and men confirmed their marriage by an exchange of corn and deer meat. The Cherokees depended on the deer, turkeys, bears, rabbits, and other game that men killed and on the corn, beans, squash, and other crops that women raised. Farming as well as hunting, therefore, was essential to the Cherokee way of life long before Europeans arrived. In fact, the ancestors of modern Cherokees were growing crops well before the beginning of the Christian era, and by 1000, when most English people lived on coarse bread and ale, the Cherokees ate a varied and balanced diet of meat, corn, and other vegetables.

A Cherokee homestead consisted of several buildings clustered around a small plaza. Large rectangular houses with wooden sides and roofs provided shelter in summer months while small, round houses with thick mud-plastered walls provided a snug refuge from winter winds. Corncribs and other storage buildings stood nearby. Several generations of a family lived together. Because the Cherokees were matrilineal—that is, they traced kinship solely through women—the usual residents of a household were a woman, her husband, her daughters and their husbands, her daughters' children, and any unmarried sons (married sons lived in their wives' households). Usually the women of the household cultivated a small garden near the homestead, but the majority of the family's produce came from the large fields where all the women worked together, moving from one family's section of the field to another's.

These homesteads might be strung out along a river in a narrow mountain valley or tightly clustered in more open terrain, but together they formed a permanent village. Although men might travel great distances on the winter hunt, the village did not relocate, and most women, children, and old men remained behind. The focal point of the village was the town house or council house, a large, circular structure with thick mud walls much like the winter houses. Town houses had to be large enough to seat the members of the village, sometimes several hundred people, because the entire town met there to conduct ceremonies and debate important issues. Cherokees arrived at decisions by consensus; that is, they discussed issues until everyone could agree or those who disagreed withdrew from the discussion or even from the meeting. Debate could last for weeks or months, and any man or woman who wanted to speak had an opportunity. This does not mean that the Cherokees considered all opinions to be equal. Indeed, if the issue was war, a prominent warrior could be expected to command more respect than a man who had never been to war. Furthermore, a woman who had lost a husband or child in a previous engagement might hold greater sway than a woman who was unrelated to previous victims. Leadership in a Cherokee community, in fact, rested with a person who could inspire followers rather than someone born to office.

War was often a concern for the Cherokees. They shared hunting grounds with many other Native peoples, and encounters in the hunting grounds often resulted in casualties. The Cherokees believed that they had a sacred duty to avenge the deaths of fallen comrades, and so war parties formed quickly following a death. If only one or two Cherokees had died, the chief responsibility for vengeance lay with the relatives of the dead, but when the deaths involved the kin of most members of a town, revenge became a concern for the entire community. War parties prepared for an expedition by fasting and singing sacred songs in the town house. When they left the village, they took care to avoid detection because the object was to return with enemy scalps or captives, not more casualties whose deaths would have to be avenged. This is why the warriors tried to stage surprise attacks and often targeted the easiest victims, including women and children.

The nature of Native warfare often struck Europeans as particularly brutal, but the Cherokees' view of the world and their place in it left them with few alternatives. They envisioned the world as composed of opposites that balanced each other. Men, for example, balanced women, and hunting balanced farming. By the same token, the Cherokees lived in a state of equilibrium with the non-Cherokees in the world, but if an outsider took the life of a Cherokee, he destroyed that state of equilibrium. For the world to be set right, one of the guilty party's people had to die. Failure to seek vengeance meant that the world remained out of kilter and placed the entire Cherokee people at risk of disease, drought, or a host of other disasters that they believed resulted from imbalance. Once a war party had exacted vengeance and restored cosmic order, however, it went home. Cherokee warriors did not conquer territory or destroy entire villages; they merely sought vengeance and order. Unfortunately, once the world had been returned to equilibrium in Cherokee eyes, it usually was out of balance from the perspective of the enemy, who would then seek to avenge the deaths of their people.

While all Cherokees worried about imbalance and sought to make things right, the individuals most concerned with exacting vengeance were the clan members of the deceased. Each Cherokee belonged to one of seven clans. Cherokees believed that the members of a particular clan descended from a distant ancestor and that, therefore, all clan members were relatives. Marriage did not alter clan affiliation. Since Cherokee clans were matrilineal, children belonged to the clan of their mother, not their father. The obligations of clan members were so strong and so scrupulously fulfilled that the Cherokees had no need for a police force or court system: Protection, restitution, and retribution came from the clan. Cherokees traveling beyond their own town could expect food and shelter from distant clan members even if they did not know the travelers. Clan members also protected a person from members of other clans and sought vengeance in the event of a relative's murder. A person's clan kin had a special obligation to avenge his or her death because the spirit of the dead could not rest until a relative quieted "crying blood" through vengeance. Because all Cherokees accepted the same view of a balanced cosmos, clans stood back from the guilty party and did not retaliate for his or her death. Failure to restore balance, after all, threatened them as well.

Because the Cherokees tried to keep their world in harmony, religious observances focused on the maintenance of a pure and balanced world. The Cherokees did not separate religious observance from the ordinary tasks of daily life. Bathing, farming, hunting, and eating all had religious dimensions. People bathed daily for spiritual purification as well as for physical cleanliness. The women sang sacred songs as they hoed their corn, and the men observed important rituals, such as asking the deer's pardon and offering its liver to the fire, when they killed game lest the spirits of the dead animals cause disease. Because the Cherokees believed that you are what you eat, stickball (lacrosse) players did not eat rabbit meat because rabbits are easily confused, and pregnant women did not eat squirrel because the baby might go up instead of down during delivery, like a squirrel on a tree. Cherokees extinguished fire with soil instead of water because water represented the underworld and fire the upper world, two spiritual realms that balanced each other and that the earth mediated. Men secluded themselves when they were most male—before and after going to war—and women when they were most female—during menstruation and childbirth—for fear that they might overwhelm their opposite and upset the precarious balance.

The greatest challenge to the Cherokee world and belief system came with the arrival of Europeans. Well before the Cherokees saw their first white man, they probably felt the effects of the unseen enemy that accompanied him—disease. Long separated from Europe and Asia, the Cherokees and other Native peoples had little immunity to deadly European diseases such as smallpox, typhus, and even measles. When pathogens—disease-causing germs or viruses—reached the Cherokee country, people had neither the physical ability to fight off the diseases nor the knowledge of how to treat them. Numbering more than thirty thousand before the introduction of European diseases, the Cherokee population plummeted to perhaps as few as sixteen thousand in 1700. In addition to the decline in total population, the Cherokees no doubt lost many valued elders and their wisdom. The high death toll also perhaps undermined their confidence in traditional beliefs and in their conception of a harmonious world.

EARLY CONTACT WITH BRITISH COLONISTS

The British were not the first non-Indians to enter Cherokee territory. The Cherokees may have had brief or limited contact with Hernando de Soto in 1540 and with other Spanish explorers in the years that followed. Furthermore, they probably encountered runaway African slaves from British colonies well before they met the colonists. About 1700, however, the Cherokees began sustained contact with the British, and soon they became major players in Britain's commercial and imperial schemes. Despite the terrible losses from epidemics, the Cherokees remained a powerful people in the Southeast and an important strategic ally.

British traders traveled into the Cherokee country for two major commodities—deerskins and war captives. A great demand existed in Europe for deerskins, which were used to make leather goods such as stylish men's breeches. War captives became slaves either in the southern colonies or in the West Indies, where they worked alongside Africans. In exchange for these commodities, traders provided a variety of British goods, including guns and ammunition, metal knives, hoes, hatchets, fabrics, kettles, rum, paint, and jewelry. These goods became so desirable and even necessary to the Cherokees that hunting and war escalated. By midcentury, the slave trade had declined, but the deerskin trade continued to flourish.

The demise of the Indian slave trade did not mean that warfare declined. Indeed, the British, as well as the Spanish and French, who also had colonies in North America, discovered how useful Native allies could be and began to employ warriors in their colonial rivalries. Sometimes these alliances contradicted traditional Native enmities. In the 1740s, for example, the British engineered an alliance between the Cherokees and the Iroquois, who lived in upstate New York and western Pennsylvania, although the two peoples were traditional enemies. In the 1750s, the British built two forts in the Cherokee country, Fort Prince George in what is today upcountry South Carolina and Fort Loudoun in eastern Tennessee, to protect Cherokee towns while warriors were away fighting the enemies of the British Crown.

The Cherokees entered the French and Indian War (1756–1763) on the side of the British, but attacks on Cherokees by white frontiersmen and duplicity by colonial officials ultimately led many Cherokees to shift their allegiance to the French. In 1760, Cherokee warriors placed Fort Loudoun under siege and defeated a force of sixteen hundred British soldiers sent to relieve the garrison. Fort Loudoun surrendered. Contrary to the terms of the surrender, however, the garrison destroyed or hid guns and ammunition, and so instead of giving the men safe conduct as originally promised, the Cherokees attacked, killed twenty-nine of the soldiers, and took the others prisoner. The following year, a British force invaded, and soldiers destroyed fifteen Cherokee towns, including cornfields, granaries, and orchards. In the invasion and the famine that followed, thousands of Cherokees died.

Between the French and Indian War and the American Revolution, British hunters and settlers pushed westward. Hunters like Daniel Boone competed with Indians for game in the hunting grounds, and settlers began to encroach on Cherokee territory, particularly in the Holston River valley of northeastern Tennessee. The Cherokees welcomed the British king's Proclamation of 1763, which prohibited settlement west of the Appalachians. This should have made the Holston valley off limits, but the proclamation was only a paper blockade and the settlers ignored it. Cherokees began to regard the colonists, not the Crown, as their enemy, and when the American Revolution erupted in 1776, most Cherokees sided with the British.

The Cherokees gave refuge to fleeing Loyalists, and warriors raided the frontiers of Georgia, South Carolina, North Carolina, and Virginia. In late summer 1776, these colonies mounted a four-pronged invasion.

The Cherokees, who had not recovered from their losses in the French and Indian War, offered little resistance. Men, women, and children fled to the forests as the invading armies destroyed houses, fields, and granaries. At one town alone in upcountry South Carolina, the soldiers destroyed six thousand bushels of corn. The destruction so late in the year left no stores for the winter and no time to replant. The soldiers killed most Cherokee captives on the spot, and many collected the seventy-five-pound bounty the South Carolina legislature offered for the scalps of Cherokee warriors. This invasion ended Cherokee participation in the American Revolution, except for a small group that moved west to the region near present-day Chattanooga. Called the Chickamaugas because many lived on a stream of that name, they continued to fight intermittently until 1794.

At the end of the American Revolution, the Cherokees faced an uncertain future. The American colonists had destroyed more than fifty towns, laid waste to fields, and killed livestock. The Cherokee population, which had recovered somewhat from the early epidemics, once again declined dramatically as many who managed to survive the invasions died of exposure and starvation. Furthermore, between the outbreak of hostilities in 1776 and the final defeat in 1794, the Cherokees surrendered more than twenty thousand square miles of their domain. Most village sites remained in Cherokee hands, but the cession of such a vast expanse of hunting grounds jeopardized a Cherokee economy dependent on the deerskin trade. What would the Cherokees do?

THE U.S. "CIVILIZATION" PROGRAM

In 1783, British and American diplomats signed the Peace of Paris, ending the American Revolution. The treaty recognized the independence of the United States and conveyed to the new nation all of England's rights and claims to the land within its boundaries. The territory of the Cherokee Nation, along with the lands of many other tribes, fell within those borders. One of the first and most important challenges for the United States was to define its authority and determine a set of policies for dealing with the tribes. Since most of them had allied with the British during the Revolutionary War, the first step was to make peace.

Congress's approach to the problem rested on the same theories that had governed the diplomats in Paris. According to international law, England had owned the American colonies by right of discovery, a concept that gave Christian European governments the right to claim and occupy the lands of non-Christian and "uncivilized" peoples, and by right of conquest, by which England had acquired France's right of discovery claims at the conclusion of the French and Indian War. This meant that while the British government recognized and accepted the rights of colonists and Indians to own and use their lands, govern themselves, shape their societies, and develop local economies, the ultimate and overarching authority was always the sovereign authority of England. When England lost the Revolutionary War, the United States won, by right of conquest, England's rights, which included sovereign authority over all the land and people within its domain.

Congress extended this logic to its relations with the Indians. Victory in the Revolutionary War gave the new nation the same rights of conquest relative to the tribes. If England had lost its lands in America, England's Indian allies, the enemies of the United States, had lost theirs as well. It made no difference if their lands and villages had not been invaded and destroyed by American armies or if Native American warriors had not been wiped out in battle; they had lost the war along with England and should be dealt with as defeated enemies.

During the 1780s, until powerful Indian resistance forced change, Congress aggressively pursued this "conquered nations" Indian policy north of the Ohio River. South of the river, the "conquered nations" policy belonged to the states. Southern colonial charters, except for South Carolina's, extended west to the Mississippi River and beyond. Those states argued that England's authority had passed to them, not Congress, and they quickly began to act on their assertions. In 1783, the North Carolina legislature granted a large block of Cherokee lands in present Tennessee to any of its citizens who would move there, and Georgia forced the Cherokees to cede a large tract for its citizens. The actions of both states outraged the Cherokees, who argued that the British government had no legal authority to dispose of their country in the Peace of Paris, that North Carolina and Georgia could not presume to take Cherokee land and offer it to their citizens, and that any Americans occupying the land without the Cherokees' permission should leave. Many Cherokee leaders believed that the best way to deal with American pretensions was through peaceful negotiations, but the Chickamaugas fought until their final defeat in 1794 to protect their land from North Carolina's and Georgia's claims.

The northern Indians reacted similarly to American right of conquest claims, and Congress had its hands full with warfare in the Ohio country. Fearful that the aggressive expansionism of North Carolina and Georgia would widen the war in the South, Congress adopted a different policy there. Making no right of conquest claims against the Cherokees and the other southern nations, Congress instead sought to negotiate peace treaties that would end the fighting and restrain the states. To that end it appointed commissioners to meet with Indian delegations at Hopewell, South Carolina.

The Treaty of Hopewell, signed with the Cherokees on November 28, 1785, established relations between them and the United States. Primarily a peace treaty between the two nations, it contained several provisions designed to ensure friendly relations in the future. Because the main concern of the Cherokees was the continued encroachment of Georgians and North Carolinians, the treaty also defined the Cherokees' boundaries and recognized their right to expel unwanted intruders. Both states protested the treaty, citing the Indian article of the Articles of Confederation, which denied Congress the power to conduct relations with tribes within the boundaries of the states, but Congress argued that the threat of war overrode state claims. Congressional authority was undeniably ambiguous, however, and the Treaty of Hopewell was, for the most part, a failure. Neither Georgia nor North Carolina respected it; they continued to expand into Cherokee country, and the Cherokees continued to resist.

By the end of the 1780s, two things had happened to change the relations between the United States and Native Americans that had important implications for the Cherokees. In the first instance, the United States abandoned its assertion that the tribes were conquered enemies that had forfeited their rights to their lands. This decision, caused largely by continued Native resistance to the encroachment of settlers into their territories, reflected the realization that Native military power could be neither ignored nor countered without an enormous investment in lives and money. A new, peaceful way had to be found to conduct relations with Native peoples. Such a resolution of the crisis in the North proved impossible because neither the United States nor the tribes were willing to compromise their goals, but in the South, where the policy had always been to end the fighting, the change meant increased government efforts to restrain the expansionist states of Georgia and North Carolina.

The second event of importance was the reorganization of the U.S. government under the Constitution. Without ambiguity, the Constitution placed sole authority over Indian affairs in the hands of Congress and the president. This, in conjunction with its design of a federal system that subordinated the states to the national government in important areas, gave the United States the means to devise and execute an Indian policy that could control the actions of the states and their citizens.

The task of making the new system workable fell to President George Washington's first secretary of war, Henry Knox. The only high official to remain in office through the transition from the Articles of Confederation to the Constitution, Knox brought to the new government several years' experience in Indian matters and clear ideas about how relations with the tribes should be conducted. He believed that the tribes were sovereign, independent nations and that the United States should recognize and respect their rights to autonomous self-government within their borders. He was convinced that the encroachment of settlers and others onto their lands was the primary cause of warfare on the frontier and that the only way to bring lasting peace to Indian relations was to exert legislative controls over aggressive U.S. citizens. Furthermore, Knox thought that the federal government had a moral obligation to preserve and protect Native Americans from the extinction he believed was otherwise inevitable when "uncivilized" people came into contact with "civilized" ones. Knox also fully concurred with the general American view that as the population of the United States grew, Indians must surrender their lands to accommodate the increased numbers. These views added up to a policy aptly described by one historian as "expansion with honor," the central premise of which was that U.S.-Indian policy should make expansion possible without detriment to the Indians.

Knox's Indian policy, which the president fully embraced, began to take shape in the first months of the Washington administration. The initial step was to win agreement to the concept that the tribes were sovereign nations and that the United States should deal with them through the negotiation of treaties ratified, as the Constitution directs, by a two-thirds vote of the Senate. In the first Indian Trade and Intercourse Act, passed in 1790, Congress approved this idea by requiring that all purchases of land from Indians must be arranged through treaties negotiated by tribal leaders and federal commissioners appointed by the president. Because the Constitution prohibited states from negotiating treaties, Knox accomplished his goal of excluding the states from conducting relations with the Indians. In this way, he hoped to end the fighting on the frontier that was caused by state expansionism.

With the means to bring peace to Indian relations at hand, Knox addressed the longer-term problem of ensuring the Indians' survival. Along with many people of their generation, Knox and Washington believed that the obviously "uncivilized" characteristics of Indian life existed because Native people knew no better. In other words, their "inferiority" was cultural, not racial. Indians, therefore, were fully capable of becoming "civilized" and assimilating into American society as functioning citizens. This would reverse their otherwise inevitable extinction and free the United States from the moral stigma of having been instrumental in their destruction.

To most Americans, "civilization" was not an abstract concept. Rather, "civilization" meant contemporary American culture. To be "civilized," Native Americans must dress, think, act, speak, work, and worship the way rural U.S. citizens, ideally, did. All they needed was a little time to learn how, and the proper role of government was to encourage their instruction.

This new Indian policy of Knox and Washington began almost immediately to influence U.S. relations with the Cherokees. The failure of the Treaty of Hopewell to end the encroachment of settlers and the resulting warfare between them and the Cherokees was, to Knox, "disgraceful." But the thousands of settlers who had entered the Cherokee Nation in violation of the treaty could hardly be removed. Instead, Knox and Washington believed that the United States should negotiate a new treaty with the Cherokees, buy the land the settlers illegally occupied, survey a new boundary, strictly prohibit any further encroachment, and take the first steps toward "civilizing" the Cherokees. The Treaty of Holston was concluded in July 1791 and contained the provisions Knox required, including the following: "That the Cherokee nation may be led to a greater degree of civilization, and to become herdsmen and cultivators, instead of remaining in a state of hunters, the United States will, from time to time, furnish gratuitously the said nation with useful implements of husbandry." Congress included a section in the 1793 Trade and Intercourse Act that extended to all the tribes this policy of donating agricultural implements and tools, draft animals, and other "civilized" goods to Indians and called for the appointment of people to explain and demonstrate their use. Thus the "civilization" program, a central feature of the expansion with honor policy devised by Knox and Washington, came into being at a time when the Cherokees desperately needed some alternative to their collapsed economy of deerskin trading.

A NEW CHEROKEE WORLD

The Cherokees embraced the government's program with enthusiasm, but they also decided to adapt "civilization" to Cherokee needs and goals. When Moravians requested permission to establish a mission in 1800, for example, the Cherokee headmen welcomed a school but expressed no interest in the gospel. When two years passed and a school had not been opened, they threatened to expel the missionaries. The Moravians shifted their emphasis to education to comply with Cherokee demands, and in 1804 they commenced classes at the mission. However important religion may have been to the missionaries, the Cherokees apparently had little interest in Christianity—the Moravians did not make their first convert until nine years after they began their work—but they recognized that the missionaries had other things to offer.

The Moravians, Protestant German immigrants who had established a town at Salem, North Carolina, had relatively little competition for Cherokee souls during nearly two decades of ministry. In 1817, however, missionaries arrived from the interdenominational (but mostly Presbyterian and Congregationalist) American Board of Commissioners for Foreign Missions, headquartered in Boston. Soon Baptist missionaries joined them, and the Methodists arrived in 1822. These Protestant missionaries differed over various theological interpretations, but they agreed that Christianity and "civilization" were inextricably linked: One could not be truly "civilized" without being Christian and vice versa. Consequently, they not only taught their students to read the Bible and pray but also taught them how to dress, eat, keep house, cook, and farm. The division of labor, of course, was European, not Cherokee: Boys rather than girls farmed, and girls learned to be subservient.

Although the number of missionaries increased, they never had enough spaces in their classrooms for all Cherokee children. Not all parents, however, wanted their children to attend mission schools. The students who did enroll generally came from two types of families. Many were the children of British traders or Loyalists and Cherokee women. The matrilineal Cherokees regarded these people as wholly Cherokee, of course, because their mothers were Cherokee, but they were often bicultural—that is, they moved comfortably in both Cherokee and Anglo-American societies. In addition to these bicultural children of mixed ancestry, other Cherokees sent their children to school because they foresaw the end of a Cherokee lifestyle of hunting and subsistence farming. Headmen who had achieved prominence in eighteenth-century warfare and wealth in the deerskin trade sought new avenues for the aggression, competition, and achievement they had enjoyed in these outmoded ways. Therefore, they looked to the "civilization" program and mission schools to prepare them and their children for a new Cherokee world.

This new world required a redefinition of the most basic principles of Cherokee life. Men could no longer do the things that identified them as men—hunt and fight—but culturally, many could not bring themselves to do what women did—farm. Yet farming was exactly what the "civilization" program prescribed for men. At the same time, many Cherokee women were reluctant to give up farming, especially since agriculture now commanded so much attention. As a result, the Cherokees tried to accommodate to changed circumstances and the "civilization" program as best they could without sacrificing their most basic categories. Many women continued to hoe the corn while their husbands tended livestock, a corollary perhaps to hunting. Men harnessed their horses to plows at planting time, but they had always helped the women prepare the field. Women now spun thread and wove cloth, but they had always been responsible for their family's clothing. For many, perhaps most, Cherokees, the pattern of life changed little.

For other Cherokees, however, "civilization" led to a far more significant transformation. With missionaries and U.S. agents as their guides, and southern planters as their models, these Cherokees began to imitate an Anglo-American way of life. Like their white southern counterparts, Cherokee planters bought African American slaves, raised cotton and other crops for sale in the regional markets, and accumulated capital. The wealthiest Cherokees invested in taverns along the roads that began to crisscross the country, opened stores, and operated ferries and toll roads. The women in these households did not normally toil in the fields. Instead, African American slaves or white sharecroppers performed the agricultural labor that traditionally had been theirs. These Cherokee planters became an economic elite, and they ultimately dominated political affairs.

Cherokee law had been informal and clan-based, but the advent of disparities in wealth and concern over the protection of property led to the creation of a written law code. The first recorded law, in 1808, established a national police force to prevent horse stealing and to protect the property of widows and orphans. In particular, the law enabled men to bequeath their wealth to their wives and children in defiance of the matrilineal tradition. Gradually other laws appeared on the books. Some dealt with criminal matters, but many involved the regulation of property: Laws set interest rates, awarded contracts for ferries and toll roads, and established licensing procedures for hiring non-Cherokees.

Another body of laws also began to emerge that strengthened the authority of the national government. The Cherokees' second written law, in 1810, shifted the responsibility for avenging certain kinds of deaths from the clans to the national government. In 1817, the Cherokees enacted articles of government giving only the National Council the authority to cede lands. Subsequent legislation provided for apportionment of representation among districts, a standing committee with executive powers, and a supreme court. Finally, in 1827, the Cherokees wrote a constitution that provided for a bicameral legislature, a chief executive, and a judicial system.

The centralization of power came about in part because wealthy Cherokees wanted to protect their property but primarily because they wanted to preserve the Nation. The Cherokees held their land in common, so individuals could not sell property on which they lived. Cherokee leaders wanted to make sure that everyone — Cherokees and non-Cherokees — knew who had the authority to sell land. The Council restricted the sale of improvements — houses and barns that individuals built on commonly held land — and revoked the citizenship of those who chose to move west. The Cherokee constitution was in one sense the culmination of the "civilization" program, but in another sense it marked the zenith of Cherokee nationalism in the East. The preamble delineated the boundaries of the Nation, thereby linking the governing document to the Cherokee homeland: Without the land, the Nation did not exist. In 1829 the Council committed to writing a law imposing the death penalty on anyone who sold that land without authority.

Another expression of Cherokee nationalism was the invention and adoption of a system for writing the Cherokee language. In the early 1820s, an untutored Cherokee named Sequoyah devised a syllabary for writing Cherokee. He developed a symbol for each sound (or syllable), and anyone who spoke Cherokee reportedly could memorize the eighty-six symbols (soon reduced to eighty-five) in a matter of days. Many Cherokees did learn to read and write, and even today, mastery of the Sequoyah syllabary is a source of great pride for individual Cherokees. In 1828, the Cherokee Nation began publication of the *Cherokee Phoenix*, with columns printed in English and in Cherokee. Because of this newspaper, we have a remarkable view of early Cherokee history. The *Phoenix* also represents the crowning glory of a Cherokee "civilization" shaped in part by the U.S. government's program and the efforts of Protestant missionaries but largely directed by the Cherokees themselves.

PRESSURE FOR REMOVAL

When Henry Knox and President Washington designed the expansion with honor policy that incorporated a commitment to "civilizing" the Indians, they had assumed that as Native people learned to be "civilized," they would enter American society as fully equal citizens. They had not anticipated that the view would quickly develop that Indian "deficiencies" were caused by racial, not cultural, characteristics. This new pattern of racist thought rejected the idea that Indians could ever be fully "civilized" and insisted that one cannot change through education characteristics determined by race. Therefore, the reasoning continued, there could be no place in American society for Native people and, furthermore, it made no sense to pursue an Indian policy that aimed to achieve an impossible goal. Such thinking came to influence U.S. relations with Native Americans in the 1820s and was used during congressional debate in 1830 to justify "removal" of the eastern Indians to land farther west to make room for a burgeoning population of American citizens. For example, Senator John Forsyth of Georgia, arguing in support of the Indian Removal Act in 1830, characterized Indians as "a race not admitted to be equal to the rest of the community; not governed as completely dependent; treated somewhat like human beings, but not admitted to be freemen; not yet entitled, and probably never will be entitled, to equal civil and political rights." Attitudes like this obviously had profound implications for the Cherokees, widely credited with being the most "civilized" of any of the Indian tribes.

In part, the issue was land. After the War of 1812, an agricultural boom, the transportation revolution, and the development of a national market brought rapid changes to the country between the Appalachian Mountains and the Mississippi River. In the North, grain and livestock farmers spread through the Ohio River valley. Indiana and Illinois became states in 1816 and 1818, and their combined population increased from barely 37,000 in 1810 to almost half a million in 1830. South of the Ohio, the expansion of cotton plantation agriculture led to the admission to the Union of Mississippi and Alabama in 1817 and 1819. Their total population jumped from 40,000 in 1810 to 445,000 in 1830. And the older states of Ohio, Tennessee, and Georgia, all with land within their borders that belonged to Indians, filled up. Their population rose from 745,000 in 1810 to over two million in 1830. Such enormous growth, occurring in just two decades, vastly increased the pressure on the tribes to sell more of their land. The demand for the land of the southern Indians was particularly intense. The Cherokees, Creeks, Choctaws, and Chickasaws held thousands of square miles, much of it astonishingly fertile, within the borders of Georgia, Alabama, Mississippi, and Tennessee. These cotton states shared the economic and social system of plantation agriculture and slavery. Southerners defined and justified their slave system by racism and were thus particularly responsive to a theory that held that Indians were racially inferior. These two phenomena—a sharply intensified demand for Indian land fed by burgeoning populations and the development of the idea that the Indians were racially rather than culturally inferior and therefore unchangeable—came together in the 1820s to create an atmosphere of extreme tension.

After the War of 1812, just as the pressure on the southern tribes to sell their land intensified, tribal leaders became increasingly reluctant to sell. Exercising their rights as sovereigns, national councils rebuffed federal commissioners sent to negotiate treaties of cession with the argument that they had already sold too much land and had no more to spare. Andrew Jackson, the commander of the army's southern district at that time and a frequent negotiator of Indian treaties, suggested that the sensible way to get land from tribes that refused to sell was to take it. Negotiating treaties with Indians was "absurd," he argued. Their nations were not sovereign and the United States should not pretend they were. Congress should treat the Indians as subjects and "legislate their boundaries," by which he meant that Congress should exercise its right of eminent domain and seize the millions of acres they "wandered" over and hunted on. Indians should be allowed to keep only their villages and fields, which they obviously owned because they had invested their labor in them. Then Congress could populate the country with American citizens who would develop it and use it properly. If the tribes resisted the confiscation of their territories, Jackson pointed out, the "arm of government" was strong enough to force their compliance. Congress rejected Jackson's recommendations, but many agreed that some radical change in policy was in order.

Clearly, however, the issue was more complicated than the lust for land. No state could demand all the land owned by Indians and ignore the question of what was to happen to them after they had sold out. If the popular ideology denied the possibility of "civilization" and assimilation, the only logical alternative was expulsion. No one seriously suggested the third possibility, extermination. Expulsion, or removal, as it came to be called, was an idea that dated back to 1803 when President Thomas Jefferson had contemplated the acquisition of Louisiana. He toyed with the notion that eastern Indians might exchange their lands for comparable tracts west of the Mississippi and even suggested it to the Cherokees and Choctaws, but he never made removal a key feature of his Indian policy. Like Knox and Washington, he believed that Indians could be "civilized" and would ultimately blend into American society. Nevertheless, in 1810 about eight hundred Cherokees did migrate to the Arkansas River valley in present Arkansas. Jefferson's idea, premature when he first suggested it, gained new life in the supercharged atmosphere of the 1820s.

Thomas L. McKenney, the War Department clerk mainly responsible for administering Indian policy, was especially sensitive to the mounting tension. Mushrooming populations demanding land from Indians who refused to sell meant serious trouble. Indian policy, dedicated to the acquisition of Indian land for the benefit of American citizens, was encumbered by two late-eighteenth-century concepts—tribal sovereignty and "civilization"—that a growing number of Americans rejected as outmoded, impractical, impossible, undesirable, and "absurd." By the mid 1820s, McKenney; President James Monroe and his successor, John Quincy Adams; and many others turned to removal as the solution to what McKenney nervously referred to as a "crisis in Indian affairs."

For many years, until Congress acted with legislation in 1830, government officials attempted to convince tribal leaders to agree to removal. Treaties with the Cherokees in 1817 and 1819, the Choctaws in 1820, and the Creeks in 1826 all contained provisions to encourage groups to move west. The government set aside land in the region west of Arkansas, later called Indian Territory, where the Indians could rebuild their societies free from the demands of encroaching settlers and expansionist states. Some of the Indians accepted the offer and migrated, including a number of Cherokees. But most rejected the idea of abandoning their homelands for a strange and distant place and refused to move. By the end of the 1820s, state and federal officials realized that the voluntary migration of small groups of Native Americans would not achieve the government's goals.

Andrew Jackson won election to the presidency in 1828 with almost unanimous support from southern voters, who believed he would expel the Indians. He urged Congress to adopt the removal plan recommended by his predecessors and made support of the plan a measure of loyalty to the Democratic Party. During the winter of 1829–1830, while public debate raged, Congress considered Jackson's removal bill.

The impetus for the legislation came directly out of the history of the tangled relations between the Cherokees and the state of Georgia. In 1802, Georgia ceded to the United States the land between its current western boundary and the Mississippi River, which was included in its colonial charter. In return, the United States pledged to purchase for Georgia all the Indian lands remaining within the state. The lands in question belonged to the Creeks and the Cherokees. By 1827, the Creeks were out of Georgia but the Cherokees remained. Indeed, the Cherokees drafted their constitution and by every statement and action indicated that they had no intention of leaving. Georgia politicians had long been impatient with what they charged was unreasonable delay by the United States in fulfilling its obligation under the 1802 agreement and intensified their demands for speedy action. Presidents Monroe and Adams countered repeatedly that they were moving as fast as they could: The law required that land could be purchased only by treaty, and federal policy respected the sovereign right of the Indian nations to refuse to sell. There was, therefore, nothing more they could do.

Jackson's election encouraged the Georgia legislature to take control of the situation. Shortly after Jackson's victory, Georgia reaffirmed and expanded its policy of extending state civil and criminal jurisdiction over the Cherokee Nation. Jackson refused to interfere, arguing that Georgia had a sovereign right to govern all the territory within its borders. This exchange took place in early 1829, formed the backdrop for the debate on removal, and focused the arguments directly on the Cherokees.

Jackson built his defense of removal on the twin themes of the sovereign rights of Georgia over the Cherokees and the moral imperative to protect Indians from the deleterious effects of exposure to American frontier settlers. Such contact, he explained, had always resulted in the degradation and ultimate demise of the Indians and only their isolation in a safe and distant haven could save them. If they remained in Georgia, they would have to be subject to the laws of the state because whatever power he had to protect Indians from outside interference applied only to the encroachment of individual citizens, not to the actions of a sovereign state. This line reflected an extremely narrow interpretation of the constitutional provisions of federal supremacy in Indian affairs and the treaty stipulations that obligated the United States to defend the territories of the Native nations from external force.

The president encountered substantial opposition to his position from U.S. citizens, particularly those who lived in the Northeast. The missionaries who worked among the Cherokees and the organizations that supported them offered evidence of Cherokee "civilization" and compelling arguments against removal. Most persuasive was Jeremiah Evarts, the corresponding secretary of the American Board of Commissioners for Foreign Missions, who published a series of essays in the Washington *National Intelligencer* in 1829 under the pseudonym William Penn. Other papers reprinted the Penn essays, ministers used them in their sermons, and outraged citizens, mainly in the Northeast, were moved to sign petitions urging their congressmen to oppose removal. The essays also influenced the debates in Congress, where politicians quoted their arguments or challenged their assertions.

But public skepticism about the efficacy of "civilizing" Indians and a fever for more land, plus party loyalty in Congress, won the day. The Indian Removal Act passed. Signed by the president on May 28, 1830, it created the machinery that expelled to a distant territory some one hundred thousand Indians, including sixteen thousand Cherokees.

CHEROKEE RESISTANCE AND CAPITULATION

The Cherokees mounted a strong defense of their rights. After agreeing to a land cessation in 1819, the National Council announced that the Cherokees would cede no more land. The Nation maintained that resolve in the face of Georgia legislation that suspended the Cherokees' political and judicial systems, curtailed their civil rights, and essentially banished missionaries and other supporters from their territory. Ultimately, the Cherokees turned to the U.S. Supreme Court to protect their rights. In 1832, when the Court ruled in favor of Cherokee sovereignty in *Worcester v. Georgia*, the state refused to respond to the Court's decision. Furthermore, Georgia went ahead with a land lottery, enacted into law in 1830, that provided for the distribution of Cherokee land to Georgia's citizens. Thousands of Georgians streamed into the Cherokee country and dramatically increased the turmoil and suffering in the Cherokee Nation. No one seemed to have the power and the will to help the Cherokees.

The Cherokees had been united in their opposition to removal, but now the situation appeared hopeless to some of them. A small group began to coalesce around the Cherokee statesman Major Ridge, a highly respected veteran of the Creek War of 1813–1814 and a successful planter, and his New England–educated son and nephew, John Ridge and Elias Boudinot. These men concluded that the Cherokees had no alternative but to negotiate with the United States to exchange their land in the east for a new homeland west of the Mississippi. This defection horrified Principal Chief John Ross and the majority of Cherokees. The Cherokee government took steps to silence the group forming around Ridge, which came to be called the "Treaty Party," for fear that the United States would seize the opportunity to make a treaty with a disgruntled minority. The National Council moved to impeach the Ridges from their seats in the Council and forced Boudinot to resign as editor of the *Cherokee Phoenix*, a position he had held since it began publication. The Cherokee government was struggling to preserve a consensus by forcing the withdrawal of the minority opposition.

Although the Treaty Party acted partly out of concern for the suffering of the Cherokee Nation, some members had less than pure motives for trying to subvert the Cherokee national government. Most members of the Treaty Party were fairly well-to-do Cherokees, but they did not fall into the elite class composed of Principal Chief Ross, his brother, and several other prominent leaders. Since the Cherokee government controlled much of the economic activity in the Nation, some suspected Ross and others of using political power to promote their own economic interests. Furthermore, several Treaty Party members had been defeated in the 1830 elections, and John Ridge believed that only the subsequent ban on elections, caused by the extension of Georgia law over the Nation, prevented him from defeating Ross in a contest for principal chief. A willingness to negotiate also brought members of the Treaty Party some tangible rewards—the Georgia governor exempted the property of the Ridges and Boudinot from the land lottery. A fair share of jealousy, thwarted ambition, and self-interest, therefore, motivated the Treaty Party.

While Ross's position may very well have enhanced his family's fortune, as principal chief he understood something about the nature of Cherokee politics that members of the Treaty Party failed to recognize. Despite major changes in the structure of Cherokee government since the days of town councils in which everyone participated, political ethics remained relatively unchanged. Cherokees still believed that leaders should represent a consensus. This is precisely what Ross did: The vast majority of Cherokees opposed removal and wanted to resist the United States and Georgia at any cost. If Ross had followed any other course, he would have lost his mandate to govern.

The federal and state governments welcomed the defection of the Treaty Party. John Ridge led a delegation to Washington to negotiate a removal treaty in 1835 but found himself confronting John Ross's delegation. Both delegations returned to the Cherokee Nation, and in October 1835 at its annual meeting at Red Clay, within the borders of Tennessee, the National Council rejected Ridge's treaty. Not to be denied, the U.S. treaty commissioner proposed a December treaty conference at the abandoned Cherokee capital of New Echota in Georgia. The Ross delegation returned to Washington, and only the Treaty Party appeared at the New Echota meeting, where a removal treaty was negotiated. The Treaty of New Echota provided for the cession of all the Nation's lands in the East, additions to Cherokee lands west of the Mississippi in what is today northeastern Oklahoma, payment of five million dollars to the Cherokees, arrangement of transportation to the West, and subsistence aid from the U.S. government for one year.

The majority of Cherokees, led by John Ross, protested the Treaty of New Echota and petitioned the U.S. Senate to reject the treaty. Despite the pleas, the Senate ratified it in the spring of 1836. The treaty gave the Cherokees two years to prepare for removal. Most people could not believe that the battle had been lost. They continued to plant their corn as Ross struggled to have the treaty abrogated. When U.S. soldiers arrived in the spring of 1838, few Cherokees had made preparations to go west. The troops began rounding up people and placing them in stockades. The summer heat, poor water supplies, disease, and inadequate provisions quickly took their toll on those awaiting deportation to the West. Seeing his people's suffering, Ross finally accepted the inevitability of removal and secured permission for the Cherokees to conduct their own emigration that fall. Except for scattered families and a small group of Cherokees whose 1819 treaty rights permitted them to stay in North Carolina, the remaining Cherokees moved west in the winter of 1838–1839 on what has come to be known as the Trail of Tears (see Map, p. 22).

Were the Cherokees "uncivilized savages" as so many people maintained? What reasons did people advance in favor of removal of the Indians? What arguments refuted their line of reasoning? How did the Cherokees themselves respond to removal? The documents in this volume will help you explore these and other issues. The selections also will introduce you to the kinds of sources historians use in writing about Cherokee removal and direct you toward additional primary sources and secondary literature. While you learn about the Cherokees and their removal, you also can learn how to go about researching their past.

Map. *Trail of Tears (Opposite).*
Removal policy extended not just to the Cherokees but to many eastern Indian nations. This map shows the locations of the five large southern nations before and after removal.

Adapted from *Historical Atlas of Oklahoma*, Third Edition, by John W. Morris, Charles R. Goins, and Edwin C. McReynolds. Copyright © 1965, 1976, 1986 by the University of Oklahoma Press. Reprinted by permission. All rights reserved.

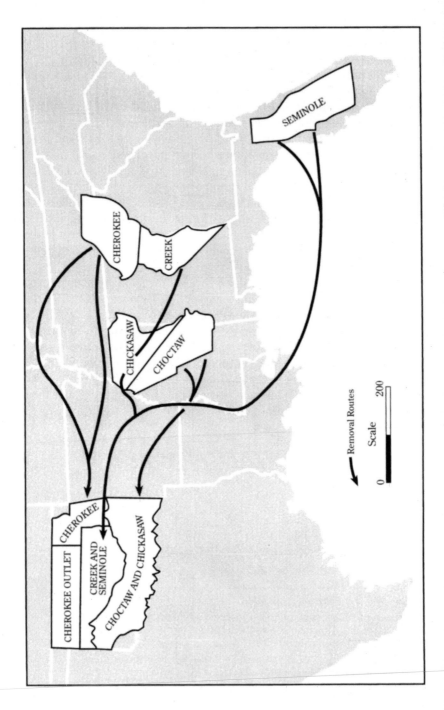

PART TWO

The Documents

1

Cherokee "Civilization"

In the early nineteenth century, the Cherokees experienced major changes in their society. For most of the eighteenth century, the deerskin trade and war had dominated their lives. With the depletion of the deer population, the collapse of the deerskin market, and the negotiation of peace treaties with the United States, the Cherokees began adapting to new economic and political realities. At the same time, the U.S. government sought to develop a new relationship with the Cherokees, one that promoted peace and held the promise of future land cessions.

President George Washington and his secretary of war, Henry Knox, developed the "civilization" program to accomplish that goal. In 1796, Washington addressed a letter to "Beloved Cherokees." In it, he pointed out that "you now see that the game with which your woods once abounded, are growing scarce, and you know that when you cannot find a deer or other game to kill, you must remain hungry." The president, however, had a plan to relieve the Cherokees' suffering. He urged Cherokee men to increase their herds of cattle and hogs and to raise sheep as well, and he instructed them to plant cotton, wheat, and flax in addition to their native corn. He promised that the U.S. agent to the Cherokees, Silas Dinsmoor, would provide plows so that the men could increase production and spinning wheels and looms so that the women could make clothing. The president also suggested that Cherokee towns send representatives to an annual meeting, the forerunner of the Cherokees' National Council, where they could meet with U.S. agents and "talk together on the affairs of your nation." Washington stressed that the attempt to "civilize" the Cherokees was an experiment: "If it succeeds, the beloved men of the United States will be encouraged to give the same assistance to all the Indian tribes within their boundaries. But if it should fail they may think it vain to make any further attempts to better the condition of any Indian tribe."

The "civilization" program rested on an image of Indians as hunters who derived their livelihood from vast game preserves and ignored the fact that Cherokee women had been farming for hundreds of years. But if the United States could convert Indian men into farmers, the Indians no longer would need their hunting grounds and would sell them to the United States. Therefore, the "civilization" program struck at the most basic way in which societies organize themselves—according to gender—and proposed to redefine the roles of men and women. Furthermore, the "civilization" program had to teach Indians to appreciate the value of private property and the marketability of land. The Cherokees, like most Native peoples, held their land in common, and each person was free to use as much as he or she needed so long as that use did not infringe on the rights of others. By promoting individual ownership and commerce, U.S. officials hoped eventually to convince Indians that land was a commodity to be bought and sold freely. "Civilization" eventually encompassed a broader cultural transformation including Christianity, formal education, and republican government, but the change in economic values remained at its core.

Washington's complete letter was published in the *Cherokee Phoenix* (March 20, 1828). For Cherokee "civilization" specifically, see Henry Thompson Malone, *Cherokees of the Old South: A People in Transition* (Athens: University of Georgia Press, 1956); and Mary Young, "The Cherokee Nation: Mirror of the Republic," *American Quarterly* 33 (1981): 502–24. For the "civilization" program's origins, see David Nichols, *Red Gentlemen and White Savages: Indians, Federalists, and the Search for Order on the American Frontier* (Charlottesville: University of Virginia Press, 2008), and *Engines of Diplomacy: Indian Trading Factories and the Negotiation of American Empire* (Chapel Hill: University of North Carolina Press, 2016).

Becoming "Civilized"

Wills and court cases are important sources of information for historians. In addition to disposing of possessions and recording disputes, these documents often imply much about how people lived. Public documents are particularly significant in recovering information about ordinary people who never kept journals or wrote personal letters. Young Wolf was such a person. Although Young Wolf's name, among others, appears several times on official Cherokee documents, he did not leave personal papers. He was not a major figure in Cherokee history, yet his life and the one personal document that survives—his will—tell us much about

*changing Cherokee culture in the early nineteenth century and an emerg-
ing sentiment in favor of removal.*

*Young Wolf first appeared in the historical record as a patriot. In 1808,
he joined other young Cherokee leaders in opposing a private cession for
mining iron ore that the U.S. agent and some self-serving older chiefs had
promoted. The young chiefs demanded that the full National Council ratify
any land cession. By 1816, Young Wolf apparently had reversed his position on land cessions. He and fourteen others negotiated with Andrew
Jackson, a federally appointed treaty commissioner, for the sale of 2.2 million acres in northern Alabama. When the Cherokee Council repudiated
their actions, they claimed to have signed under duress and insisted that
they thought the entire Council would be given a chance to ratify the treaty.*

*By this time, Young Wolf clearly supported the cession of lands in the
East and emigration to the West. The Cherokee Council, however, opposed
cession and emigration. In 1817, the Council passed a law that revoked
the citizenship of anyone who did enroll to go west. Despite this law, Young
Wolf enrolled for emigration in 1818, but he did not actually go. In 1820,
the deadline passed for emigration with assistance from the federal government. Left in the East without the rights of Cherokee citizenship, including
the use of common land, Young Wolf and other enrollees conspired to cede
additional land in Alabama. The Council discovered the conspiracy in
1821 and indicted the leaders, including Young Wolf, for treason, but no
record of a trial survives. Not long after this, Young Wolf died.*

*Young Wolf left a will that he had written in 1814. The will is very
revealing. First of all, Young Wolf had abandoned a number of traditional Cherokee practices. The Cherokees were matrilineal; that is, they
traced kinship through women. Young Wolf's children would have been
members of their mother's clan, not his, and their inheritance would have
come from their mother or her brother, not from Young Wolf. If Young
Wolf had continued to follow traditional lines of descent, his property
would have passed to his sister's children. How does he deviate from
matrilineal descent in his will? Can you find any remnants of matrilineal descent in the will?*

*In his will, Young Wolf tells how he managed to accumulate his prop-
erty. He lived in a period when men could no longer follow their traditional pursuits of hunting and war. Native and non-Native hunters had
depleted southern forests of deer, the free-ranging livestock of white settlers
competed with the remaining animals for food, and colonial merchants
increasingly turned from the export of deerskins to the export of cotton
after the invention of the cotton gin in 1793. Furthermore, the United
States pursued a policy of peace with Native southerners, and except*

for brief campaigns in the Creek War of 1813–1814, few opportunities to fight existed. With little else left to do, many men turned to livestock herding. Since the common method of herding was to release cattle and hogs into the forests to forage for food, the labor pattern for herding was not much different from that for hunting: Men simply rounded up their animals in the fall and drove them to market rather than killing them and taking their skins to traders. The deerskin trade had taught many Cherokee men to be astute traders, and they simply applied these lessons to the trade in livestock. How does Young Wolf fit this pattern?

Young Wolf's will and the controversy that followed his death reveal a departure from the traditional division of labor. Women had been the farmers in Cherokee households; men had hunted. Why then did Young Wolf own farming equipment? And why did he leave these tools to his son? It is possible, of course, that Young Wolf had begun to farm himself. What is more likely is that in spring, he broke the fields with a horse and plow, a task compatible with the traditional participation of men in planting. The routine hoeing probably fell to his wife and daughters or to his African American slaves. Like other Cherokees in the late eighteenth and early nineteenth centuries, Young Wolf had acquired African American slaves. Slaves permitted Cherokee men to become responsible for farming without actually doing it themselves. When Young Wolf died, his wife did not support herself by farming but conformed to Anglo-American expectations of women. How did she make a living by relying on the "domestic arts"—cooking and housekeeping?

The introduction of significant amounts of privately held property produced controversy in the Cherokee Nation and in the Young Wolf household. The very first written Cherokee law focused on the protection of private property. Following Young Wolf's death, two of his daughters argued with their mother over property. Had there been no slavery and no value attached to slaves, perhaps this family would not have engaged in a dispute so serious that it reached the National Council. Furthermore, the growing concern with all types of property and, in particular, the increasing material value placed on land overshadowed other attachments. Long before his daughters considered their material gain ahead of familial ties, Young Wolf came to regard land as a commodity to be bought and sold. Its value as a commodity had come to outweigh all spiritual association with or patriotic feelings for the Cherokee homeland.

Most wills and court cases are located in county courthouses or, if they are very old, in state archives. Because of the destruction of the Cherokee government in the East, Cherokee records are scattered. These particular documents found their way to the Newberry Library, a private library in Chicago that is supported by grants and contributions, by way of John Howard Payne, an Anglo-American writer most famous for the lyrics to "Home Sweet Home." Payne visited the Cherokees in 1835 to collect material for a book. Several Cherokee leaders and missionaries assisted him, and in the turmoil of the period they entrusted him with important documents. Payne never wrote his book, but the documents he preserved and the interviews he conducted provide an important source for scholars who write about nineteenth-century Cherokees. Some of these papers have been published in William L. Anderson, Anne F. Rogers, and Jane L. Brown, eds., The Payne-Butrick Papers, *2 vols. (Lincoln: University of Nebraska Press, 2010). The editors have altered punctuation and capitalization, but they have retained original spellings.*

1

YOUNG WOLF

Last Will and Testament

1814

BIG SPRING, MARCH 12, 1814

In the name of God in men.[1] I, Young Wolf, being in real good sense at this present time, do make my last Will and Testimony and bequeath and leave loving daughter, Ann, that Negro Woman named Tabb, and also leave to my loving son, Dennis, a Negro man named Ceasar. Also I leave a yearly income for Dennis in the Turnpike Company to get equal shear with the rest of the company & also leave to my loving wife one year-old heifer, & her increase from that time must be her own. Also one mare I let her have and the increase of them must be hers. Also I leave to my son Dennis my house & plantation & all the farming tools. If any contest should arise after my decease about my property, I leave

---

[1]Young Wolf, or the person who wrote this will for him, had some sense of the proper Anglo-American form for wills in the early nineteenth century but little understanding of some of the words. Consequently, there is an amusing malapropism (ludicrous misuse of a word) in the first sentence. Wills normally began "In the name of God Amen."

Charles Hicks, Rattling Gourd and The Hair,[2] to be my executors on my whole estate. And through friendship to Elijah Hicks, I do give my brace of pistols to him. Also if death should take place with any one of my children, the property to said deceasd must be equally divided among the other children. Also to my mother that raised me, I leave a black horse, a three-year-old which the Crawler has in the army.[3]

By my being careful & by own industry, I have gathered a smart chance of property, and my first start was from herding my brother's cattle. I recvd one calf which I took my strt from, except my own industry, & with cow and calf which I sold, I bought two sows & thirteen pigs. Sometime after I was able to purchase three mares, & the increase of them since is amounted to thirty more or less & from that start I gathred money enough to purchase a negro woman named Tabb, also a negro man named Ceasar. Also I leave to my loving Daughter Neecootia, one good sorrel mare and colt.

Young Wolf

N.B. Also I make my will agreeable to the laws of the Cherokee Nation which my executors understands perfectly well.
Test.
William Murdock

I do certify that the above is a true copy of the original will of Young Wolf, deceased.

A. McCoy
Clk, Nl. Committee

New Town
6th Novr. 1824

[2]Rattling Gourd and The Hair were brothers of Young Wolf. The Hair later took their father's surname and became Hair Conrad. His descendants were known as Conrads. Rattling Gourd's descendants used Rattlinggourd as a surname, and Young Wolf's descendants used Wolf. Charles Hicks, a highly regarded leader who became principal chief just before his death in 1827, was involved in the effort to prevent the mining of iron ore. Elijah Hicks was his son.

[3]The Crawler was with the Cherokees who accompanied Andrew Jackson on his campaign against the Creeks in the Creek War (1813–1814).

2

CHEROKEE COMMITTEE

Ruling on Young Wolf's Estate

1824

FORTVILLE, 25TH MAY 1824

Whereas complaint has been lodged against Mrs. Jane Wolf, now Mrs. Williams, by the heirs of Young Wolf, deceased, by refusing to surrender bills of sales for Negroes given to the heirs by said Young Wolf, deceased, it appears also that there is some design to wrong the said Heirs out of their property,[1] it is the request of the undersigned that Thomas Starr & Daniel McCoy[2] take charge of Bills of Sales of property, and also take into their hands the education of Anna and Dennis Wolf, until the National Council and Committee shall be convened and act thereon. Given under my hand & seal & date above.

Ch. R. Hicks

The National Committee have deliberated the subject matter of the written order, and upon a full investigation, it appears from the will of Young Wolf, deceased, that Mr. Charles R. Hicks, Rattling Gourd & The Hair were chosen as executors, and that the house & farm were left to his only son, Dennis, and that the executors thought best to let Jane Wolf, the widow of the deceased, occupy the house and farm and manage and conduct the same according to her own discretion.

And it further appears that the said Janey Wolf did manage and conduct the place with economy & propriety & in consequence thereby has accumulated considerable money, by keeping a house of entertainment for travellers, which enabled her to purchase some Negroes; and that she also has raised her children with that maternal regard which is peculiar to the trait of a kind mother, and that the two oldest daughters

---

[1]Apparently, the will was introduced in this case to show that Young Wolf did not leave slaves to two older daughters who had married and moved away from home. They claimed that the slaves their mother had given them actually had been bequeathed to them by their father. If the slaves had been inherited, the daughters would have been entitled to the slaves' children. If their mother had given them only the use of the slaves but reserved any children for herself, they would have lost their case.

[2]These men are Jane Wolf Williams's sons-in-law. Nannie (Neecootia) Wolf married Thomas Starr and Margaret Wolf married Daniel McCoy.

being of age and married and settled off to themselves; and that the said Janey Wolf put into the hands of each of those daughters a Negro woman which she had bought with money accumulated as before stated, and intended making a right of those Negro women to them, after getting some of their increase, for the benefit of her two youngest children, which are not yet of age; and the eldest daughters being desirous to get their mother to make a transfer of bills of sales for those Negro women, was to embrace all their increase; and the mother's refusing to do so having produced a misunderstanding and controversy between the mother and two daughters which has led to this order.

The National Committee are of opinion that justice forbids coercion on the mother to transfer bills of sale for those Negroes, contrary to her own free will and consent.

Therefore, it is decreed that the order herein be disannulled.

By order of the National Committee

Jno. Ross, President

A. McCoy
Clerk, Nl. Committee

A Cherokee View of "Civilization"

In the 1820s, a new generation of Cherokee leaders began to emerge. The sons of prominent warriors and traders, these young men had received an English education from private tutors or missionaries and entrée into business and politics from their fathers. They moved comfortably in an Anglo-American world and aspired to the same kinds of success as the sons of white southern planters. John Ridge was an important member of this Cherokee upper class.

The son of a warrior, The Ridge, John benefitted from his father's early move from hunting and fighting to farming. The Ridge had cleared a large expanse of land in the Oothcaloga Valley in northern Georgia before the turn of the nineteenth century. He built a log house with a chimney, planted corn and cotton, and began to buy African American slaves. He became involved in national politics as a promoter of "civilization" and as a patriot who helped execute the unscrupulous chief Doublehead for an illegal land sale. Participation in the Creek War of 1813–1814 enhanced his stature as a Cherokee leader and brought him a commission as major, a title that he subsequently took as his first name.

John Ridge was born in 1803, and in 1810 his father enrolled him and his older sister Nancy in the Moravian mission school at Springplace. This was John's first introduction to the English language. He remained at Springplace until 1814 when his father employed a private tutor. Then in 1817, John and Nancy enrolled in the Brainerd Mission of the American Board of Commissioners for Foreign Missions. The next year, John briefly attended an academy in Knoxville, Tennessee, and then traveled to Cornwall, Connecticut, to enroll in the American Board's Foreign Mission School. While he was a student in Connecticut, John fell in love with Sarah Northrup, daughter of the school's steward. They married in 1824. Two years later, Ridge's fellow student and cousin Elias Boudinot wed another young woman from Cornwall. The town's outrage over these two interracial marriages forced the school to close.

Following the completion of his formal education and his marriage, John Ridge accepted a position as a secretary for the Creek Indians, the Cherokees' neighbors to the south, in their negotiations with the federal government. This position took the young Cherokee man to Washington, where he came to the attention of Albert Gallatin, a prominent statesman who had served in Thomas Jefferson's cabinet. Gallatin was in the process of collecting information about American Indians, particularly their languages, and he enlisted Ridge in his research efforts. In addition to collecting vocabularies for several Indian languages, Ridge provided Gallatin with information about the Cherokees. The following letter was written in response to a list of questions Gallatin gave Ridge. Two versions of the letter survive. The one printed here, which is in the Payne papers at the Newberry Library, is the draft; the letter Gallatin actually received is in the New-York Historical Society. The two are virtually identical, but the editors have chosen the draft because it contains more spontaneous responses—and perhaps more accurate descriptions—than the final version. If you would like to compare the letters, see "John Ridge on Cherokee Civilization in 1826," edited by William C. Sturtevant, Journal of Cherokee Studies 7 (1981): 79–91. The editors have modernized spelling and punctuation to make the letter more readable.

John Ridge was particularly interested in charting culture change among the Cherokees. How had the economy changed? What new crops and animals had been introduced? How had the division of labor changed? What did men do? What did women do? Ridge suggested that among poorer Cherokees, women still farmed. How did he explain their work in the fields? Can you think of other reasons why women might have continued to farm? How had government changed? In what ways did the new Cherokee political organization incorporate the Anglo-American

principle of balance of power? How did the Cherokee government com-
pare with that of the United States? What was John Ridge's attitude
toward traditional religion? How might you explain his attitude? How
did he regard the "civilization" program?

If you are interested in learning more about John Ridge and his fam-
ily, see Thurman Wilkins, Cherokee Tragedy: The Story of the Ridge
Family and the Decimation of a People *(New York: Macmillan, 1970).*
John Demos's The Heathen School: A Story of Hope and Betrayal in
the Age of the Early Republic *(New York: Vintage, 2013) and Theresa*
Strouth Gaul's To Marry an Indian: The Marriage of Harriet Gold and
Elias Boudinot in Letters, 1823–1839 *(Chapel Hill: University of North*
Carolina Press, 2005) address the issue of Ridge and Boudinot's inter-
racial marriages.

3

JOHN RIDGE

Letter to Albert Gallatin

February 27, 1826

The Cherokee Nation is bounded on the North by east Tennessee &
North Carolina, east by Georgia, south by the Creek Nation & state of
Alabama, & west by west Tennessee. The extreme length of the Nation
must be upwards of 200 miles & extreme breadth about 150. At a rough
conjecture, it has been supposed to contain about 10,000,000 of acres
of land. It is divided into eight districts or Counties by a special act of
the National Council, & their boundaries are distinctly designated and
defined. A census of the Nation was taken last year (1825) by order of
the Council to ascertain the amount of property and Taxable persons
within the Nation. The correctness of this may be relied on, and the
population proved to be 13,583 native citizens, 147 white men married
in the Nation, 73 white women, and 1,277 African slaves, to which if we
add 400 cherokees who took reservations in North Carolina & who are
not included in the census & who have since merged again among us,
the Cherokee Nation will contain 15,480 inhabitants.[1] There is a scanty

---

[1] The reservations to which Ridge refers were tracts of land (often 640 acres) within
cessions that the United States deeded to individual Indians. The U.S. government originally intended to give private reservations to those Indians who wanted to become citizens and assimilate into Anglo-American society, but in practice officials often awarded

instance of African mixture with the Cherokee blood, but that of the white may be as 1 to 4, occasioned by intermarriages which has been increasing in proportion to the march of civilization.[2] The above population is dispersed over the face of the Country on separate farms; villages, or a community, having a common enclosure to protect their hutches [cabins], have disappeared long since, & to my knowledge, there is but one of this character at Coosawattee, the inhabitants of which are gradually diminishing by emigration to the woods, where they prefer to clear the forest & govern their own individual plantations. In this view of their location, it really appears that they are farmers and herdsmen, which is their real character. It is true that there are distinctions now existing & increasingly so in the value of property possessed by individuals, but this only answers a good purpose, as a stimulus to those in the rear to equal their neighbors who have taken the lead. Their principal dependence for subsistence is on the production of their own farms. Indian corn is a staple production and is the most essential article of food in use. Wheat, rye & oats grow very well & some families have commenced to introduce them on their farms. Cotton is generally raised for domestic consumption and a few have grown it for market & have realized very good profits. I take pleasure to state, tho' cautiously, that there is not to my knowledge a solitary Cherokee to be found that depends upon the chase for subsistence and every head of a family has his house & farm. The hardest portion of manual labor is performed by the men, & the women occasionally lend a hand to the field, more by choice and necessity than any thing else. This is applicable to the poorer class, and I can do them the justice to say, they very contentedly perform the duties of the kitchen and that they are the most valuable portion of our Citizens. They sew, they weave, they spin, they cook our meals and act well the duties assigned them by Nature as mothers as far as they are able & improved. The African slaves are generally mostly held by Half breeds and full Indians of distinguished talents. In this class the principal value of property is retained and their farms are conducted in the same style with the southern white farmers of equal ability in point of property. Their houses are usually of hewed logs, with brick chimneys & shingled roofs, there are also a few excellent Brick houses & frames.

---

these private reservations to prominent individuals as an inducement to sign cessions. The holders often sold this property, pocketed the money, and moved onto common land within the Cherokee Nation; unscrupulous whites defrauded others of their reservations, and they too moved into the Nation.

[2]The Census of 1835 documents the racial composition of the Cherokee Nation. The census lists 12,776 Cherokees, or 77.7 percent, as "full bloods," that is, of only Cherokee ancestry.

Their furniture is better than the exterior appearance of their houses would incline a stranger to suppose. They have their regular meals as the whites, Servants to attend them in their repasts, and the tables are usually covered with a clean cloth & furnished with the usual plates, knives & forks &c.[3] Every family more or less possess hogs, Cattle & horses and a number have commenced to pay attention to the introduction of sheep, which are increasing very fast. The horse is in general use for purposes of riding, drawing the plough or wagon.

Domestic manufactures is still confined to women who were first prevailed to undertake it. These consist of white or striped homespun, coarse woolen Blankets & in many instances very valuable & comfortable, twilled & figured coverlets. Woolen & cotton Stockings are mostly manufactured for domestic use within the Nation. I can only say that these domestic cloths are preferred by us to those brought from the New England. Domestic plaids our people are most generally clothed with them, but calicoes, silks, cambricks, &c. Handkerchiefs & shawls &c. are introduced by Native merchants, who generally trade to Augusta in Georgia. The only trade carried on by the Cherokees with the adjoining States, is in hogs & horned Cattle. Skins formerly were sold in respectable quantities but that kind of trade is fast declining & getting less reputable. Cherokees on the Tennessee river have already commenced to trade in cotton & grow the article in large plantations and they have realized very handsome profit. All those who have it in their power, are making preparations to grow it for market & it will soon be the staple commodity of traffic for the Nation.

You will be able more fully to ascertain their state of improvement by giving the out lines of their Government. Having been honored with a seat in its National Councils, I have better acquaintance with this branch of your enquiry, than any other. . . . In short, these Chiefs organized themselves into Standing body of Legislators who meet in October annually at New Town [New Echota], their seat of Government.

They are composed of two departments, the National Committee & the Representative Council. The former consist of 13 members including their President & have a Clerk to record their proceedings. They control & regulate their monied concerns: powers to inspect the Books of the Treasury, & acknowledge claims, power to Legislate & Negative the sets of the other Branch of the Legislative Council. The Representatives have also their Secretary, consist of 45 members including their Speaker. They have power to Legislate & Negative the proceedings

---

[3]Cherokees traditionally ate only when they were hungry, a practice many Anglo-Americans considered to be "savage."

of the Nat. committee fill their own vacancies & the vacancies in the Committee, to elect the two head chiefs, or their executive in conjunction with the National Committee. All laws of course are passed with the concurrences of these two departments & approved of by the head Chiefs. Their laws at present are written in the English Language. . . .

These Branches of our Legislature are composed of men chosen from the eight districts heretofore mentioned in as satisfactory proportion as circumstances will allow. The Judiciary of our Nation is more perfect than the Legislature, having less obstacles to make it so than the latter. It is independent [and has the] Power to bring any Chief before it of any grade, to pass sentence & put it in execution. There is a Court of Justice in every district & its district Judge, who presides over two Districts. Every Court has a Jury and its district officers, Sheriff constables &c. to attend it. A plaintiff or defendant can object to any Jury to sit on his trial or suit & if reasonable, he is indulged by the laws of his Country. There is also a Supreme Court of the Nation held once annually at New Town when all appeals from the district Courts are finally decided. . . . We have as yet not prisons and Justice is quickly awarded. The thief as soon as convicted & sentence passed is tied to the first Tree & on the naked skin is impressed, his receipt, for release. We have not as yet many written laws, it being the policy of our Government to regulate itself to the capacity and state of improvement of our people. I will give you a sketch of a few of these laws.

1. Law to regulate our Citizens agreeable to the Intercourse laws of the U. States for the purpose of Securing peace on the frontiers.

2. A law prohibiting the introduction of Intoxicating liquors by the whites.

3. Regulating intermarriages with the whites, making it necessary for a white man to obtain license & be married by a Gospel minister or some authorized person.

4. Against Renting land & introducing white people without a special written permission of the Legislative Council. Penalty: Expulsion of the white people so introduced as intruders, a fine of $500 on the aggressor and one hundred stripes on the naked back.

5. Giving indefeasible title to Lands improved—houses &c.—to the Citizens with power to sell or transfer them among each other, but not to Citizens of the adjoining States.

6. Regulating Taxes and defining the duties of collectors.

7. Law, prohibiting the sale of any more Lands to the United States except it be done by the concurrences of the Nat. Committee & Council; Penalty: disgrace & death to the offender.

8. A law to protect the orphan & widow to the father's [and] husband's property after death.

9. Regulating the Salary of the two head Chiefs, District & circuit Judges, the pay of the members of the Legislative Council & their clerks during active service and officers of the Nation generally.

10. Regulating the Judicial Courts of the Nation, defining their Powers.

11. against stealing.

12. against murder.

13. Defining the power of the Chiefs and that only exercised in a body in their Legislative capacity at the times appointed by law, and in the recess to be on a level with private Citizens.

. . . Property belonging to the wife is not exclusively at the control & disposal of the husband, and in many respects she has exclusive & distinct control over her own, particularly among the less civilized & in fact in every class & grade of intelligence, the law is in favor of the females in this respect.[4] Rules & customs in the transfer of property are adopted & respected from the adjoining states in the absence of any law to regulate this branch of our trade. Property descends from parents, equally to the children; if none, to the next relatives &c. But if a will is made, it is respected to the fullest extent & every person, possessed of property, is entitled to dispose of his or her property in this way. . . .

We attempted to pass a law regulating marriage, but as nearly all the members of our Legislature, tho' convinced of the propriety, had been married under the old existing ceremony, [and] were afraid it would reflect dishonor on them, it failed. Time will effect the desired change in this system & it is worthy of mention, even now, that the most respectable

---

[4]In 1826, the states followed English common law with respect to married women's property. Under this legal tradition, married women had no right to property, even property they had before they married. When a woman married, her husband gained title to everything she owned. In 1839, Mississippi became the first state to enact legislation to protect the property rights of married women. The Cherokee law that protected married women's property may have been a holdover from traditional practices in which women controlled houses and fields, but the Council probably enacted this law to prevent white men from marrying Cherokee women solely to gain control of their property, which the Nation regarded as commonly owned.

portion of our females prefer, tho' not required by law to be united in marriage attended by the solemnities of the Christian mode. . . . In regard to Intemperance, we are still as a nation grossly degraded. We are however on the improve. Five years ago our best chiefs during their official labors would get drunk & continue so for two or three days. It is now not the case & any member who should thus depart from duty would now be expelled from the Council. Among the younger class, a large number are of fine habits, temperate & genteel in their deportment. The females aspire to gain the affection of such men & to the females we may always ascribe the honor of effecting the civilization of man.

There are about 13 Schools established by missionaries in the Nation and may contain 250 students. They are entirely supported by the humane Societies in different parts of the U. States. The Nation has not as yet contributed to the support of these Schools. Besides this, some of our most respectable people have their children educated at the academies in the adjoining states. Two cherokee females have recently completed their Education, at the expense of their father, at a celebrated female Academy in Salem, North Carolina. They are highly accomplished & in point of appearance & deportment; they would pass for the genteel & wellbred ladies in any Country.

I know of some others who are preparing for an admission in the same institution. I suppose that there are one third of our Citizens, that can read & write in the English Language. George Guess a Cherokee who is unacquainted with the English has invented 86 characters, in which the cherokees read & write in their own Language and regularly correspond with their Arkansas friends. This mode of writing is most extensively adopted by our people particularly by those who are ignorant of the English Language. A National Academy of a high order is to be soon established by law at our seat of Government.[5] The edifice will be of Brick & will be supported by the Nation. It is also in contemplation to establish an English & Cherokee printing press & a paper edited in both languages at our seat of Government. In our last Session, $1500 was appropriated to purchase the press and regulations adopted to carry the object into effect.[6] We have also a Society organized called the "Moral & Literary Society of the Cherokee Nation." A library is attached to this Institution.

[5]The plan to establish a national academy materialized only after removal. In the 1850s the Cherokees opened the Cherokee Male Seminary and the Cherokee Female Seminary, publicly supported institutions of higher education.

[6]The Cherokee Nation began publication of a bilingual newspaper, the *Cherokee Phoenix*, in 1828 with Ridge's cousin, Elias Boudinot, as editor.

Provision has been made by our Delegation at this place, in a Treaty with John C. Calhoun, the Sec'y of War in 1819, to afford aid to education in our Nation, by Reserving twelve miles square of Land to be sold by the President & by him invested to draw interest & applied as he shall think proper. This tract has not been sold as yet, owing as I have understood in the unfavorable condition of the market at this time.

Having given a view of the present of civilization of the Cherokee Nation, it may not be amiss to relate the time & manner when it was first introduced. About the year 1795 Missionaries were sent by the United Abraham Or Moravians to the Cherokees & established a Station called Spring place in the center of Nation.[7] At or about that time, Col. Silas Dinsmore was appointed by Genl. Washington as Agent of the Nation, who from the Indian Testimony itself labored indefatigably in Teaching the Cherokees the art of agriculture by distributing hoes & ploughs & giving to the women Spinning wheels, cards & Looms. It appears when this change of Hunter life to a civilized one was proposed by the Agent to the Chiefs in Council, that he was unanimously laughed at by the Council for attempting [to] introduce white peoples' habits among the Indians, who were created to pursue the chase. Not discouraged here, the Agent turned to Individuals & succeeded to gain some to pay their attention to his plan by way of experiment, which succeeded. An anecdote is related of a Chief who was heartily opposed to the Agent's view. He came to Col. Dinsmore & said, "I don't want you to recommend these things to my people. They may suit white people, but will do [nothing] for the Indians. I am now going to hunt & shall be gone six moons & when I return, I shall expect to hear nothing of your talks made in [my] absence to induce my people to take hold of your plan." But in his absence the Agent induced his wife & daughters to Spin & weave with so much assiduity as to make more cloth in value, than the Chief's Hunt of six months amounted to. He was astonished & came to the Agent with a smile, accusing him for making his wife & daughters better hunters than he & requested to be furnished a plough & went to work on his farm.

In the meantime, the Moravians opened their School for the Indians, cleared a farm, cultivated a garden & planted an orchard. The Venerable Rev. John Gambold & his amiable Lady were a standing monument of Industry, Goodness & friendship. As far as they had means, they converted the "Wilderness to blossom as the Rose." There the boys & girls were taught to read & write, & occasionally labor in the Garden & in the

---

[7]The Moravians actually established their mission in 1800.

field. There they were first taught to sing & pray to their Creator, & here Gospel Worship was first Established. Never shall I forget father Gambold & mother Mrs. Gambold. By them the clouds of ignorance which surrounded me on all sides were dispersed. My heart received the rays of civilization & my intellect expanded & took a wider range. My superstition vanished & I began to reason correctly

> "Curious to view the Kings of ancient days,"
> "The mighty dead that live in endless praise."[8]

I draw to a close. Solemn & gloomy is the thought that all the Indian nations who once occupied America are nearly Gone! Powerful in War & Sage in peace, the Chiefs now sleep with their heroic deeds silent, in the bosom of the Earth! It was not their destiny to become great. Their Council fires could not be united into one, as the Seat of a great empire. It was for strangers to effect this, and necessity now compels the last Remnants to look to it for protection. It is true we Govern ourselves, but yet we live in fear. We are urged by these strangers to make room for their settlements & go farther west. Our National existence is suspended on the faith & honor of the U. States, alone. Their convenience may cut this asunder, & with a little faint struggle we may cease to be. All Nations have had their rises & their falls. This has been the case with us. Within the orbit the U. States move the States & within these we move in a little circle, dependent on the great center. We may live in this way fifty years & then we shall by Natural causes merge in & mingle with the U. States. Cherokee blood, if not destroyed, will wind its courses in beings of fair complexions, who will read that their ancestors became civilized under the frowns of misfortunes & causes of their enemies.

[8]From Alexander Pope's translation of *The Odyssey*.

Christian Missions

The United States employed an agent to reside among the Cherokees and teach them the skills of "civilization," but much of the responsibility for "civilizing" the Cherokees fell to missionaries. The U.S. government subsidized Christian missions because the scope of mission work extended far beyond preaching the gospel: Missionaries set up schools and model farms and even served as U.S. postmasters. The peaceful partnership of missionaries and government agents, however, had a relatively brief tenure. As you will discover in later documents, some missionaries ultimately embraced the Cherokee cause and joined the struggle against land cession and removal.

Indian missions became a major concern of most Protestant denominations in the early nineteenth century as a wave of revivalism swept the United States and reinvigorated Protestantism. Those who responded to revivalism emphasized the salvation experience that resulted from God's grace and the convert's faith, and they became known as evangelicals. Many evangelical Christians believed that they could transform the world into a Christian commonwealth. They embarked on a crusade to convert non-Christians, particularly those who had never heard the gospel, around the globe. Native Americans became a special mission target for many groups, in part because they were closer to home and cheaper to reach.

Although the first permanent missionaries to the Cherokees, the Moravians, were not particularly touched by the revivalism of the period, the Presbyterians (American Board), Baptists, and Methodists who followed them were. While conversion to Christianity was the foremost concern of the missionaries, they linked Christianization to "civilization." With financial assistance from the U.S. government and encouragement from Cherokee leaders, they established mission stations, which served several purposes. First, the buildings housed the families of missionaries, and the surrounding fields fed them. Second, they provided a site for services and a base from which itinerant ministers could travel. Third, they afforded educational opportunities for Cherokee children who boarded at the mission stations or attended day schools. And finally, the mission family, farm, houses, and lifestyle—even to the point of table manners and dress—served as a model for Cherokees to emulate.

Although most Cherokees found an English education desirable, few had much use for Christianity. By 1835, only about 10 percent of the population belonged to a church. While this is roughly the same percentage of church membership as in the white South, the failure to join a church meant radically different things for Cherokees and whites. Most white southerners subscribed to some version of Christian doctrine even if they did not place their names on church rolls. Most unchurched Cherokees, however, were not nominal Christians: They rejected basic Christian doctrines, preferring their own religious beliefs.

While missionaries were often dismayed at the difficulty of converting adult Cherokees, they held out great hope for the children. To convert children, missionaries believed that they must also "civilize" them. Children had to be separated from their own culture, and frequently this meant separating them from their parents. Children often lived in dormitories or with mission families, and the missionaries carefully supervised their activities. Children learned not only to read and write, add and subtract, and sing and pray, but also how to live like Anglo-Americans. The missionaries taught boys to farm and girls to keep house, and they tried to teach all Cherokee children that "civilization" was preferable to traditional Cherokee culture.

One of the most successful schools, Brainerd Mission, was located at present-day Chattanooga. The American Board of Commissioners for Foreign Missions established Brainerd in 1817. Headquartered in Boston, the American Board was an interdenominational organization composed largely of Presbyterians and Congregationalists. Brainerd Mission depended heavily on contributions from white Christians for its operating expenses, and the missionaries encouraged the students to correspond with benefactors. Several letters written by young Cherokee women at Brainerd survive. They are part of the John Howard Payne papers at the Newberry Library. The letters reprinted here, along with others, have been edited by Theda Perdue and published in the Journal of Cherokee Studies *4 (1979): 4–9.*

In reading these letters, pay particular attention to the daily regimen, the response of the students to Christianity, and the students' attitudes toward nonmission Cherokees. How did students spend their days? What success were missionaries having in converting them? What was the relationship of these students to their families? How did the students regard Cherokee culture?

For more information about Indian missions in general, see Robert F. Berkhofer Jr., Salvation and the Savage: An Analysis of Protestant Missions and American Indian Response *(Lexington: University of Kentucky Press, 1965). William G. McLoughlin's studies of missionaries to the Cherokees are well worth reading:* Cherokees and Missionaries, 1789–1839 *(New Haven, Conn.: Yale University Press, 1984), and* The Cherokees and Christianity, 1794–1870: Essays on Acculturation and Cultural Persistence, *ed. Walter H. Conser Jr. (Athens: University of Georgia Press, 1994). Also see Robert Sparks Walker,* Torchlights to the Cherokees: Brainerd Mission *(New York: The Macmillan Company, 1931). Important sources include Joyce B. Phillips and Paul Gary Phillips,* The Brainerd Journal: A Mission to the Cherokees, 1817–1823 *(Lincoln: University of Nebraska Press, 1998); Rowena McClinton, ed.,*

The Moravian Springplace Mission to the Cherokees, *2 vols. (Lincoln: University of Nebraska Press, 2007); and C. Daniel Crews and Richard W. Starbuck, eds.,* Records of the Moravians Among the Cherokees, *5 vols. (Tahlequah, Okla.: The Cherokee National Press, 2010–2014).*

4

ELIZABETH TAYLOR

Letter to Miss Abigail Parker
June 26, 1828

As we often write to our teachers friends she has requested me to write a few lines to you. She wishes me to give you an idea of the customs of the Cherokees, as she has not time. I am willing to do it because I think when christians know how much we need the means of knowledge, they will feel the importance of sending missionaries. —The unenlightened parts of this nation assemble for dances around a fire. The one that goes before sings; a woman follows after having herself adorned with shells which make a rattling noise when she dances. The others follow after, dancing around a fire in a ring, and keep up their amusements all night. In like manner the men dance the night before their ball plays. The next day when the two parties are collected at the ball ground, the side that excels receives horses, kegs, guns, clothing &c. from the other party. When they wish it to rain, they will send for a conjurer who will throw a black cat into the water, hang up a serpent &c.

Likewise when they are sick, they get one to blow and throw cold water on them and mutter over talk that cannot be understood. . . . Every year when the green corn, beans, &c are large enough to eat, they dance one night and torture themselves by scratching their bodies with snakes teeth before they will eat any.

When they go to each others houses, they will stand and peep through the fence, till some one goes out and inquires what they wish. Their living consist chiefly of pounded corn, sweet potatoes, and some meat. Their dishes are made by themselves of clay, first hardned by burning, then glazed by the smoke of meal bran; eight or ten will often get around one of these on the ground, with one wooden spoon, one will take a mouthful and pass it on to the other.

Many about this station are more civilized. Some come to meeting and appear as well as white people. Others dress in the Indian manner with maucassins for shoes, and handerchiefs round their heads for turbans.

But I have learned that the white people were once as degraded as this people; and that encourages me to think that this nation will soon become enlightened.

5

SALLY M. REECE

Letter to Reverend Daniel Campbell
July 25, 1828

First I will tell you about the Cherokees. I think they improve. They have a printing press, and print a paper which is called the Cherokee Phoenix. They come to meeting on Sabbath days. They wear clothes which they made themselves.

Some though rude, have shoes and stockings. They keep horses, cows, sheep, and swine. Some have oxen. They cultivate fields. They have yet a great many bad customs but I hope all these things will soon be done away. They have thought more about the Saviour lately. I hope this nation will soon become civilized and enlightened. There are 25 girls in school at Brainerd. Mary Ann and Electa goes to school. They are not Cherokees. They are the daughters of Mr. John Vail, one of the missionaries.

I am now under the care of Mr and Mrs Fernal. They live down to the creek when Mr Dean used to live. Catharine my sister stays there too. My parents comes here to meeting on Sabbaths. My Father thinks is a great privelege to learn to read. He can read but Mother cannot. I should like to tell you how my Father's house is situated. It is surrounded with hills. There are trees in the door yard. I take pleasure in sitting under them to attend to my work. And [there is] an orchard back of the house. A road [runs] between the house and field where the travellers pass. They very often call to stay all night. I help Mother to take care of my Brothers and sisters. My Father works in the field. Mother spins and weaves.

6

NANCY REECE

Letter to Reverend Fayette Shepherd
December 25, 1828

I will tell you something of our happy school, so you may know how we shall feel if we should be separated from each other, and from our teachers and other missionaries. Miss. Ames has twenty-nine scholars one more is expected which will make the school full. The studies in our school are Reading, Spelling, Writing, Geography, Arithmetick, two have begun to study grammar. Eight new scholars have entered school this year. Part of them cannot talk english, and Miss Ames is obliged to have me interpret for her. I have a class of the younger children in Sabbath school. I ask those children who do not talk english if they understood the sermon that was read and they say they do not but when my father comes on sabbath days he talks in Cherokee. Then they tell me a great [deal] he says. I try to tell them how to spend the sabbath day and tell them where they will go when they die if they are not good. When they first enter school if they are asked these questions, they often say they don't know.

When school hours are over, the girls attend to domestick concerns and learn to make their own clothes and the clothes of the boys so they can do such work when they go home, to assist their parents. They can then take care of their houses and their brothers and sisters and perhaps can learn their parents something that they do not understand.

We have a society on Saturdays we work two hours to try to get some money for the heathen who have not had missionaries as we have. Miss Sargent generally comes in and reads to us.

The boys chop wood and in the summer help about the farm and some that have left school are learning the black smiths trade. Miss Sargent goes into their school room evenings to teach them, and sometimes they set with her in her room. . . .

I do not think that all the people are friends to the Cherokees. Miss. Ames has been reading a part of the Presid. message. Perhaps he does not like the laws of the Indian tribes for he says "This state of things requires that a remedy should be provided." Miss. Ames has been talking to the scholars and she felt bad and told them that they must get a good education soon as they can, so they can teach if they should be removed where they could not attend school and says that we must try to get religion for all the instructors ought to be christians. It seems that it will be a trying season to us and the missionaries if we should be separated from them, but she says if God suffers it to be, we ought not to complain, for it will be for the best. I have been talking to the children about it and one says "if the white people want more land let them go back to the country they came from," another says "they have got more land than they use, what do they want to get ours for?"

Quantifying Cherokee "Civilization"

In 1835, the U.S. government commissioned an accounting of Cherokees east of the Mississippi, their property and productivity, and their skills. The Census of 1835 contains the names of 2,637 Cherokees whom the census taker assumed to be the heads of households. The census recorded a total of 16,542 Cherokees, of whom 77.27 percent were "full blooded," 201 intermarried whites, and 1,592 African American slaves. These people cultivated 44,000 acres and raised well over half a million bushels of corn. Slightly more than half the households in the Nation had at least one reader of Cherokee, while 18 percent had an English reader. The census entries printed here represent only a tiny fraction of the total number of Cherokees listed on the census.

These particular people lived in the Long Savannah community of what became Hamilton County, Tennessee. This community was typical of most in the Cherokee Nation. Wealthy Cherokees lived near much poorer Cherokees, and people with no Anglo-American ancestry lived in the same community with intermarried whites and their descendants. Long Savannah had slaveholders and nonslaveholders, farmers and craftsmen, people who were literate and those who were not. In other words, however economically stratified and culturally divided the Cherokees had become by 1835, few Cherokees lived in isolation from those who had different values and lifestyles. As you examine the census, pay particular attention to the relationship between variables—for example, slave ownership and agricultural productivity.

A census can give us more than merely statistical information. For example, the designer of this census thought that enumerating the amount of wheat a person grew was important, yet in the Long Savannah community only Adam Seabolt produced any. Everyone else who farmed grew corn. The remainder of the census follows this pattern. Why was wheat production included as a variable, and what can this tell us about the Cherokees? Missionaries and other promoters of "civilization" encouraged the Cherokees to grow wheat because they considered wheat, the grain most widely grown in Europe, to be a "civilized" crop and far preferable to corn, a grain native to the Americas. The vast majority of Cherokees, including descendants of Europeans, and intermarried whites clearly disagreed. The cultivation of wheat by a few people like Seabolt, however, may reflect their acceptance of Anglo-American culture and "civilization."

The census also reveals Anglo-American attitudes about the proper role of women. Five members of the Long Savannah community listed as heads of household were women — Lizy Ratley, Ootiah, Peggy Waters, Polly Gritts, and Betsey Goins. Ootiah and Polly Gritts had three acres each under cultivation while Betsey Goins cultivated twenty-two acres. They produced sixty, fifteen, and one hundred bushels of corn, respectively. Nevertheless, the census suggests that no farmers over eighteen, a separate category on the census, lived in their households. The households of Ootiah and Polly Gritts included males under eighteen, but only another adult woman lived with Betsey Goins. Could it be that the census taker simply refused to acknowledge women farmers? Perhaps so. Anglo-Americans in the nineteenth century believed that a woman's proper place was in the home, not the field. The "cult of domesticity," as this belief is sometimes called, may have blinded the census taker to the traditional Cherokee practice of women farming. The farmers counted on the census are men; the weavers and spinners are women.

Several categories need further explanation.

"Houses" is ambiguous. Presumably this includes not only dwellings but barns, stables, springhouses, smokehouses, corncribs, and other structures.

The Long Savannah community had no mill, but Alex Drumgolds operated one on nearby Candy's Creek, and so people may have had lumber sawn or grain ground there. Or they may have used logs for construction and pounded their corn with traditional mortars and pestles.

Ferrymen such as William Reese were essential to commerce because streams and rivers cut across the Cherokee Nation and no bridges existed. The National Council awarded contracts to operate ferries.

"Mechanics" were skilled craftsmen such as blacksmiths, carpenters, or manufacturers of saltpeter, an essential component of gunpowder.

The "Readers in Cherokee" were literate in the Sequoyah syllabary. Most of these people learned to read from parents or neighbors because mission schools taught English rather than Cherokee. While the emphasis on English literacy reflected a cultural bias, missionaries had little choice: few of them ever mastered the Cherokee language.

The fact that looms are far larger, harder to transport, and more expensive than spinning wheels may explain why "Spinners" outnumbered "Weavers."

The terms "Half-Breed" and "Quadroon" (one-quarter Cherokee) are now considered pejorative as well as ethnocentric. According to the matrilineal Cherokees, whether a person was a Cherokee or not depended on the status of the mother. If your mother was a Cherokee, you were Cherokee regardless of who your father was. Therefore, no one could be "half" Cherokee. In 1825, the Cherokee Council passed a law extending Cherokee citizenship to the children of white mothers and Cherokee fathers, but more than likely, many traditional Cherokees continued to regard these children as white. The concern with blood quantum reflected racist nineteenth-century thinking that linked ancestry and culture. However outdated such views may be, these distinctions remain a part of U.S.-Indian policy today.

The categories on the census appear in a somewhat different (and more logical) order than in the original. The editors have omitted several columns that appear on the original because there were no "Mixed Catawbas," "Mixed Spaniards," "Mixed Negroes," "Reservees" (Indians given personal reservations by the U.S. government), or "Descendants of Reservees" in this community.

Like many Cherokee records, the Census of 1835 is housed at the National Archives in Washington, D.C., and is available on microfilm and online. If you would like further information, see William G. McLoughlin and Walter H. Conser Jr., "The Cherokees in Transition: A Statistical Analysis of the Federal Cherokee Census of 1835," Journal of American History 64 (1977): 678–703.

7

The Census of 1835

HEAD OF HOUSEHOLD	1. William Reese	2. Roman Nose Johnson	3. Turnover	4. Lizy Ratley	5. Ooyeakee	6. Dry	7. Wallace Ratley	8. Deer Coming	9. Ootiah	10. Johnson	11. Whirlwind	12. The Hunter	13. Moses
READERS IN CHEROKEE		2	5	1	1	1			1			3	
READERS IN ENGLISH	1					1							
SPINNERS		4	1	3	4	4	1	1	2	1	1	3	1
WEAVERS		1		1	3	4	1	1				1	
MECHANICS OVER 18 YEARS			1		1	1		2		1	1		
FARMERS OVER 18 YEARS		1	2		4	2	1	2		1	4	3	1
FULL BLOODED		1	2		6	8		5	7	2	8	10	5
QUADROONS													
HALF-BREEDS	1	6	4	8	6		4						
WHITES CONNECTED BY MARRIAGE													
TOTAL SLAVES													
FEMALE SLAVES													
MALE SLAVES													
TOTAL CHEROKEE	1	7	6	8	12	8	4	5	7	2	8	11	5
FEMALES OVER 18		1	1	1	3	3	1	2	1			3	2
FEMALES UNDER 18		2	5	3	2	1			2		3	4	
MALES OVER 18	1	2		2	4	2	2		1	1	4	3	1
MALES UNDER 18		2		2	3	2	1	2	3		1	1	2

14. The Dog	3	2		1	3				3	2	1		1	1	1
15. Peggy Waters	3	1	1	2	6				6	1		2	2	2	
16. The Doctor	2	1	1	1	5				5	1		1	1	1	
17. William Read	1		1	1	1	2	1	1		1	1		1	1	1
18. Pigeon		3	2	4	10	1			10	3	1		2	2	
19. Big Jim		1	1	1	2		1		1	1	1	1	1		
20. Path Killer	2		2		4				4	2	1				
21. Polly Gritts	1		2	1	4	1		3		1	1	2	1		
22. John Blythe	1	1	2		4	1	1		4		1	1	1	2	
23. James Vann	2	1	1		4	5	9	14	1	4		1	2	1	2
24. Adam Seabolt		2	2	5		1		1	4	1	1		2	3	2	1
25. Betsey Goins		2	2	2		1			1	1		1	2	1	
26. Wilson Nivens	3	3	1	7		1	1		7	1		1	1	2	1	3

United States. National Archives. Census of 1835. Reference group 75.

HEAD OF HOUSEHOLD	FARMS	ACRES IN CULTIVATION	HOUSES	MILLS	FERRY BOATS	BUSHELS WHEAT RAISED	BUSHELS CORN RAISED	BUSHELS WHEAT SOLD	BUSHELS CORN SOLD	FOR HOW MUCH	BUSHELS CORN BOUGHT	FOR HOW MUCH
1. William Reese	1	30	3		1		200					
2. Roman Nose Johnson	1	30	8				300		150	75.00	47	23.00
3. Turnover	1	5	1								30	15.00
4. Lizy Ratley	1		1								50	25.00
5. Ooyeakee	1	50	5				400				10	5.00
6. Dry	1	40	6				450					
7. Wallace Ratley	1	15	2				200					
8. Deer Coming	1	15	4				300					
9. Ootiah	1	3	2				60					
10. Johnson	1	4	1									
11. Whirlwind	1	20	2				200		100	50.00		
12. The Hunter	1	6	1				50		10	5.00		

13. Moses	1	10	4		30				
14. The Dog	1	30	3		450	150	37.50		
15. Peggy Waters	1	40	5						
16. The Doctor	1	6	1		30				
17. William Read	1	20	4					100	33.00
18. Pigeon	1	3	2		15			8	4.00
19. Big Jim	1	11	4		200				
20. Path Killer	1	35	7		300	100	50.00		
21. Polly Gritts	1	3	1		15				
22. John Blythe	1	55	5	15	500	150	75.00	20	6.00
23. James Vann	1	100	20		2000	20	9.00		
24. Adam Seabolt	1	35	8	20	350	200	85.00		
25. Betsey Goins	1	22	5		100			20	7.50
26. Wilson Nivens	1	100	14		1000	100	50.00		

United States. National Archives. Census of 1835. Reference group 75.

Who Is an Indian?

"Race" is a complex concept rooted in culture rather than biology. Human beings are fundamentally the same biologically but have superficial physical differences, such as height, skin and hair color, and shape of eyes. Those differences take on increased significance when societies attach behavioral meanings to them in order to achieve certain goals. Differences are exaggerated and even fabricated. Europeans, for example, linked the dark skin that seemed to separate them from Africans to the learned behavior of slaves. To justify using an enslaved workforce, they imagined that the obsequiousness, indolence, and inclination to run away that they attributed to slaves were as indelible as skin color. Similarly, because white southerners wanted Indian land, they attributed a number of characteristics to Indians. In particular, they linked savagery and the violent, unsettled, untutored, heathen existence it implied to physical characteristics, such as skin color, that revealed ancestry. An Indian with light skin presumably had European ancestry and, therefore, was less likely to exhibit savage behavior than an Indian with darker skin. Even people sympathetic to Indians tended to believe that the capacity of Indians to change was limited. They expressed surprise when someone who "looked" like an Indian behaved in "civilized" ways or when someone who did not "look" like an Indian pursued a course contrary to that of whites.

Major Ridge and John Ross, who are pictured here, provide an example. Charles Bird King painted their portraits, along with those of more than a hundred other Indian leaders, at the behest of Thomas L. McKenney, who served as U.S. Superintendent of the Indian Trade (1816–1822) and U.S. Superintendent of Indian Affairs (1824–1830). The purpose of the paintings was to make "a permanent record of the features of the more prominent Indians of the various tribes." McKenney and a coauthor, James Hall, published the portraits along with biographical sketches of their subjects. McKenney was sympathetic to American Indians and supported the "civilization" program, but he also was an advocate of removal.

One thing McKenney and Hall noted in their biographies of Ridge and Ross was their ancestry. Ridge's father was a "full blooded Cherokee" and his mother was "a respectable Cherokee woman of half-blood." Ridge was mostly Indian, that is, and was expected to act accordingly. As a child, Ridge learned to hunt, at twelve he underwent the ritual that prepared him spiritually to be a warrior, and at fourteen he joined his first war party. By the 1820s, however, he had embraced the "civilization" pro-gram: "Major Ridge is one of the very few individuals who, after being reared in the habit of the savage, have embraced the employments and comforts of civilised life. In youth we have seen him pursuing the chase for a livelihood, and seeking the war path with all the Indian avidity for bloodshed and plunder. Gradually withdrawing from these occupations, he became a cultivator of the soil, a legislator, and a civil magistrate; exhibiting in each capacity a discretion and dignity of character, worthy of a better education."

John Ross had different ancestry that was largely Scottish. His only Cherokee ancestor was his grandmother, "a half-blood Cherokee." As a child, Ross cried so bitterly when his grandmother dressed him in a suit that she permitted him to don a "calico frock [hunting shirt] and leg-gings, and moccasins." But being an Indian was a childhood diversion, distinct from the entrepreneur that Ross's father intended his son to be. After time with a private tutor, Ross left the Cherokee Nation for school in Kingston, Tennessee, and a job clerking in a store there. When he returned, he worked for the U.S. agent distributing goods to Cherokees and then enlisted in the army to fight against the Creeks. After the war, public service took up much of Ross's time.

Ross and Ridge served the Cherokee Nation together, Ross as president of the National Committee and Ridge as speaker of the Council. Although they parted ways over the issue of removal, many Cherokees regarded both as patriots. Both had many admirers among whites as well. How do these portraits convey similar status? Note also that there are significant differences in the portraits. In what ways (and there is more than one) does the painter racialize these portraits? According to racialist thinking, who might have been expected to support removal, which many whites advocated and most Cherokees opposed? Who actually signed the removal treaty? Did "race" play a role?

For the entire work from which I have quoted, see Thomas L. McKenney and James Hall, The Indian Tribes of North America, *3 vols. (Philadel-phia: E. C. Biddle and D. Rice and J. G. Clark, 1836, 1842–1844). If you are interested in reading further on race, you can begin with the Ameri-can Anthropological Association's Statement on "Race" (May 17, 1998) and Robert L. Anemone, "Race as a Cultural Construction,"* Race and Human Diversity: A Bicultural Approach *(Upper Saddle River, N.J.: Pren-tice Hall, 2011), 163–83. To learn more about southern Indians with European ancestry, see Theda Perdue,* "Mixed Blood" Indians: Racial Con-struction in the Early South *(Athens: University of Georgia Press, 2003).*

8

Major Ridge (1771?–1839)

National Anthropological Archives, Smithsonian Institution (43, 113-B).

9

John Ross (1790–1866)

National Anthropological Archives, Smithsonian Institution (988-B).

The Cherokee Constitution of 1827

At its October meeting in 1826, the Cherokee National Council voted to call a convention for the following year to adopt a constitution. Cherokee government had evolved over the previous fifty years from a national council loosely composed of representatives from traditional towns to a formal government with three branches. In separate pieces of legislation over several years, the council created eight electoral districts that sent representatives to its annual meetings, an executive committee that managed national affairs in the interim, and a supreme court that heard appeals from district courts. By 1826, council members apparently thought the time had come to establish a comprehensive governing document. They scheduled an election for delegates, in which only Cherokee men could vote, for May 1827.

Not all Cherokees were happy with the decision to draft a constitution. Cherokee government had become less inclusive, and Cherokee leaders increasingly came from an elite group of wealthy men who promoted acculturation, both in the laws they passed and the ways they lived. The government in which they disproportionately served had limited political participation by moving most decision making from clans and local councils to the National Council. The National Council enacted a number of laws that promoted social change, including reordering descent from matrilineal to patrilineal, abolishing clan vengeance, and discouraging polygamy. With a combination of repressive tactics and conciliatory overtures, the Council ultimately thwarted the opposition, and plans proceeded for the constitutional convention.

The men who convened at New Echota, the Cherokee capital in the summer of 1827, were no more representative of the Cherokees than the U.S. founding fathers were of Americans. They were more likely to be wealthy, literate, and Christian than the average Cherokee. But like other Cherokees, they were patriots who sought to protect the Nation, its lands, and its sovereignty. They fully understood the symbolism of July 4, the opening day of the convention, and the document they produced exhibited substantial familiarity with not only the U.S. Constitution but the constitutions of the states as well. Like those documents, the Cherokee constitution reflected a profound belief in republicanism, a representative form of government in which those eligible to vote elected individuals to make laws to protect their life, liberty, and property.

As you read the Cherokee constitution, note the differences as well as the similarities between it and the U.S. Constitution. In the Cherokee constitution, Article 1 defined the boundaries of the Cherokee Nation while Article 2 confirmed the common ownership of Cherokee land. Article 4 provided for three counselors elected by the legislature to advise the principal chief and assistant principal chief, a feature that did not separate the executive and legislative branches to quite the extent that the U.S. Constitution did. What other overlaps between branches do you see? Article 6 is the equivalent of the Bill of Rights, but it does not include all the same provisions as the U.S. Constitution. What differences can you identify? What does the Cherokee constitution have to say about women and African Americans? What is the relationship between church and state as set forth in this document?

The constitution caused an uproar in Georgia. The governor regarded it as an attempt to legitimize the sovereignty of the Cherokee Nation, which lay largely within the state's boundaries, and demanded that President John Quincy Adams denounce it. Adams insisted that, as an instrument of local government, the constitution did not change the Cherokee Nation's relationship with the federal government and refused to act. The constitution provided Georgia with an additional legal argument to bolster its case, grounded in racism and greed, for Cherokee removal. But it also gave the Cherokees an institutional structure for resisting removal and an elected government to lead the fight. In August 1828, Cherokee voters went to the polls to choose their representatives under the new constitution. For the office of principal chief, they chose John Ross, the man who would guide them through the removal crisis, the rebuilding in the West, and the Civil War.

The Cherokees published several editions of their constitution and laws. This one appeared in Laws of the Cherokee Nation: Adopted by the Council at Various Periods. Printed for the Benefit of the Nation *(Tahlequah, Cherokee Nation: Cherokee Advocate Printing Office, 1852). The editors have corrected obvious typographical errors. The publisher Scholarly Resources has reprinted the laws and constitutions of many tribes, including the Cherokees; these documents are, therefore, available in many libraries. For more information on the political history of the Cherokees in this period, see William G. McLoughlin,* Cherokee Renascence in the New Republic *(Princeton, N.J.: Princeton University Press, 1986), and Theda Perdue, "The Conflict Within: The Cherokee Power Structure and Removal,"* Georgia Historical Quarterly *73 (1989): 467–91. For an explanation of why the Cherokees were so successful in establishing a centralized republican government, see Duane Champagne,* Social Order and Political Change: Constitutional Governments among the Cherokee, the Choctaw, the Chickasaw, and the Creek *(Palo Alto, Calif.: Stanford University Press, 1992).*

10

Constitution of the Cherokee Nation

Formed by a Convention of Delegates from the Several Districts, at New Echota

July 1827

We, the representatives of the people of the Cherokee Nation, in Convention assembled, in order to establish justice, ensure tranquility, promote our common welfare, and secure to ourselves and our posterity the blessings of liberty; acknowledging with humility and gratitude the goodness of the sovereign Ruler of the Universe, in offering us an opportunity so favorable to the design, and imploring His aid and direction in its accomplishment, do ordain and establish this Constitution for the Government of the Cherokee Nation.

ARTICLE 1.—Sec. 1.—The boundaries of this Nation, embracing the lands solemnly guarantied and reserved forever to the Cherokee Nation by the Treaties concluded with the United States, are as follows, and shall forever hereafter remain unalterably the same, to wit:

Beginning on the north bank of Tennessee river at the upper part of the Chickasaw old field, thence along the main channel of said river, including all the islands therein, to the mouth of the Hiwassee river, thence up the main channel of said river, including islands, to the first hill which closes in on said river about two miles above Hiwassee Old Town, thence along the ridge which divides the waters of the Hiwassee and Little Tillico, to the Tennessee river at Tallassee, thence along the main channel, including islands, to the junction of the Cowee and Nanteyalee, thence along the ridge in the fork of said river, to the top of the blue ridge, thence along the blue ridge to the Unicoy Turnpike road, thence by a straight line to the main source of the Chestatee, thence along its main channel, including islands, to the Chattahoochy, and thence down the same to the Creek boundary at Buzzard Roost, thence along the boundary line which separates this and the Creek Nation, to a point on the Coosa river opposite the mouth of Wills creek, thence down along the south bank of the same to a point opposite to Fort Strother, thence up the river to the mouth of Wills creek, thence up along the east bank of said creek to the west branch thereof, and up the same to its source, and thence along the ridge which separates the Tombeccee and Tennessee waters to a point on the top of said ridge, thence due north to Camp Coffee on Tennessee river, which is opposite the Chickasaw Island, thence to the place of beginning.

Sec. 2.—The sovereignty and Jurisdiction of this Government shall extend over the country within the boundaries above described, and the lands therein are, and shall remain, the common property of the Nation; but the improvements made thereon, and in the possession of the citizens of the Nation, are the exclusive and indefeasible property of the citizens respectively who made; or may rightfully be in possession of them; *Provided*, that the citizens of the Nation, possessing exclusive and indefeasible right to their respective improvements, as expressed in this article, shall possess no right nor power to dispose of their improvements in any manner whatever to the United States, individual states, nor individual citizens thereof; and that whenever any such citizen or citizens shall remove with their effects out of the limits of this Nation, and become citizens of any other Government, all their rights and privileges as citizens of this Nation shall cease; *Provided nevertheless*, That the Legislature shall have power to re-admit by law to all the rights of citizenship, any such person or persons, who may at any time desire to return to the Nation on their memorializing the General Council for such readmission. *Moreover*, the Legislature shall have power to adopt such laws and regulations, as its wisdom may deem expedient and proper, to prevent the citizens from monopolizing improvements with the view of speculation.

ARTICLE II.—Sec. 1—The power of this Government shall be divided into three distinct departments; the Legislative, the Executive, and Judicial.

Sec. 2.—No person or persons belonging to one of these Departments shall exercise any of the powers properly belonging to either of the others, except in the cases hereinafter expressly directed or permitted.

ARTICLE III.—Sec. 1.—The Legislative power shall be vested in two distinct branches; a Committee and a Council, each to have a negative on the other, and both to be styled the General Council of the Cherokee Nation; and the style of their acts and laws shall be.

"RESOLVED by the Committee and Council, in General Council convened."

Sec. 2.—The Cherokee Nation, as laid off into eight Districts, shall so remain.

Sec. 3.—The Committee shall consist of two members from each District, and the Council shall consist of three members from each District, to be chosen by the qualified electors of their respective Districts, for two years; and the elections to be held in every District on the first Monday in August for the year 1828, and every succeeding two years thereafter; and the General Council shall be held once a year, to be convened on the second Monday of October in each year, at New Echota.

Sec. 4.—No person shall be eligible to a seat in the General Council, but a free Cherokee male citizen, who shall have attained to the age of twenty-five years. The descendants of Cherokee men by all free women, except the African race, whose parents may have been living together as man and wife, according to the customs and laws of this Nation, shall be entitled to all the rights and privileges of this Nation, as well as the posterity of Cherokee women by all free men. No person who is of negro or mulatto parentage, either by the father or mother side, shall be eligible to hold any office of profit, honor or trust under this Government.

Sec. 5.—The electors and members of the General Council shall, in all cases except those of treason, felony, or breach of the peace, be privileged from arrest during their attendance at election, and at the General Council, and in going to, and returning from the same.

Sec. 6.—In all elections by the people, the electors shall vote *viva voce*. Electors for members to the General Council for 1828, shall be held at the places of holding the several courts, and at the other two precincts in each District which are designated by the law under which the members of this Convention were elected; and the District Judges shall superintend the elections within the precincts of their respective Court Houses, and the Marshals and Sheriffs shall superintend within the precincts which may be assigned them by the Circuit Judges of their respective Districts, together with one other person, who shall be appointed by the Circuit Judges for each precinct within their respective Districts; and the Circuit Judges shall also appoint a clerk to each precinct.—The superintendents and clerks shall, on the Wednesday morning succeeding the election, assemble at their respective Court Houses and proceed to examine and ascertain the true state of the polls, and shall issue to each member, duly elected, a certificate, and also make an official return of the state of the polls of election to the Principal Chief, and it shall be the duty of the Sheriffs to deliver the same to the Executive; *Provided nevertheless*, The General Council shall have power after the election of 1828, to regulate by law the precincts and superintendents and clerks of elections in the several Districts.

Sec. 7.—All free male citizens, (excepting negroes and descendants of white and Indian men by negro women who may have been set free,) who shall have attained to the age of eighteen years, shall be equally entitled to vote at all public elections.

Sec. 8.—Each house of the General Council shall judge of the qualifications and returns of its own members.

Sec. 9.—Each house of the General Council may determine the rules of its proceedings, punish a member for disorderly behaviour, and with the concurrence of two thirds, expel a member; but not a second time for the same cause.

Sec. 10.—Each house of the General Council, when assembled shall choose its own officers; a majority of each house shall constitute a quorum to do business, but a smaller number may adjourn from day to day and compel the attendance of absent members in such manner and under such penalty as each house may prescribe.

Sec. 11.—The members of the Committee shall each receive from the public Treasury a compensation for their services which shall be two dollars and fifty cents per day during their attendance at the General Council; and the members of the Council shall each receive two dollars per day for their services during their attendance at the General Council:—*Provided,* That the same may be increased or deminished by law, but no alteration shall take effect during the period of service of the members of the General Council, by whom such alteration shall have been made.

Sec. 12.—The General Council shall regulate by law, by whom and in what manner, writs of elections shall be issued to fill the vacancies which may happen in either branch thereof.

Sec. 13.—Each member of the General Council before he takes his seat, shall take the following oath or affirmation, to wit:

"I, A. B., do solemnly swear, (or affirm, as the case may be,) that I have not obtained my election by bribery, treats or any undue and unlawful means used by myself, or others by my desire or approbation, for that purpose; that I consider myself constitutionally qualified as a member of _____ and that, on all questions and measures which may come before me, I will so give my vote, and so conduct myself, as may in my judgment, appear most conducive to the interest and prosperity of this Nation; and that I will bear true faith and allegiance to the same; and to the utmost of my ability and power observe, conform to, support and defend the Constitution thereof."

Sec. 14.—No person who may be convicted of felony before any court of this Nation, shall be eligible to any office or appointment of honor, profit or trust within this nation.

Sec. 15.—The General Council shall have power to make all laws and regulations, which they shall deem necessary and proper for the good of the Nation, which shall not be contrary to this Constitution.

Sec. 16.—It shall be the duty of the General Council to pass such laws as may be necessary and proper, to decide differences by arbitrators to be appointed by the parties, who may choose that summary mode of adjustment.

Sec. 17.—No power of suspending the laws of this Nation shall be exercised, unless by the Legislature or its authority.

Sec. 18.—No retrospective law, nor any law impairing the obligations of contracts shall be passed.

Sec. 19.—The legislature shall have power to make laws for laying and collecting taxes, for the purpose of raising a revenue.

Sec. 20.—All bills making appropriations shall originate in the Committee, but the Council may propose amendments or reject the same.

Sec. 21.—All other bills may originate in either house, subject to the concurrence or rejection of the other.

Sec. 22.—All acknowledged Treaties shall be the Supreme law of the land.

Sec. 23.—The General Council shall have the sole power of deciding on the construction of all Treaty stipulations.

Sec. 24.—The Council shall have the sole power of impeaching.

Sec. 25.—All impeachments shall be tried by the Committee;—when sitting for that purpose, the members shall be upon oath or affirmation; and no person shall be convicted without the concurrence of two thirds of the members present.

Sec. 26.—The Principal Chief, assistant principal Chief, and all civil officers, under this Nation, shall be liable to impeachment for any misdemeanor in office; but Judgment, in such cases, shall not extend further than removal from office, and disqualification to hold any office of honor, trust or profit, under this Nation. The party whether convicted or acquitted, shall, nevertheless, be liable to indictment, trial, judgment and punishment, according to law.

ARTICLE IV.—Sec. 1. The Supreme Executive Power of this Nation shall be vested in a Principal Chief, who shall be chosen by the General Council, and shall hold his office four years; to be elected as follows,—The General Council by a joint vote, shall, at their second annual session, after the rising of this Convention, and at every fourth annual session thereafter, on the second day after the Houses shall be organized, and competent to proceed to business, elect a Principal Chief.

Sec. 2.—No person, except a natural born citizen, shall be eligible to the office of Principal Chief; neither shall any person be eligible to that office, who shall not have attained to the age of thirty-five years.

Sec. 3.—There shall also be chosen at the same time, by the General Council, in the same manner for four years, an assistant Principal Chief.

Sec. 4.—In case of the removal of the Principal Chief from office, or of his death, resignation, or inability to discharge the powers and duties of the said office, the same shall devolve on the assistant principal Chief, until the inability be removed, or the vacancy filled by the General Council.

Sec. 5.—The General Council may, by law, provide for the case of removal, death, resignation or inability of both the Principal and assistant Principal Chiefs, declaring what officer shall then act as Principal Chief, until the disability be removed, or a Principal Chief shall be elected.

Sec. 6.—The Principal Chief, shall, at stated times, receive for their services,—a compensation—which shall neither be increased nor diminished during the period for which they shall have been elected; and they shall not receive, within that period, any other emolument[1] from the Cherokee Nation, or any other government.

Sec. 7.—Before the Principal Chief enters on the execution of his office, he shall take the following oath, or affirmation; "I do solemnly swear (or affirm) that I will faithfully execute the office of Principal Chief of the Cherokee Nation, and will, to the best of my ability, preserve, protect and defend, the Constitution of the Cherokee Nation."

Sec. 8.—He may, on extraordinary occasions, convene the General Council at the Seat of Government.

Sec. 9.—He shall from time to time give to the General Council information of the State of the Government, and recommend to their consideration such measures as he may think expedient.

Sec. 10.—He shall take care that the laws be faithfully executed.

Sec. 11.—It shall be his duty to visit the different districts, at least once in two years, to inform himself of the general condition of the Country.

Sec. 12.—The assistant Principal Chief shall, by virtue of his office, aid and advise the Principal Chief in the Administration of the Government, at all times during his continuance in office.

Sec. 13.—Vacancies that may happen in offices, the appointment of which is vested in the General Council, shall be filled by the Principal Chief, during the recess of the General Council, by granting Commissions which shall expire at the end of the next Session.

Sec. 14.—Every Bill which shall have passed both Houses of the General Council, shall before it becomes a law, be presented to the Principal Chief of the Cherokee Nation. If he approve, he shall sign it, but if not, he shall return it, with his objections, to that house in which it shall

[1] Profit.

have originated, who shall enter the objections at large on their journals, and proceed to reconsider it. If, after such reconsideration, two thirds of that House shall agree to pass the bill, it shall be sent, together with the objections, to the other house, by which it shall likewise be reconsidered, and if appoved by two thirds of that house, it shall become a law. If any bill shall not be returned by the Prin'l Chief within five days (Sundays excepted) after it shall have been presented to him, the same shall be a law, in like manner as if he had signed it; unless the General Council by their adjournment prevent its return, in which case it shall be a law, unless sent back within three days after their next meeting.

Sec. 15.—Members of the General Council and all officers Executive and Judicial, shall be bound by oath to support the Constitution of this Nation, and to perform the duties of their respective offices with fidelity.

Sec. 16.—In case of disagreement between the two houses with respect to the time of adjournment, the Principal Chief shall have power to adjourn the General Council to such a time as he thinks proper, *provided*, it be not to a period beyond the next Constitutional meeting of the same.

Sec. 17.—The Principal Chief shall, during the sitting of the General Council, attend to the Seat of Government.

Sec. 18.—There shall be a Council to consist of three men to be appointed by the joint vote of both Houses, to advise the Principal Chief in the Executive part of the Government, whom the Principal Chief shall have full power, at his discretion, to assemble; and he, together with the assistant Principal Chief, and the Counsellors, or a majority of them may, from time to time, hold and keep a Council for ordering and directing the affairs of the Nation according to law.

Sec. 19.—The members of the Council shall be chosen for the term of one year.

Sec. 20.—The resolutions and advice of the Council shall be recorded in a register and signed by the members agreeing thereto, which may be called for by either house of the General Council; and any counsellor may enter his dissent to the resolution of the majority.

Sec. 21.—The Treasurer of the Cherokee Nation shall be chosen by the joint vote of both Houses of the General Council for the term of two years.

Sec. 22.—The Treasurer shall, before entering on the duties of his office, give bond to the Nation with sureties to the satisfaction of the Legislature, for the faithful discharge of his trust.

Sec. 23.—No money shall be drawn from the Treasury, but by warrant from the Principal Chief, and in consequence of appropriations made by law.

Sec. 25.—It shall be the duty of the Treasurer to receive all public monies, and to make a regular statement and account of the receipts and expenditures of all public monies at the annual Session of the General Council.

ARTICLE V.—Sec. 1.—The Judicial Powers shall be vested in a Supreme Court, and such Circuit and Inferior Courts, as the General Council may, from time to time ordain and establish.

Sec. 2.—The Supreme Court shall consist of three Judges, any two of whom shall be a quorum.

Sec. 3.—The Judges of each shall hold their Commissions four years, but any of them may be removed from office on the address of two thirds of each house of the General Council to the Principal Chief, for that purpose.

Sec. 4.—The Judges of the Supreme and Circuit Courts shall, at stated times, receive a compensation, which shall not be diminished during their continuance in office, but they shall receive no fees or perquisites of office, nor hold any other office of profit or any other power.

Sec. 5.—No person shall be appointed a Judge of any of the Courts before he shall have attained to the age of thirty years, nor shall any person continue to execute the duties of any of the said offices after he shall have attained to the age of seventy years.

Sec. 6.—The Judges of the Supreme and Circuit Courts shall be appointed by a joint vote of both houses of the General Council.

Sec. 7.—There shall be appointed in each District, under the Legislative authority, as many Justices of the Peace as it may be deemed the public good requires, whose powers, duties and duration in office, shall be clearly designated.

Sec. 8.—The Judges of the Supreme Court and Circuit Courts shall have complete criminal Jurisdiction in such cases and in such manner as may be pointed out by law.

Sec. 9.—Each Court shall choose its own Clerks for the term of four years; but such Clerks shall not continue in office unless their qualifications shall be adjudged and approved of by the Judges of the Supreme Court, and they shall be removable for breach of good behaviour at any time, by the Judges of their respective courts.

Sec. 10.—No Judge shall sit on trial of any cause, where the parties shall be connected with him by affinity or consanguinity, except by consent of the parties. In case all the Judges of the Supreme Court shall be interested in the event of any cause, or related to all, or either of the parties, the Legislature may provide by law for the selection of three men of good character and knowledge, for the determination thereof, who shall be specially commissioned by the Principal Chief for the case.

Sec. 11.—All writs and other process shall run in the name of the Cherokee Nation, and bear test, and be signed by the respective clerks.

Sec. 12.—Indictments shall conclude, "against the peace and dignity of the Cherokee Nation."

Sec. 13.—The Supreme Court shall hold its session annually at the seat of Government to be convened on the second Monday of October in each year.

Sec. 14.—In all criminal prosecutions, the accused shall have the right of being heard, of demanding the nature and cause of the accusation against him, of meeting the witnesses face to face, of having compulsory process for obtaining witnesses in his favor: and in prosecutions by indictment or information, a speedy public trial by an impartial jury of the vicinage;[2] nor shall he be compelled to give evidence against himself.

Sec. 15.—The people shall be secure in their persons, houses, papers and possessions, from unreasonable seizures and searches, and no warrant to search any place or to seize any person or things, shall be issued without describing them as nearly as may be, nor without good cause, supported by oath, or affirmation. All prisoners shall be bailable by sufficient securities unless for capital offences, where the proof is evident, or presumption great.

ARTICLE VI.—Sec. 1.—Whereas, the ministers of the Gospel are, by their profession, dedicated to the service of God and the care of souls, and ought not to be diverted from the great duty of their function, therefore, no minister of the gospel, or public preacher of any religious persuasion, whilst he continues in the exercise of his pastoral functions, shall be eligible to the office of Principal Chief, or a seat in either house of the General Council.

Sec. 2.—No person who denies the being of a God, or a future state of rewards and punishment, shall hold any office in the civil department of this Nation.

Sec. 3.—The free exercise of religious worship, and serving God without distinction shall forever be allowed within this Nation; *Provided*, That this liberty of conscience shall not be so construed as to excuse acts of licentiousness, or justify practices inconsistent with the peace or safety of this Nation.

Sec. 4.—Whenever the General Council shall determine the expediency of appointing delegates or other public Agents for the purpose of transacting business with the Government of the United States; the power to recommend, and by the advice and consent of the Commit-

[2]Neighborhood.

tee, shall appoint and commission such delegates or public agents accordingly, and all matters of interest touching the rights of the citizens of this Nation, which may require the attention of the government of the United States, the Principal Chief shall keep up a friendly correspondence with that Government, through the medium of its proper officers.

Sec. 5.—All commissions shall be in the name and by the authority of the Cherokee Nation, and be sealed with the seal of the Nation, and signed by the Principal Chief.

The Principal Chief shall make use of his private seal until a National seal shall be provided.

Sec. 6.—A Sheriff shall be elected in each District by the qualified electors thereof, who shall hold his office for the term of two years, unless sooner removed. Should a vacancy occur subsequent to an election, it shall be filled by the Principal Chief as in other cases, and the person so appointed shall continue in office until the next general election, when such vacancy shall be filled by the qualified electors, and the Sheriff then elected shall continue in office for two years.

Sec. 7.—There shall be a Marshal appointed by a joint vote of both houses of the General Council, for the term of four years, whose compensation and duties shall be regulated by law, and whose jurisdiction shall extend over the Cherokee Nation.

Sec. 8.—No person shall for the same offence be twice put in jeopardy of life or limb, nor shall any person's property be taken or applied to public use without his consent; *Provided*, That nothing in this clause shall be so construed as to impair the right and power of the General Council to lay and collect taxes. All courts shall be open, and every person for an injury done him in his property, person or reputation, shall have remedy by due course of law.

Sec. 9.—The right of trial by jury shall remain inviolate.

Sec. 10.—Religion, morality and knowledge being necessary to good government, the preservation of liberty, and the happiness of mankind, schools and the means of education shall forever be encouraged in this Nation.

Sec. 11.—The appointment of all officers, not otherwise directed by this Constitution, shall be vested in the Legislature.

Sec. 12.—All laws in force in this Nation at the passing of this Constitution, shall so continue until altered or repealed by the Legislature, except where they are temporary, in which case they shall expire at the times respectively limited for their duration; if not continued by an act of the Legislature.

Sec. 13. — The General Council may at any time propose such amendments to this Constitution as two thirds of each house shall deem expedient; and the Principal Chief shall issue a proclamation, directing all the civil officers of the several Districts to promulgate the same as extensively as possible within their respective Districts, at least nine months previous to the next general election, and if at the first session of the General Council after such general election, two thirds of each house shall, by yeas and nays, ratify such proposed amendments they shall be valid to all intents and purposes, as parts of this Constitution; *Provided*, That such proposed amendments shall be read on three several days, in each house as well when the same are proposed as when they are ratified.

Done in Convention at New Echota, this twenty-sixth day of July, in the year of our Lord, one thousand eight hundred and twenty-seven; In testimony whereof, we have each of us, hereunto subscribed our names.

JNO. ROSS, *Pres't Con.*

Jno. Baldrige, Geo. Lowrey, Jno. Brown, Edward Gunter, John Martin, Joseph Vann, Kelechulee, Lewis Ross, Thomas Foreman, Hair Conrad, James Daniel, John Duncan, Joseph Vann, Thomas Petitt, John Beamer, Ooclenota, Wm. Boling, John Timson, Situwakee, Richard Walker,

A. McCOY, *Sec'y to Con.*

2

Georgia Policy

One of the most important keys to understanding the policy of Indian removal and its relation to the Cherokees lies in Georgia. No state agitated more consistently or aggressively for the expulsion of Native people from within its borders, no legislature sent more resolutions to Congress, no congressional delegation worked harder, and no press devoted more space to its support. The reasons for this are complicated, confused, and to a degree unclear.

The immediate history of Georgia's campaign for Indian removal begins in 1802 when the state and the federal government negotiated an arrangement by which Georgia surrendered its colonial charter claims to the region that now includes the states of Alabama and Mississippi. In compensation, Georgia received $1.25 million in cash, congressional agreement to assume responsibility for the legal and financial tangles left by the Yazoo grants of the 1790s, and a pledge that the U.S. government would acquire all the lands held by Indians within the new boundaries of the state as rapidly as it could be done "peaceably" and on "reasonable terms." Embarrassed by the Yazoo frauds in which land companies had bribed the state legislature to award them vast tracts of land at a fraction of its value, the Georgia legislature immediately devised a lottery system for disposing of the land it expected to receive from the Cherokees and Creeks. Giving the land away by lottery removed it as a financial temptation to corrupt another legislature, thwarted speculation schemes, and created in the populace a universal enthusiasm for acquiring land from the Indians that no politician could ignore.

But because the United States recognized Indian tribes as sovereign nations and conducted relations with them by treaties, the government could not force tribal leaders to sell their land. And tribal leaders often refused to sell. Thus, as Georgia politicians became quick to point out, Indians remained within the borders claimed by Georgia, and the United States was failing to abide by the 1802 compact. Indeed, in each treaty, the United States guaranteed to the Creeks and Cherokees the lands they refused to sell, causing some Georgians to charge that the government was worse than irresponsible, it was actually impeding the fulfillment of the compact. By the mid-1820s, the political leaders of Georgia had created an atmosphere so volatile and threatening that the Creeks, who owned several million acres of rich agricultural land in the Chattahoochee River valley, were forced to sell out and relocate. Some moved west, but most settled on the unsold portion of their nation that lay within the borders of Alabama.

Georgia politicians learned an important lesson from their role in the expulsion of the Creeks. Intense, single-minded pressure exerted on both the Indians and the federal government could force a treaty of cession and removal. Georgia's governor in the mid-1820s, George M. Troup, had orchestrated a campaign of bluster, threat, and audacity that had both acquired the rich Creek lands for the people of his state and enhanced his popularity with the voters.

The strides the Cherokees had made toward "civilization" convinced many Georgians that the Indians were strengthening their hold on their land. Well-educated Cherokees not only were more difficult to trick or intimidate, they also shared many of the economic and social values of the Georgians. They understood the productive worth of their land, and the marketplace held many of the same financial attractions. Furthermore, it was hard for Georgians to point to Cherokee planters and businessmen and claim that God intended that "uncivilized" Indian hunters should give way to "civilized" white farmers.

The federal program to "civilize" the Cherokees made many Georgians nervous, but the Cherokees' 1827 constitution outraged them. In Article 1, the constitution defined the borders of the Nation and in legal language proclaimed its sovereignty, that is, its exclusive right to govern people within those borders. In the body of the document, the framers drew up a government that was hardly distinguishable in form from that of Georgia. Ratified and in operation by mid-1828, the constitutional government was certainly not the work of people who were contemplating removal anytime soon.

The Cherokee Nation included the northwest corner of the territory claimed by Georgia and thereby blocked Georgia's access to the Tennessee River, which emptied into the Ohio and the Mississippi. Economic development theorists argued that Georgia's full potential could never be reached until it could tap that vast inland market. Wilson Lumpkin, a prominent Georgia politician, congressman, and governor between 1831 and 1835, participated in a survey of the region and became an enthusiast for the construction of railroads to link the agricultural heartland of the state to the river network of the north and west. But nothing could be done as long as the Cherokees remained in place.

The economic and social order of Georgia, as well as of the other states of the South, rested on plantation agriculture and slavery and was rationalized by a racial conceptualization of society that defined whites as free and blacks as unfree. The debate over slavery expansion that led to the Missouri Compromise in 1821 had revealed deep divisions over slavery in the nation, and southerners were searching for ways to defend the institution and their way of life. Fearful that Congress might fall under the control of antislavery forces, they saw two immediate ways to block such a threat. One was to replace Indians with free white voters who would increase southern representation in the House of Representatives. Race-conscious southerners would not consider Indians, as people of color, eligible for citizenship and voting rights no matter how "civilized" they might be. The other solution was to embrace the principle of state sovereignty based on a strict interpretation of the Constitution. This step offered a host of possibilities; in the case of Indian removal the states could challenge federal claims to exclusive authority in Indian relations, extend state civil and criminal jurisdiction into Indian country, outlaw tribal governments, and confiscate tribal land. In these and other ways, a state could use its legal institutions to make life for Indians so miserable that they would gladly sell their lands and flee to the West. A state could justify such action by claiming its sovereignty over all the people and land within its boundaries even though those boundaries included Indian land.

All of these ideas and forces came together in Georgia by the late 1820s and were directed with full force against the Cherokees. Claiming sovereign jurisdiction over the Cherokee Nation, the Georgia legislature passed a series of laws beginning in 1828 that subjected the Cherokees to Georgia law. In 1829, soon after the inauguration of Andrew Jackson, the Cherokee National Council petitioned the president for protection from Georgia's legislation. Citing provisions in the treaties and the Trade and Intercourse Acts, the council called on Jackson to fulfill his obligation to protect them from encroachment and interference in their domestic affairs. Jackson responded by defending Georgia's claim to sovereignty and offered the Cherokees two choices: Accept Georgia law or move west. The Supreme Court ruled against Georgia in *Worcester v. Georgia* in 1832, but Georgia refused to acknowledge the ruling and Jackson clearly had no intention of forcing the state to comply. Georgians accelerated their campaign and forced many Cherokees from their homes. The president's unwillingness to intercede left the Cherokees at Georgia's mercy.

While the Jackson administration was eager to remove all of the southern tribes, the articles and essays, memorials and petitions, debates and discussions focused on the Cherokees. They had become the object of everyone's attention, in part because Georgia made them so.

Georgia's Indian policy in the 1820s and 1830s has not been the subject of systematic inquiry in recent years, but material useful for further study does exist. Ulrich B. Phillips, "Georgia and States Rights: A Study of the Political History of Georgia from the Revolution to the Civil War, with Particular Regard to Federal Relations," *Annual Report of the American Historical Association for 1901* (Washington, D.C.: Government Printing Office, 1902, 2: 3–224; reprint edited by Louis Filler, Yellow Springs, Ohio: Antioch Press, 1968), is an important place to begin, although the interpretation is unabashedly pro-Georgia. Michael D. Green, *Politics of Indian Removal: Creek Government and Society in Crisis* (Lincoln: University of Nebraska Press, 1982), discusses the controversy between Georgia and the Creeks that set the stage for Cherokee removal. Mary Young, "The Exercise of Sovereignty in Cherokee Georgia," *Journal of the Early Republic* 10 (1990): 43–63, considers Georgia policy relative to the Cherokees. For a good legal history, see Tim Alan Garrison, *The Legal Ideology of Removal: The Southern Judiciary and the Sovereignty of Native American Nations* (Athens: University of Georgia Press, 2002).

The Georgia Laws

Resolutions of the Georgia General Assembly in 1826 and 1827 asserted that by virtue of its colonial charter, Georgia held complete sovereign dominion over all the land and people within its borders, including the Cherokees. This claim implied that under the Constitution, the federal government had no authority in dealing with the Cherokees except to regulate commerce. Therefore, if the United States failed to acquire the Cherokee Nation for Georgia under the Compact of 1802, the state was within its sovereign rights simply to take it.

These resolutions were not empty threats. Rather, they were designed to put both the United States and the Cherokee Nation on notice that Georgia would not relax its demand that the Cherokees be expelled. The legislature did not threaten to invade the Cherokee Nation with an armed force, but it clearly believed that it had the right to do so if it wished. For example, the assembly resolved in 1827 "that the Indians are tenants at [Georgia's] will, and [Georgia] may at any time she pleases, determine that tenancy by taking possession of the premises." But because the state was anxious not to "disturb the public tranquility . . . she will not attempt to improve her rights by violence until all other means of redress fail." Rather, the assembly instructed the governor to send copies of its report and resolutions to both the president and the Cherokees so that all would understand that "if the United States will not redeem her pledged honor; and if the Indians continue to turn a deaf ear to the voice of reason and friendship, we now solemnly warn them of the consequences. The lands in question belong to Georgia. She must and she will have them."

The next year, 1828, produced no treaty of cession and in December the General Assembly enacted legislation to attach the Cherokee Nation to five Georgia counties, thus putting the Cherokees and their lands under state jurisdiction. To go into effect June 1, 1830, this extension law also disallowed all laws enacted by the Cherokee National Council. Everyone understood the political and constitutional implications of Georgia's action and eagerly awaited the president's reaction. President Jackson recognized Georgia's claim to sovereignty over the Cherokee Nation and upheld the extension law. But Georgia still had no treaty of cession. Frustrated by continued delay and encouraged by Jackson's supportive Indian policy, the assembly enacted a second, more comprehensive jurisdiction law. In part, this act responded to legislation passed by the Cherokee Council in 1829 that revoked the Cherokee citizenship of people who enrolled to emigrate west.

In December 1830, the General Assembly further tightened the grip on the Cherokee Nation by making it illegal for the Cherokee government to meet and act. To go into effect February 1, 1831, this law also prescribed that whites living in the Cherokee Nation take an oath of allegiance to Georgia and established the Georgia Guard, a special police force empowered to enforce Georgia law within the Cherokee Nation. The acts printed here, along with the 1826 and 1827 resolutions and the 1828 law, come from Acts of the Georgia General Assembly, *published annually in Milledgeville, then the state capital.*

As you read these laws, remember that their purpose was to force the Cherokees to the treaty table by using the political power of the state to make life for the Cherokees so miserable that they would be happy to flee. How did these laws affect the Cherokee Nation's government? How did they challenge Cherokee sovereignty?

11

GEORGIA STATE ASSEMBLY

Laws Extending Jurisdiction over the Cherokees
December 19, 1829, and December 22, 1830

An act to add the Territory lying within the chartered limits of Georgia, and now in the occupancy of the Cherokee Indians, to the counties of Carroll, DeKalb, Gwinnett, Hall and Habersham, and to extend the laws of this State over the same, and to annul all laws and ordinances made by the Cherokee nation of Indians, and to provide for the compensation of officers serving legal process in said Territory, and to regulate the testimony of Indians, and to repeal the ninth section of the act of eighteen hundred and twenty-eight, upon this subject. . . .

Sec. 6. *And be it further enacted*, That all the laws both civil and criminal of this State be, and the same are hereby extended over said portions of territory respectively, and all persons whatever residing within the same, shall, after the first day of June next, be subject and liable to the operation of said laws, in the same manner as other citizens of this State or the citizens of said counties respectively, and all writs and processes whatever issued by the courts or officers of said courts, shall extend over, and operate on the portions of territory hereby added to the same respectively.

Sec. 7. *And be it further enacted*, That after the first day of June next, all laws, ordinances, orders and regulations of any kind whatever, made, passed, or enacted by the Cherokee Indians, either in general council or in any other way whatever, or by any authority whatever of said tribe, be, and the same are hereby declared to be null and void and of no effect, as if the same had never existed; and in all cases of indictment or civil suits, it shall not be lawful for the defendant to justify under any of said laws, ordinances, orders or regulations; nor shall the courts of this State permit the same to be given in evidence on the trial of any suit whatever.

Sec. 8. *And be it further enacted*, That it shall not be lawful for any person or body of persons by arbitrary power or by virtue of any pretended rule, ordinance, law or custom of said Cherokee nation, to prevent, by threats, menaces or other means, to endeavor to prevent any Indian of said nation residing within the chartered limits of this State, from enrolling as an emigrant or actually emigrating, or removing from said nation;

nor shall it be lawful for any person or body of persons by arbitrary power or by virtue of any pretended rule, ordinance, law or custom of said nation, to punish in any manner, or to molest either the person or property, or to abridge the rights or privileges of any Indian for enrolling his or her name as an emigrant or for emigrating, or intending to emigrate from said nation. . . .

Sec. 10. *And be it further enacted*, That it shall not be lawful for any person or body of persons, by arbitrary power, or under colour of any pretended rule, ordinance, law or custom of said nation to prevent, or offer to prevent, or deter any Indian, head man, chief or warrior of said nation residing within the chartered limits of this State, from selling or ceding to the U.States, for the use of Georgia the whole or any part of said territory, or to prevent or offer to prevent any Indian, head man, chief or warrior of said nation, residing as aforesaid, from meeting in council or treaty, any commissioner or commissioners on the part of the United States, for any purpose whatever. . . .

Sec. 15. *And be it further enacted*, That no Indian or descendant of any Indian residing within the Creek or Cherokee nations of Indians, shall be deemed a competent witness in any court of this State to which a white person may be a party, except such white person resides within the said nation.

An act to prevent the exercise of assumed and arbitrary power, by all persons under pretext of authority from the Cherokee Indians, and their laws, and to prevent white persons from residing within that part of the chartered limits of Georgia, occupied by the Cherokee Indians, and to provide a guard for the protection of the gold mines, and to enforce the laws of the State within the aforesaid territory.

Be it enacted by the Senate and House of Representatives of the State of Georgia, in General Assembly met, and it is hereby enacted by the authority of the same, That after the first day of February, eighteen hundred and thirty-one, it shall not be lawful for any person, or persons, under colour or pretence, of authority from said Cherokee tribe, or as head men, chiefs, or warriors of said tribe, to cause or procure by any means the assembling of any council, or other pretended Legislative body of the said Indians, or others living among them, for the purpose of legislating, (or for any other purpose whatever.) And persons offending against the provisions of this section, shall be guilty of a high misdemeanor, and subject to indictment therefor, and on conviction, shall be punished by confinement at hard labour in the Penitentiary for the space of four years.

Sec. 2. *And be it further enacted by the authority aforesaid,* That after the time aforesaid, it shall not be lawful for any person or persons under pretext of authority from the Cherokee tribe, or as representatives, chiefs, headmen, or warriors of said tribe, to meet, or assemble as a council, assembly, convention, or in any other capacity, for the purpose of making laws, orders, or regulations for said tribe. And all persons offending against the provisions of this section, shall be guilty of a high misdemeanor and subject to an indictment, and on conviction thereof, shall undergo an imprisonment in the Penitentiary at hard labour for the space of four years. . . .

Sec. 6. *And be it further enacted by the authority aforesaid,* That none of the provisions of this act, shall be so construed as to prevent said tribe, its headmen, chiefs, or other representatives from meeting any agent or commissioner, on the part of this State or the United States, for any purpose whatever.

Sec. 7. *And be it further enacted by the authority aforesaid,* That all white persons residing within the limits of the Cherokee nation, on the first day of March next, or at any time thereafter, without a license or permit, from his Excellency the Governor, or from such agent as his Excellency the Governor, shall authorise to grant such permit or license, and who shall not have taken the oath hereinafter required, shall be guilty of an high misdemeanor, and upon conviction thereof, shall be punished by confinement in the Penitentiary at hard labour, for a term not less than four years. . . .

Sec. 11. *And be it further enacted by the authority aforesaid,* That his Excellency the Governor, be, and he is hereby empowered, should he deem it necessary, either for the protection of the mines, or for the enforcement of the laws of force within the Cherokee nation, to raise and organise a guard, to be employed on foot, or mounted as occasion may require, which shall not consist of more than sixty persons, which guard shall be under the command of the commissioner or agent appointed by the Governor, to protect the mines, with power to dismiss from the service, any member of said guard, on paying the wages due for services rendered, for disorderly conduct, and make appointments to fill the vacancies occasioned by such dismissal.

Georgia and the Supreme Court

The Cherokees resisted Georgia's encroachment on their territory and sovereignty by challenging the state in the U.S. Supreme Court. The first case to reach the Supreme Court was Cherokee Nation v. Georgia *(1831). The Georgia Guard had arrested George Tassel, a Cherokee citizen, for murdering another Cherokee within the Cherokee Nation. A Georgia court tried and convicted Tassel of violating Georgia law, which the state had extended over Cherokee territory and citizens. The Cherokee Council contended that Georgia laws had no validity within the Cherokee Nation and sought an injunction against their enforcement. The Cherokees engaged as their lawyer William Wirt, who had served as attorney general in the presidential administrations of James Monroe and John Quincy Adams. Georgia did not wait for the case to run its course and executed Tassel. The Supreme Court ultimately declined to rule on the issue at stake—the enforcement of Georgia law within the Cherokee Nation—because the Cherokee Nation had no legal standing as a "foreign nation" before the Court. Chief Justice John Marshall referred to the Cherokees as a "domestic dependent nation," but he left the door open for a subsequent suit brought by a U.S. citizen who did have legal standing. Most missionaries in the Cherokee Nation were just such persons. They had come from states other than Georgia to the Cherokee Nation, and if the Cherokee argument prevailed, Georgia had no authority over them. The missionaries generally refused to take the oath of allegiance Georgia required of whites living among the Cherokees on the grounds that they were subject solely to Cherokee law while within the Nation. In July 1831 the Georgia Guard arrested eleven missionaries, including Samuel Austin Worcester and Elizur Butler of the American Board of Commissioners for Foreign Missions, and a Georgia court convicted them. Georgia finally released nine of the missionaries who either took the oath or agreed to leave the state. Worcester and Butler refused. Their cases reached the Supreme Court, which in March 1832 ruled specifically on* Worcester v. Georgia *and extended that decision to Butler as well. The Court, in a decision authored by Chief Justice Marshall, found in favor of Worcester and decreed that Georgia law was not valid within the Cherokee Nation, but Georgia refused to follow the Supreme Court's order to release the missionaries. In his annual message, delivered in November 1832, Georgia Governor Wilson Lumpkin denounced the "fallibility, infirmities, and errors of this Supreme tribunal." In December, the missionaries decided to end legal proceedings to force Georgia's compliance, and in January 1833 they appealed to the governor for a pardon, which he granted.*

Since World War II, the Worcester *case has become one of the cornerstones of federal Indian law. Having languished for nearly a century and a half, Marshall's opinion on the nature of Cherokee sovereignty in 1832 has provided the tribes with the arguments necessary to reaffirm their sovereign status today. The key element in the* Worcester *decision is the doctrine of retained sovereignty—the idea that a nation retains all those attributes of sovereignty it does not voluntarily surrender. In other words, according to Marshall, a tribe came to the treaty table with full sovereignty, surrendered certain specified attributes of sovereignty in exchange for particular benefits, and held on to all the sovereign rights and powers it did not agree to give up.*

The following selection is an excerpt from John Marshall's opinion in Worcester v. Georgia, *printed in Richard Peters, ed.,* Report of Cases Argued and Adjudged in the Supreme Court of the United States: January Term, 1832 *(Philadelphia, Pa.: Thomas, Cowperthwait & Co., 1845). The United States prints Supreme Court decisions in an ongoing government publication,* United States Reports. *Before 1875, Supreme Court decisions are cited by the name of the reporter, and each reporter has his own series of volumes beginning with volume 1. The first Cherokee case,* Cherokee Nation v. Georgia, *is cited as 5 Peters 1–80 (the fifth volume of the series edited by Richard Peters, pages 1 through 80).* Worcester v. Georgia *is cited as 6 Peters 515–97. You can find a good introduction to laws and court decisions regarding Native Americans in Charles F. Wilkinson,* American Indians, Time, and the Law *(New Haven, Conn.: Yale University Press, 1987). The best discussion of the Cherokee cases remains Joseph C. Burke, "The Cherokee Cases: A Study in Law, Politics, and Morality,"* Stanford Law Review *21 (February 1969): 500–31. A more recent study is Jill Norgren,* The Cherokee Cases: The Confrontation of Law and Politics *(New York: McGraw-Hill, 1996).*

What right, according to Marshall, did Native Americans have to their land? What rights did European discoverers have to Native land? What evidence does Marshall cite in support of Cherokee sovereignty?

12

U.S. SUPREME COURT

Worcester v. Georgia

March 1832

Mr. Chief Justice Marshall delivered the opinion of the Court.

This cause, in every point of view in which it can be placed, is of the deepest interest.

The defendant is a state, a member of the Union, which has exercised the powers of government over a people who deny its jurisdiction, and are under the protection of the United States.

The plaintiff is a citizen of the state of Vermont, condemned to hard labour for four years in the penitentiary of Georgia; under colour of an act which he alleges to be repugnant to the Constitution, laws, and treaties of the United States. . . .

The indictment charges the plaintiff in error, and others, being white persons, with the offence of "residing within the limits of the Cherokee nation without a license," and "without having taken the oath to support and defend the constitution and laws of the state of Georgia.". . .

The indictment and plea in this case draw in question, we think, the validity of the treaties made by the United States with Cherokee Indians; if not so, their construction is certainly drawn in question; and the decision has been, if not against their validity, "against the right, privilege, or exemption, specially set up and claimed under them." They also draw into question the validity of a statute of the state of Georgia, "on the ground of its being repugnant to the Constitution, treaties, and laws of the United States, and the decision is in favour of its validity.". . .

The Indian nations had always been considered as distinct, independent political communities, retaining their original natural rights, as the undisputed possessors of the soil, from time immemorial, with the single exception of that imposed by irresistible power, which excluded them from intercourse with any other European potentate than the first discoverer of the coast of the particular region claimed; and this was a restriction which those European potentates imposed on themselves, as well as on the Indians. The very term "nation," so generally applied to them, means "a people distinct from others." The Constitution, by declaring treaties already made, as well as those to be made, to be the supreme law of the land, has adopted and sanctioned the previous treaties with the Indian nations, and consequently admits their rank among those powers who are capable of making treaties. The words "treaty" and "nation" are words of our own language, selected in our diplomatic and legislative proceedings, by ourselves, having each a definite and well understood meaning. We have applied them to Indians, as we have applied them to the other nations of the earth. They are applied to all in the same sense.

Georgia, herself, has furnished conclusive evidence that her former opinions on this subject concurred with those entertained by her sister states, and by the government of the United States. Various acts of her legislature have been cited in the argument, including the contract of cession made in the year 1802, all tending to prove her acquiescence in the universal conviction that the Indian nations possessed a full right to the lands they occupied, until that right should be extinguished by the United States, with their consent: that their territory was separated from that of any state within whose chartered limits they might reside, by a boundary line, established by treaties: that, within their boundary, they possessed rights with which no state could interfere; and that the whole power of regulating the intercourse with them was vested in the United States. A review of these acts, on the part of Georgia, would occupy too much time, and is the less necessary, because they have been accurately detailed in the argument at the bar. Her new series of laws, manifesting her abandonment of these opinions, appears to have commenced in December, 1828. . . .

The Cherokee nation, then, is a distinct community, occupying its own territory, with boundaries accurately described, in which the laws of Georgia can have no force, and which the citizens of Georgia have no right to enter, but with the assent of the Cherokees themselves, or in conformity with treaties, and with the acts of Congress. The whole intercourse between the United States and this nation, is, by our Constitution and laws, vested in the government of the United States. . . .

The forcible seizure and abduction of the plaintiff in error, who was residing in the nation with its permission, and by authority of the President of the United States, is also a violation of the acts which authorize the chief magistrate to exercise this authority. . . .

It is the opinion of this Court that the judgment of the Superior Court for the county of Gwinnett, in the state of Georgia, condemning Samuel A. Worcester to hard labour in the penitentiary of the state of Georgia, for four years, was pronounced by that Court under colour of a law which is void, as being repugnant to the Constitution, treaties, and laws of the United States, and ought, therefore, to be reversed and annulled.

Dispossessing the Cherokees

While the state laws extending jurisdiction into the Cherokee Nation had as their general purpose to harass the Indians to the treaty table and out of the state, the body of legislation enacted by the Georgia General Assembly between 1828 and 1835 covered a range of specifics that applied both to government and to property. As the Cherokees clung to their homes, farms, and businesses despite the pressures to leave, politicians devised new schemes to turn up the heat. Many Georgians were reluctant to infringe on the rights of the Cherokees to their improved property, however, and so most improvements remained relatively secure for a while.

Many of the leading men in the Cherokee government were wealthy businessmen and planters. If they could be dispossessed, Georgians came to think, they would surely agree to removal. The problem of how to do so was solved when a federal agent realized that many of the wealthiest, including Principal Chief John Ross, had accepted reserves (individual or personal reservations) under the terms of the treaties of 1817 and 1819. The treaty provisions in question assumed that those who took reserves intended to leave the Cherokee Nation and either become citizens in the states where their reserves were located or sell them and move west. While no one in the Cherokee Nation believed that accepting these reserved tracts had denationalized Ross and the others, the politicians claimed that it had, which meant that they had no legal or moral right to the property they had subsequently acquired in the Nation. Acting on this argument, in December 1833 the Georgia General Assembly passed a law that authorized the confiscation of their improvements.

The legislators went after these people for two reasons. One was that the politicians could concoct an argument that permitted them to increase the pressure while blaming the victims for the action. The other was that the victims of this policy composed a substantial segment of the Cherokee economic and political elite. As the leadership class, they were the ones who led Cherokee resistance to removal. Furthermore, the pro-removal advocates in Georgia and Washington had claimed for years that this privileged elite blocked the desire of the mass of Cherokees, who really wanted to move west where they could continue their hunting lifestyle, in order to protect their property. If they were stripped of their possessions, the leaders supposedly would have no reason to block the removal of their people.

The following selection, part of a memorial submitted by the Cherokee Nation to Congress on June 22, 1836, is one of dozens of statements and petitions drafted by Cherokee leaders in a frantic hope that somehow they could convince the government to rescind its policy to remove them. Signed by John Ross, John Martin, James Brown, Joseph Vann, John Benge, Lewis Ross, Elijah Hicks, and Richard Fields, delegates sent to Washington by the National Council, this petition describes something of the hardship and terror Cherokees experienced daily as the laws of Georgia did their work. Men of wealth, these Cherokees represented the most "civilized" element of their Nation. But being "civilized" did not protect them from a policy rationalized as a measure to save helpless and "degenerate" Indians from the evils of American culture. Instead, their property targeted them for special attack. Mary Young's article "The Exercise of Sovereignty in Cherokee Georgia" (cited on p. 74) provides further information on this topic. Also see Sarah Hill, "To Overawe the Indians and Give Confidence to the Whites: Preparations for the Removal of the Cherokee Nation from Georgia," Georgia Historical Quarterly 95 (2011): 465–97.

The "Memorial of Protest of the Cherokee Nation" was printed in the United States Congressional Serial Set *as House Document 286, 24th Cong., 1st sess. The serial set is a varied collection of documents that Congress began to publish in 1817. Virtually anything that congressional committees or individual representatives and senators wished to include was printed, and historians have found it to be an enormously valuable source of primary records. It is one of the few places, for example, where documents produced by Native people, such as this memorial, can be found quite easily. This collection normally is housed in the government documents section of a library. Some libraries have the serial set in its original bound (book) form, while others have it on microfiche or provide access to a digitized format. For an index to material in the serial set relevant to Indians, see Stephen L. Johnson,* Guide to American Indian Documents in the Congressional Serials Set, 1817–1899 *(New York: Clearwater Publishing Company, 1977).*

13

Memorial of Protest of the Cherokee Nation
June 22, 1836

It is the expressed wish of the Government of the United States to remove the Cherokees to a place west of the Mississippi. That wish is said to be founded in humanity to the Indians. To make their situation more comfortable, and to preserve them as a distinct people. Let facts show how this *benevolent* design has been prosecuted, and how faithful to the spirit and letter has the promise of the President of the United States to the Cherokees been fulfilled—that *"those who remain may be assured of our patronage, our aid, and good neighborhood."* The delegation are not deceived by empty professions, and fear their race is to be destroyed by the mercenary policy of the present day, and their lands wrested from them by physical force; as proof, they will refer to the preamble of an act of the General Assembly of Georgia, in reference to the Cherokees, passed the 2d of December, 1835, where it is said, "from a knowledge of the Indian character, and from the present feelings of these Indians, it is confidently believed, that the right of occupancy of the lands in their possession should be withdrawn, *that it would be a strong inducement to them to treat with the General Government, and consent to a removal to the west*; and whereas, the present Legislature openly avow that their primary object in the measures intended to be pursued, *are founded on real humanity to these Indians*, and with a view, in a distant region, to perpetuate them with their old identity of character, *under the paternal care of the Government of the United States*; at the same time frankly disavowing *any selfish or sinister motives towards them in their present legislation."* This is the profession. Let us turn to the practice of *humanity*, to the Cherokees, by the State of Georgia. In violation of the treaties between the United States and the Cherokee nation, that State passed a law requiring all white men, residing in that part of the Cherokee country, in her limits, to take an oath of allegiance to the State of Georgia. For a violation of this law, some of the ministers of Christ, missionaries among the Cherokees, were tried, convicted, and sentenced to hard labor in the penitentiary. Their case may be seen by reference to the records of the Supreme Court of the United States.

Valuable gold mines were discovered upon Cherokee lands, within the chartered limits of Georgia, and the Cherokees commenced working them, and the Legislature of that State interfered by passing an act, making it penal for an Indian to dig for gold within Georgia, no doubt "*frankly disavowing any selfish or sinister motives towards them.*" Under this law many Cherokees were arrested, tried, imprisoned, and otherwise abused. Some were even shot in attempting to avoid an arrest; yet the Cherokee people used no violence, but humbly petitioned the Government of the United States for a fulfilment of treaty engagements, to protect them, which was not done, and the answer given that the United States could not interfere.

Georgia discovered she was not to be obstructed in carrying out her measures, "*founded on real humanity to these Indians,*" she passed an act directing the Indian country to be surveyed into districts. This excited some alarm, but the Cherokees were quieted with the assurance it would do no harm to survey the country. Another act was shortly after passed, to lay off the country into lots. As yet there was no authority to take possession, but it was not long before a law was made, authorizing a lottery for the lands laid off into lots. In this act the Indians were secured in possession of all the lots touched by their improvements, and the balance of the country allowed to be occupied by white men. This was a direct violation of the 5th article of the treaty of the 27th of February, 1819. The Cherokees made no resistance, still petitioned the United States for protection, and received the same answer that the President could not interpose.

After the country was parcelled out by lottery, a horde of speculators made their appearance, and purchased of the "fortunate drawers," lots touched by Indian improvements, at reduced prices, declaring it was uncertain when the Cherokees would surrender their rights, and that the lots were encumbered by their claims. The consequence of this speculation was that, at the next session of the Legislature, an act was passed limiting the Indian right of occupancy to the lot upon which he resided, and his actual improvements adjoining. Many of the Cherokees filed bills, and obtained injunctions against dispossession, and would have found relief in the courts of the country, if the judiciary had not been prostrated at the feet of legislative power. For the opinion of a judge, on this subject, there was an attempt to impeach him, then to limit his circuit to one county, and when all this failed, equity jurisdiction was taken from the courts, in Cherokee cases, by acts passed in the years 1833 and 1834.

The Cherokees were then left at the mercy of an interested agent. This agent, under the act of 1834, was the notorious William N. Bishop, the captain of the Georgia Guard, aid to the Governor, clerk of a court, postmaster, &c. and his mode of trying Indian rights is here submitted:

Murray county, Georgia, January 20, 1835

Mr. John Martin:

Sir: The legal representative of lots of land,

No. 95	25 district	2d section
86	25 "	2 "
93	25 "	2 "
89	25 "	2 "
57	25 "	2 "

has called on me, as States agent, to give him possession of the above described lots of land, and informs me that you are the occupant upon them. Under the laws of the State of Georgia, passed in the years 1833 and 1834, it is made my duty to comply with his request, you will, therefore, prepare, yourself to give entire possession of said premises, on or before the 20th day of February next, fail not under the penalty of the law.

Wm. N. Bishop, *States Agent*

Mr. Martin, a Cherokee, was a man of wealth, had an extensive farm; large fields of wheat growing; and was turned out of house and home, and compelled, in the month of February, to seek a new residence within the limits of Tennessee. Thus Mr. Bishop settled his rights according to the notice he had given.

The same summary process was used towards Mr. John Ross, the principal chief of the Cherokee nation. He was at Washington city, on the business of his nation. When he returned, he travelled till about 10 o'clock at night, to reach his family; rode up to the gate; saw a servant, believed to be his own; dismounted, ordered his horse taken; went in, and to his utter astonishment, found himself a stranger in his own house, his family having been, some days before, driven out to seek a new home. A thought then flitted across his mind, that he could not, under all the circumstances of his situation, reconcile it to himself to tarry all night under the roof of his own house as a stranger, the new host of that house being the tenant of that mercenary band of Georgia speculators, at whose instance his helpless family had been turned out and made homeless.

Upon reflecting, however, that "man is born unto trouble," Mr. Ross at once concluded to take up lodgings there for the night, and to console himself under the conviction of having met his afflictions and trials in a manner consistent with every principle of moral obligation towards himself and family, his country and his God. On the next morning he arose early, and went out into the yard, and saw some straggling herds of his cattle and sheep browsing about the place. His crop of corn undisposed of. In casting a look up into the wide spread branches of a majestic oak, standing within the enclosure of the garden, and which overshadows the spot where lies the remains of his dear babe, and most beloved and affectionate father, he there saw, perched upon its boughs, that flock of beautiful peafowls, once the matron's care and delight, but now left to destruction and never more to be seen. He ordered his horse, paid his bill, and departed in search of his family, after travelling amid heavy rains, had the happiness of overtaking them on the road, bound for some place of refuge within the limits of Tennessee. Thus has his houses, farm, public ferries and other property, been seized and wrested from him. . . .

Mr. Joseph Vann, also, a native Cherokee, was a man of great wealth, had about eight hundred acres of land in cultivation; had made extensive improvements, consisting, in part, of a brick house [see Document 37], costing about ten thousand dollars, mills, kitchens, negro houses, and other buildings. He had fine gardens, and extensive apple and peach orchards. His business was so extensive, he was compelled to employ an overseer and other agents. In the fall of 1833, he was called from home, but before leaving, made a conditional contract with a Mr. Howell, a white man, to oversee for him in the year 1834, to commence on the first of January of that year. He returned about the 28th or 29th of December 1833, and learning Georgia had prohibited any Cherokee from hiring a white man, told Mr. Howell he did not want his services. Yet Mr. Bishop, the State's agent, represented to the authorities of Georgia, that Mr. Vann had violated the laws of that State, by hiring a white man, had forfeited his right of occupancy, and that a grant ought to issue for his lands. There were conflicting claims under Georgia for his possessions. A Mr. Riley pretended a claim, and took possession of the upper part of the dwelling house, armed for battle. Mr. Bishop, the State's agent, and his party, came to take possession, and between them and Riley, a fight commenced and from twenty to fifty guns were fired in the house. While this was going on, Mr. Vann gathered his trembling wife and children into a room for safety. Riley could not be dislodged from his position up stairs, even after being wounded, and Bishop's party finally set fire to the house. Riley surrendered and the fire was extinguished.

Mr. Vann and his family were then driven out, unprepared, in the dead of winter, and snow upon the ground, through which they were compelled to wade, and to take shelter within the limits of Tennessee, in an open log cabin, upon a dirt floor, and Bishop put his brother Absalom in possession of Mr. Vann's house. This Mr. Vann is the same, who, when a boy, volunteered as a private soldier in the Cherokee regiment, in the service of the United States, in the Creek war, periled his life in crossing the river at the battle of the Horse Shoe. What has been his reward?

Hundreds of other cases might be added. In fact, near all the Cherokees in Georgia, who had improvements of any value, except the favorites of the United States agents, under one pretext or other, have been driven from their homes. . . .

The Cherokee delegation have thus considered it their duty to exhibit before your honorable body a brief view of the Cherokee case, by a short statement of facts. A detailed narrative would form a history too voluminous to be presented, in a memorial and protest. They have, therefore, contented themselves with a brief recital, and will add, that in reviewing the past, they have done it alone for the purpose of showing what glaring oppressions and sufferings the peaceful and unoffending Cherokees have been doomed to witness and endure. Also, to tell your honorable body, in sincerity, that owing to the intelligence of the Cherokee people, they have a correct knowledge of their own rights, and they well know the illegality of those oppressive measures which have been adopted for their expulsion, by State authority. Their devoted attachment to their native country has not been, nor ever can be, eradicated from their breast. This, together with the implicit confidence, they have been taught to cherish, in the *justice, good faith, and magnanimity of the United States*, also, their firm reliance on the generosity and friendship of the American people, have formed the anchor of their hope and upon which alone they have been induced and influenced to shape their peaceful and manly course, under some of the most trying circumstances any people ever have been called to witness and endure.

White Intruders

The Cherokees complained bitterly about white people moving onto their land, mining their gold, stealing their livestock, and evicting them from their houses and farms. The U.S. government sent soldiers to eject intruders and offer protection to the Cherokees, but the small force had little effect, except perhaps in the gold country where the soldiers were concentrated. While many intruders had no claim to Cherokee land, the status of others was less clear-cut. Confronted with Cherokee refusal to negotiate removal, Georgia began awarding Cherokee land to its citizens in an attempt to force the Cherokees out. Thousands of white settlers, who believed that they had legitimate title to land, moved into the Cherokee Nation.

Georgia had a well-established method for distributing public lands which, the state insisted, included Cherokee territory. Male residents of the state as well as widows and orphans registered for land lotteries, and certain categories of people, such as veterans, could register twice. Surveyors partitioned the land into plots and prepared plats, or maps, for each of these plots. Lottery officials pulled a name out of one hopper and a plat out of another, thereby matching winner and prize. The winner paid only a small filing fee for his or her acreage. Unlike the later federal homestead law that required people to settle the land they claimed, Georgia's lotteries placed no restrictions on the winners. Consequently, many winners did not move to their new land but sold either their chances or the property to another party, often through one of the real estate agents who appeared on the scene. Wealthy planters tended to buy up the best land and leave that of marginal quality to poorer folk. The market was speculative and volatile, and some participants lost a great deal of money.

One of those who lost money in the market that followed the lottery for Creek lands was John Brandon, husband of Zillah Haynie Brandon, whose memoir is printed here. The Creeks ceded their last land in Georgia to the federal government in 1827. The Compact of 1802 required that this land be surrendered to the state, and so Creek lands became available for distribution to the citizens of Georgia through the lottery. The lottery was so successful and popular that Georgia did not wait for the Cherokees to vacate their land before granting it to state citizens. Indeed, Georgia officials hoped a survey and lottery might hasten the Cherokees' departure. In 1830, the Georgia legislature provided for a survey of Cherokee lands in preparation for a lottery. In 1832, the same year that the Cherokees won their case before the U.S. Supreme Court, the lottery wheels began to turn in the state capital. Georgia law gave some protection to land that Cherokees actually occupied, but the process for halting eviction by a lottery winner became so complicated and expensive that few Cherokees could take advantage of it. As a result, lottery winners or those who bought land from winners swarmed into the Cherokee Nation.

John Brandon's early loss had not dampened his enthusiasm for the land lottery and the secondary market that followed. When he failed to draw a lot, he purchased another man's rights to Cherokee land. He had not met with much success in life, and land in the Cherokee Nation gave him yet another opportunity to start over. He did not hope alone. Many in Georgia sang the popular song:

All I want in this Creation
Is a pretty little wife and a big plantation
Way up north in the Cherokee Nation.

John and Zillah Brandon moved with their three small children to a Cherokee cabin in what Georgia had designated Cass (later renamed Bartow) County. When she was an elderly woman, Zillah Haynie Brandon remembered these trying times in a memoir spanning her life from 1823 to 1871, which she wrote for her children. Her original handwritten memoir is housed in the Alabama Department of Archives and History in Montgomery. In transcribing the memoir, the editors standardized punctuation and capitalization and added paragraph breaks to make the document more readable, but they retained the author's spelling.

Brandon's memoir gives us some insight into conditions in the Cherokee Nation in the period between the signing of the Treaty of New Echota (1835) and removal (1838). Many Cherokees lived in despair. Forced from their homes, uncertain of their future, they exhibited profound distrust far more than hostility. Many unfortunately turned to alcohol to ease their pain. The Cherokee Nation had strict laws against the sale of alcohol, but Georgia had suspended Cherokee law. The result was an invasion of whiskey traders who preyed on people's misery. Brandon graphically described the effects of the unregulated sale of liquor among a people who had given up hope.

Brandon's memoir also gives us a look at the mindset of the people who actually dispossessed the Cherokees. She was a religious woman, as indeed were many who forced Cherokee families from their homes. The wave of revival that swept the United States in the early nineteenth century heightened religious sensibilities, but religiosity took different forms. In many northern congregations, attention turned to social ills and the need for reform. This northern evangelicalism inspired the missionaries who came to the Cherokee Nation to establish churches and schools. In the South, evangelical religion tended to be focused inward on the individual or the family, not on the broader community. Brandon clearly was a devout woman, but her religious concerns did not extend beyond her own family except in the most general and impersonal way.

Brandon also had a very stereotypical view of Indians: All Indians, in her mind, were essentially the same. She refers twice, for example, to William McIntosh, who was executed in 1825 for illegally signing a Creek removal treaty, without realizing that McIntosh was a Creek, not a Cherokee. She also had difficulty separating the Cherokee farmers among whom she lived from the warriors about whom she had heard. She accepted the notion, common in the nineteenth century, that race determined character, and she regarded the Indian character as decidedly inferior. At the same time, the death of her Cherokee neighbor clearly moved her, particularly since she believed that she could have prevented it. She gave refuge in her home to a Cherokee woman whose husband threatened her. And she kept the gifts presented to her two young sons by neighboring Cherokees long after the little boys had become men. One of the important things that Brandon's memoir does is demonstrate that stereotypes of intruders are perhaps no more valid than stereotypes of Indians.

14

ZILLAH HAYNIE BRANDON

Memoir

1830–1838

After my marriage, your father thought proper to make an investment of all the money in his power in lands in Ga. He accordingly bought in Troop and Tolbert, from which he would, no doubt, have realized considerable profit if he had lived near them. But as it was, in view of so much land coming into market, after lying out of the use of his money for several years, he sold at a discount. He then engaged in the mercantile business in 1830, and at the close of two years, found his money all gone for goods and himself in possession of a pile of accounts and notes of no value, a low shaving[1] having been previously passed, denominated by some the poor man's law, which enabled many whose principle it was to keep from paying, to throw themselves upon its protection. So your father had to suspend business in the mercantile line.

Georgia, in the meantime, was pressing her claims for the lands ceded to her by the United States which was then in possession of the Cherokee Indians. But throwing herself upon her sovereignty, she gave it to her citizens by a state lottery. Many who had a right of claim acted like

---

[1] The practice of purchasing a note or debt for less than the amount actually owed.

Esau with his birthright.[2] They were offering to sell their chance, and your Father, thinking he might thereby mend his broken fortune, gave what money he could raise, and all the property he could spare, and by that means became interested in thirteen chances, none of which drew a single dollar's worth. As soon, however, as those lands came into market, he bought some in Cass County on the Etowah River. . . . and in December 1835, we moved to our lands in Cass. . . .

The weather was excessively cold, but on the sixth day after our departure, we arrived at the place of our destination [and] found a family of *Indians occupying our house*, which, by the way, was a very poor one without floor or loft. The Indians set about moving out, tho, with looks as magisterial as if they had been kings seated upon thrones in royal robes with a retinue about them, leaning upon the sceptres. They would not deign to look at us, much less speak to us. That, though, was characteristic of that people: they are seldom known to speak to strangers, that is, among the white people. As soon, however, as they were out, we spread carpets over the dirt floor and unloaded the wagons and went in with thankful hearts, yet at the same time suffering from unavoidable circumstances, something of which you that were with me felt, but I in its intense rigor. . . .

In sixty yards of our house there lived three families of Indians, who like their whole tribe, looked as if the very shafts of desolation was hanging around them, maddening that nation with more than death-like quiver, whose venom darts lay but half concealed in brave unconquered hearts. The tide of discord among their own nation wove a web which fettered those hands which were stained with the blood of one of their noblest chiefs, McIntosh, hung powerless while their tongues cursed the shrine upon which the white people knelt in prayer to God. And although there were many well informed and religious among that tribe, yet those nearest us were not of that class, especially the males. The women I believe were chaste and very civil, but their husbands would drink to drunkeness, and were very cruel when under the influence of the fire water. And though death had come among them and with an unpleasant brow, when on the very brink of the sable shore, warned them to drink no more, yet it seemed like a mirror held before them which lost its brilliancy in a few weeks, and then the poisoned cup was again placed to their lips.

---

[2] In Genesis 25:29–34, Esau, son of Isaac, is tricked into selling his birthright to his twin brother, Jacob.

The death referred to was an old man, the English of whose name was Peacock, being a nobleman among them. He was taken sick a month or two after we settled there. We had so far gained upon their good graces as to have a nod of their head when we spoke to them, or an occasional call when they wished to barter fish for salt or some other little matter relating to their necessities. A white woman in her degredation had some years before come in among them, and then had an Indian husband. She, after visiting the sick one day, called at my door and answered my enquiries in English. I came to the conclusion that the old man had pneumonia. I told her that I thought several things which I had in my power to supply them with would be of service to him. But she said I had better not offer to assist them, for if the means did not cure him, they would at once believe I had killed him. So as I was so much of a stranger, I did not offer them any assistance, but sincerely did I pity them when, from the want of knowledge, their sufferings were so much augmented.

A few weeks past, and one night at mid hour, we were awakened by the lamentable wail of many voices. We guessed the cause, which was proven to us as soon as daylight came, for they came in for plank to make a coffin, each family having their burying ground. Preparation was going on in sight of our house for the interment. However deep their lamentation, whenever any white person would go in, they would suppress it. But the white woman, before alluded to, told me of the closing scene, when the soul and body was about to be rent assunder. Then the heathen, the Indian, was honest with himself when his destiny was about to be sealed for eternity. He past in review over the past: the frightful rocks, the treacherous seas, the dangers he had dared. . . . Yea, with falling voice he spoke of that liberty the Great Spirit had given them, though the star that had given them light was growing dim, their glory as a nation lost. Their cause he thought was betrayed by two of their Chieftains, McIntosh and Ridge, which had sunk them into wretchedness, with a doom still darker gathering over them. But oh! One rapturious thought kindling out of woe. He said he "had lived a long time, had done much but had never done much harm." He said he "had sometimes drank too much but he had not been bad while drinking." I am thus particular in relating these things to show that truly that Spirit enlightenith every man that cometh into the world, had been doing its work even in the heart of the heathen. We stood with them as the grave closed over him without any ceremony or any burial service. Yet mentally we could say "Christ is the resurrection and the life, he that believeth in me shall never die." Glory, glory to God. How gladly we would have pointed these broken hearted people to the foot of the cross and the victory of Calvery for balm to heal their wounded spirits.

During the time they lived by us, we attended three of their burials. Their interments are pretty much like ours with the exception of the shallowness of their graves. They place in the coffin all that had been dearest to the departed, [and] all throw in a handful of dirt upon the lid. I had noticed the man about whom I have been telling you wearing a beautiful large merino shawl which I saw them pack in around his head and shoulders.

When they were sober, we were not afraid of them, but their drinking was so common a thing, a whiskey shop being kept by a white man in a quarter of a mile of us, that it was impossible to tell when we were safe. The contiguity of our habitations rendered our situation perilous. When they got drunk from home and their death like yells were heard by their families, they would look as if the cord of their souls were torn asunder. They would stand outside of their houses weeping and looking so doleful, that it would move any heart, not possessed of a demon, to pity. But presently the wives of those whose husbands were drunk would dress and take their babes and go and meet them with appearance of the soul of love and bravery, and from their husbands' savage eyes the truth was thus concealed and their secret well kept while they remained drunk. I have thought of all the women in the world, the wives of those drunken savages knew the least about a resting place.

I recollect once, while your father was on a journey, that a dozen or more Indian men came to the houses of those bordering on our yard, bringing whiskey with them, and it happened on a day when one of their wives were across the river, a quarter from her home. The first she knew of the troubles at home she heard the shrill panther-like screams which at once admonished her to get home in order, with pleasant alacrity, to attend to the nod of his lordship—her husband. But she was too late. He had taken the death drought till his anger was excited. Thinking it might endanger her life to go in, she and some lads came into our house. Her babe was snugly placed against her shoulders, cradled there by a large piece of canvas. I noticed that she did not take it down, and her distressed looks plainly told us her situation. One or two of the boys stood at the back of the chair on which she was seated, their hands placed upon it as if they intended to shield her. One of them in the meantime, watching to see if he could get a glimpse of some of the women from whom he could learn something relative to the wife's safety, after remaining a few minits, he walked boldly to the house. In a few minits, with a hurried step, he returned, telling her to fly. Quick as possible, they were again to the river, leaving us almost parilized with fear for ourselves. A resolve was instantly taken that I would take you children and go to a neighbor's for that night. So locking our door, we were off instantaneously. Having gotten about eighty steps from the house, we looked back and saw the enraged husband turn off from our door with his gun in his hand. Seeing us look at him, he gave one of his war whoops such as only rolls from the caverns of devils.

We had at that time the socity of three white families who lived in less than a half of a mile of us, one on the east of us and the other two west. The continued noise among the Indians on the evening refered to, excited the fears of our neighbors so much that when the men of one of those families came in, they asked the landlady what they should do in regard to us. She said, "By all means go and look after their safety," saying she expected they had killed me and all my children. The white man whose name was Spence, taking a Negro who was also able to measure arms with any of the Indians, came stealthily to our house. It was then getting dark, and they, acting the spy, had come to the back part of the house to see if they could hear us, but finding all was still and dark within, they redily came to the conclusion that the lady's conjectures had proven a reality. Spence, who had been living among the Indians for two or three years, having learned their language and understanding their true character, said to his companion, "Let us go round. And if they are killed," with an oath he swore, "the last one of them should die before day light." As soon as he got to the door, discovering the lock, he said, "We were safe." Like a bird we had escaped. But as anger was burning in his soul and not fearing danger and death, and the yell of havoc ringing in his ears with curses poured forth upon the whites, he burst in among them like a spirit of fire, and being armed for battle, fell on them with his stick, and after beating several of them, avenging himself for the alarm they had caused, left by telling them if their fury was not sufficiently cooled that he would return with hellish force and rend the last one of them. That led them as soon as they were sufficiently sober to scatter.

Soon after that your Father hired them to move a quarter of a mile farther from us. That however endangered his life, for although they had received pay for their possessions, one of them, in a drinking spree, came to our house to kill him, but was prevented by a young Indian man running ahead of him to give us warning, which we could not fully understand till the wife who came with her unmanageable husband bid us go away. But to our great comfort the liquor shop was demolished, and from that time, we had less to fear.

All the kindness we could show to any living people, we were assiduous to show to them. All that would relieve their sufferings or ameliorate their sorrows, that was in our power, we did for them, looking to God for his approval and reward. And at length, when the time came for their removal, their regard and kind feelings for us were made manifest, bursting the cold bars of silence that were raised like a wall of adamant around them, manifesting an unbounded preference for us by giving us those articles which were dearest to them, though of no real value to us. Two middle aged men, Duck and Etowah, gave William and John their bows and blow guns which, although nearly a score of years have passed, are still here, the former with their dressed squirrel skin strings wrapped loosely around, while the brawny hand, is far away, by which they have been so often tightened, born and nurtured in dangerous paths; whose skill and fierceness we would not dare to tempt, for whenever the fatal aim was taken and the pointed arrow flew, they were sure of their prey. Yet poor Cherokee, here lies your great bows unstrung. And although the sun has risen and set so often and torrents have flown, and streams of carnage have passed over portions of the land, and the word of the Lord demolished the thrones of the living, yet hope and courage still kindle along the track of those two boys by whom these momentoes are kept.

3

U.S. Policy

Andrew Jackson's election to the presidency in November 1828 has been widely regarded as a watershed in the history of U.S.-Indian policy. Scholars have debated his motivations with arguments ranging from his history as an Indian fighter and "hater," to claims that his main concern was national security, to assertions that he was anxious to halt the decline and extinction of the Native peoples in the East. Despite their disagreements, none have suggested that his role was unimportant.

Jackson's contemporaries also believed that his election was a turning point. The first westerner to occupy the White House (Tennessee was then considered the West), his victory dramatized the rapidly growing political power of the region west of the Appalachians. If one believed that western needs and interests differed from those of the Atlantic states, Jackson's election seemed like the dawn of a new day. Jackson also represented the coalescence of a new political movement, the Democratic party, viewed by many as an important alternative to the political philosophy and American system of John Quincy Adams, Daniel Webster, and Henry Clay. Jackson, in other words, personified change. While many welcomed a new order, others feared and resented it.

Seen in this light, the debate over Indian removal during 1829–1830 represented a larger set of issues that went to the heart of American public life. What were the proper relationships between the federal government and the states? Could the concept of shared sovereignty that marked the constitutional system be satisfactorily defined? The emerging conflict over slavery made these questions increasingly crucial, just as it polarized the attempts to answer them.

But, of course, the debate over Indian removal was also much more than a part of the ongoing dispute over constitutional interpretation. For forty years the U.S. government had followed a set of policies, including the negotiation of treaties, that recognized the sovereignty of the nations of Native Americans and had committed itself to helping them preserve and protect that status. None of Jackson's predecessors, even in their frustration over their failures to convince the tribes to do as they wished, seriously considered rejecting such recognition. But Jackson, on record for more than ten years as favoring such a step, did so in 1829 when he decided to honor Georgia's claims of jurisdiction over the Cherokees.

Probably Jackson saw Georgia's legislation, in effect nullification of congressional law, as an expedient means to achieve removal and not as an acceptable constitutional principle. His reaction to South Carolina's nullification in 1832 at least suggests that. But Georgia, Alabama, Mississippi, and Tennessee, all of which violated Native national sovereignty by extending their jurisdiction into Indian country, could do what Jackson could not. They could force the tribes to the treaty table where waiting federal officials would bargain to save them from state harassment by sending them off to the West. Critics called the scheme callous and inhumane, unconstitutional and illegal, but supporters saw it as efficient and effective as well as expedient.

Congressional implementation of Jackson's views came in the form of the Indian Removal Act, a bill that senators and representatives hotly debated. All claimed primary concern for the best interests of the Indians, but the constitutional and legal implications of removal remained central to the dispute. Indian policy became a partisan issue in the debate over removal and continued to be so during the next decade of party alignment known as the second party system.

The removal bill, enacted largely along party lines, thus aligned Congress with the president in support of Georgia's claims to sovereignty over the Cherokees. The Supreme Court's rejection of state jurisdiction in the 1832 *Worcester* decision, an important moral victory for the Cherokees, had little immediate effect. The Court neither designed nor implemented Indian policy; that was the responsibility of the president and Congress. And in 1832, in the midst of the larger debate over the nature of the federal system, there was no agreement that either must abide by the decisions of the Court. As a result, the president and Congress succeeded in achieving a dramatic restructuring of the relations among the Indian tribes, the states in which they lived, and the federal government. Andrew Jackson was instrumental in making that happen.

Scholarly study of the removal policy began with the publication of Annie H. Abel's "The History of Events Resulting in Indian Consolidation West of the Mississippi," *Annual Report of the American Historical Association for 1906* (Washington, D.C.: Government Printing Office, 1908, 1: 241–412; reprint, New York: AMS Press, 1972). For a recent scholarly study, see Theda Perdue and Michael D. Green, *The Cherokee Nation and the Trail of Tears* (New York: Penguin, 2008). Mary Young, "Conflict Resolution on the Indian Frontier," *Journal of the Early Republic* 16 (1996): 1–19, reminds us of the limited options available to Native Americans during the removal era. On the relationship between Jackson's military career, Indian warfare, and American expansion, see Fred Anderson and Andrew Cayton, *Dominion of War: Empire and Liberty in North America, 1500–2000* (New York: Penguin/Random House, 2005), chap. 5.

In Defense of the Cherokees: The "William Penn" Essays

Jeremiah Evarts, chief administrative officer of the large interdenominational missionary consortium the American Board of Commissioners for Foreign Missions, had definite ideas about the proper relation between the Indian tribes and the United States. Born in Vermont and trained as an attorney, he had become convinced early in his life that God had a special mission for the United States to lead the way in the conversion of the world to Christianity. American leadership required that the United States be a "beacon of goodness" that radiated the light of justice and morality in all of its affairs. Christian citizens were obligated, he believed, to critique their leaders if they strayed from the path and demand that they return. Otherwise, Evarts feared, God would punish the United States with disasters and destruction.

Since 1817, the American Board had maintained a significant presence in the Cherokee Nation. Several missionaries lived there, operated schools, conducted religious services, studied the language, worked on a translation of the Bible, and sent back to headquarters in Boston a steady stream of correspondence and reports on their progress. Evarts read all the reports, studied what additional sources he could find, and developed a deep and abiding respect for the Cherokees. Furthermore, with a lawyer's eye, he analyzed the history of Indian policy in all of its legislative and administrative aspects. To him, the Constitution clearly authorized Congress and the president to conduct relations with the Indians outside the involvement of the states. Treaties were the acts of sovereigns, and the policy of the United States had always been to respect the sovereign rights of the tribes. By definition, therefore, tribal sovereignty was superior to the claims of the states. In addition, neither Evarts nor his associates in New

*England were Democrats. Their view of the Union and the proper relation
of the federal and state governments convinced them that the Constitution
intended the national government to take an active, leading role in public affairs, to override and inhibit the narrow and selfish provincialism of
the states, and to set the moral tone for the country.*

*Evarts was both outraged and terrified by the events of the winter of
1828–1829. Georgia's extension of jurisdiction over the Cherokees and the
Cherokee protest to the president had elicited the response of the Jackson
administration. Though conveyed in a private letter dated April 18,
1829, from Secretary of War John Eaton to the Cherokee Council, the
news that the government would not protect the Cherokees from the
actions of Georgia law but rather would encourage the state's aggressive policy quickly made its way to Evarts's desk at the American Board
offices. Shortly thereafter, Thomas L. McKenney, the War Department
official chiefly responsible for the administration of Indian policy, wrote
Evarts to explain and justify Jacksonian policy. Unable to win the support of the American Board, McKenney approached Episcopalian and
Dutch Reformed church officials in New York; they agreed with Jackson's
arguments and in July, with McKenney's active involvement, organized
the Indian Board for the Emigration, Preservation, and Improvement of
the Aborigines of America. This organization of lay and clerical religious
leaders, McKenney hoped, would offer a persuasive alternative moral
voice to Evarts and the American Board.*

*All of this jolted Evarts, who believed that the new policy was uncon-
stitutional, illegal, immoral, and fraught with danger. Not only would the
policy run roughshod over Indian human and legal rights, it would surely
rain untold suffering and hardship onto a helpless and innocent people.
Furthermore, God would punish the United States for such immorality,
and Evarts shivered to think of the consequences.*

*Thus motivated, between August 5 and December 19, 1829, Evarts
wrote and published in the Washington* National Intelligencer *twenty-
four articles entitled "Essays on the Present Crisis in the Condition of the
American Indians." Published under the pseudonym of William Penn,
Evarts's essays constitute a propaganda masterpiece of historical, legal,
and moral analysis and interpretation of America's relations with the
Indians. The essays, reprinted in dozens of papers and published as a
separate pamphlet, responded to Jackson's position and shaped the arguments on removal that resounded in Congress and the press during the
early months of 1830.*

*The selection printed here is a summary of the "William Penn" essays
written by Evarts late in 1829 as the body of a petition that opponents*

of removal could sign and send to their congressmen. Entitled "A Brief View," this represented one of many efforts by Evarts and those of like mind to bombard Congress with expressions of popular outrage. Note the logic of Evarts's presentation. How does he mix history, law, and morality to make his points? Do his views of the Cherokees betray a paternalistic attitude?

This copy is taken from Francis Paul Prucha, ed., Cherokee Removal: The "William Penn" Essays and Other Writing *(Knoxville: University of Tennessee Press, 1981), 201–11. Prucha's introduction is an excellent discussion of Evarts and the American Board's campaign against removal. For further information, see John A. Andrew III,* From Revivals to Removal: Jeremiah Evarts, the Cherokee Nation, and the Search for the Soul of America *(Athens: University of Georgia Press, 1992).*

15

WILLIAM PENN [JEREMIAH EVARTS]

A Brief View of the Present Relations between the Government and People of the United States and the Indians within Our National Limits

November 1829

In the various discussions, which have attracted public attention within a few months past, several important positions, on the subject of the rights and claims of the Indians, have been clearly and firmly established. At least, this is considered to be the case, by a large portion of the intelligent and reflecting men in the community. Among the positions thus established are the following: which, for the sake of precision and easy reference, are set down in regular numerical order.

1. The American Indians, now living upon lands derived from their ancestors, and never alienated nor surrendered, have a perfect right to the continued and undisturbed possession of these lands.

2. Those Indian tribes and nations, which have remained under their own form of government, upon their own soil, and have never submitted themselves to the government of the whites, have a perfect right to retain their original form of government, or to alter it, according to their own views of convenience and propriety.

3. These rights of soil and of sovereignty are inherent in the Indians, till voluntarily surrendered by them; and cannot be taken away by compacts between communities of whites, to which compacts the Indians were not a party.

4. From the settlement of the English colonies in North America to the present day, the right of Indians to lands in their actual and peaceable possession, and to such form of government as they choose, has been admitted by the whites; though such admission is in no sense necessary to the perfect validity of the Indian title.

5. For one hundred and fifty years, innumerable treaties were made between the English colonists and the Indians, upon the basis of the Indians being independent nations, and having a perfect right to their country and their form of government.

6. During the revolutionary war, the United States, in their confederate character, made similar treaties, accompanied by the most solemn guaranty of territorial rights.

7. At the close of the revolutionary war, and before the adoption of the federal constitution, the United States, in their confederate character, made similar treaties with the Cherokees, Chickasaws, and Choctaws.

8. The State of Georgia, after the close of the revolutionary war, and before the adoption of the federal constitution, made similar treaties, on the same basis, with the Cherokees and Creeks.

9. By the constitution of the United States, the exclusive power of making treaties with the Indians was conferred on the general government; and, in the execution of this power, the faith of the nation has been many times pledged to the Cherokees, Creeks, Chickasaws, Choctaws, and other Indian nations. In nearly all these treaties, the national and territorial rights of the Indians are guaranteed to them, either expressly, or by implication.

10. The State of Georgia has, by numerous public acts, implicitly acquiesced in this exercise of the treaty-making power of the United States.

11. The laws of the United States, as well as treaties with the Indians, prohibit all persons, whether acting as individuals, or as agents of any State, from encroaching upon territory secured to the Indians. By these laws severe penalties are inflicted upon offenders; and the execution of the laws on this subject, is specially confided to the President of the United States, who has the whole force of the country at his disposal for this purpose.

The positions here recited are deemed to be incontrovertible. It follows, therefore,

That the removal of any nation of Indians from their country by force would be an instance of gross and cruel oppression:

That all attempts to accomplish this removal of the Indians by bribery or fraud, by intimidation and threats, by withholding from them a knowledge of the strength of their cause, by practising upon their ignorance, and their fears, or by vexatious opportunities, interpreted by them to mean nearly the same thing as a command;—all such attempts are acts of oppression, and therefore entirely unjustifiable:

That the United States are firmly bound by treaty to protect the Indians from force and encroachments on the part of a State; and a refusal thus to protect them would be equally an act of bad faith as a refusal to protect them against individuals: and

That the Cherokees have therefore the guaranty of the United States, solemnly and repeatedly given, as a security against encroachments from Georgia and the neighboring States. By virtue of this guaranty the Cherokees may rightfully demand, that the United States shall keep all intruders at a distance, from whatever quarter, or in whatever character, they may come. Thus secured and defended in the possession of their country, the Cherokees have a perfect right to retain that possession as long as they please. Such a retention of their country is no just cause of complaint or offence to any State, or to any individual. It is merely an exercise of natural rights, which rights have been not only acknowledged but repeatedly and solemnly confirmed by the United States.

Although these principles are clear and incontrovertible, yet many persons feel an embarrassment from considering the Cherokees *as living in the State of Georgia*. All this embarrassment may be removed at once by bearing in mind, that the Cherokee country is not in Georgia, in any sense affecting sovereignty, right of soil, or jurisdiction; nor will it rightfully become a part of Georgia, till the Cherokees shall first have ceded it to the United States. Whenever that event shall take place, it will immediately fall into the States of Georgia, Tennessee and Alabama; not by virtue of any compact to which the Cherokees have been a party, but in consequence of compacts now existing between these States and the United States. . . .

Again, it is supposed, that the existence of a little separate community of Indians, living under their own laws, and surrounded by communities of whites, will be fraught with some great and undefined mischief. This supposed evil is set forth under learned and hard names. It is called *an anomaly*, an *imperium in imperio*,[1] and by various other pedantic epithets. When the case is accurately examined, however, all the fog clears away, and nothing appears in the prospect but a little tract of country full of civilized Indians, engaged in their lawful pursuits, neither molesting their neighbours, nor interrupting the general peace and prosperity.

If the separate existence of the Indian tribes *were* an inconvenience to their neighbours, this would be but a slender reason for breaking down all the barriers of justice and good faith. Many a rich man has thought it very inconvenient, that he could not add the farm of a poor neighbour to his possessions. Many a powerful nation has felt it to be inconvenient to have a weak and dependent state in its neighbourhood, and has therefore forcibly joined the territory of such state to its own extensive domains. But this is done at the expense of honour and character, and is visited by the historian with his severest reprobation. . . .

And as to the learned chimera of *imperium in imperio*, it is, and always has been, one of the most common things in the world. The whole of modern Germany is nothing else but one specimen after another of *imperium in imperio*. Italy has an abundance of specimens also. As to our own country, we have governments within governments of all sizes, and for all purposes, from a school district to our great federal union. And where can be the harm of letting a few of our red neighbours, on a small remnant of their own territory, exercise the rights which God has given them? They have not the power to injure us; and, if we treat them kindly and justly, they will not have the disposition. They have not intruded upon our territory, nor encroached upon our rights. They only ask the privilege of living unmolested in the places where they were born, and in possession of those rights, which we have acknowledged and guaranteed. . . .

---

[1] "Empire within an empire" (Latin).

May a gracious Providence avert from this country the awful calamity of exposing ourselves to the wrath of heaven, as a consequence of disregarding the cries of the poor and defenceless, and perverting to purposes of cruelty and oppression, that power which was given us to promote the happiness of our fellow-men.

American Women Organize against Removal

Perhaps as many as a half-million people in the United States read Evarts's essays, and many of them, especially women, decided to take action. In the 1820s, the public role of women was limited to social, religious, and charitable activities; they could not vote or stand for office. The removal issue, however, provided women with an opportunity to focus their benevolent concerns on a political issue. Women's missionary societies had long supported Indian missions through donations of money and goods, and individual women made contributions as well: About half the donors listed in the periodical the Missionary Herald *were women. Many women regarded the treatment of the Cherokees and other Indians as immoral, and since morality was well within their purview, they felt compelled to oppose removal.*

The call to action came from Catherine Beecher, a prominent educator and writer (and sister of Harriet Beecher Stowe, author of Uncle Tom's Cabin*). In 1829, she anonymously published a widely distributed circular in which she called on women to petition Congress to defeat the impending Indian Removal Act. In response, women collected signatures on scores of petitions demanding respect for Indian rights, which they sent to Congress.*

This kind of concerted political action on a national level was new to American women, as Mary Hershberger pointed out in "Mobilizing Women, Anticipating Abolition: The Struggle against Indian Removal in the 1830s," Journal of American History *86 (1999): 15–40. Women soon began to urge the abolition of slavery and to address other injustices in American society. Opposition to Indian removal, therefore, politically empowered women in the United States and provided them with a public voice despite their disfranchisement.*

Below is an excerpt from Catherine Beecher's circular that was printed in the Christian Advocate and Journal, *December 25, 1829. This journal and other nineteenth-century publications can be found in the* American Periodical Series, *which many libraries have on microfilm and online.*

How does Beecher's tone differ from that of Jeremiah Evarts? How would you compare her depiction of Indians and their relations with Europeans to his? In what ways does she call on the moral authority of women to legitimize their taking a stand on this issue?

16

CATHERINE BEECHER

Circular

Addressed to Benevolent Ladies of the U. States

December 25, 1829

The present crisis in the affairs of the Indian nations in the United States demands the immediate and interested attention of all who make any claims to benevolence or humanity. The calamities now hanging over them threaten not only these relics of an interesting race, but, if there is a Being who avenges the wrongs of the oppressed, are causes of alarm to our whole country.

The following are the facts of the case:—This continent was once possessed only by the Indians, and earliest accounts represent them as a race numerous, warlike, and powerful. When our forefathers sought refuge from oppression on these shores, this people supplied their necessities, and ministered to their comfort; and though some of them, when they saw the white man continually encroaching upon their land, fought bravely for their existence and their country, yet often, too, the Indian has shed his blood to protect and sustain our infant nation.

As we have risen in greatness and glory, the Indian nations have faded away. Their proud and powerful tribes have gone; their noble sachems[1] and mighty warriors are heard of no more; and it is said the Indian often comes to the borders of his limited retreat to gaze on the beautiful country no longer his own, and to cry with bitterness at the remembrance of past greatness and power.

Ever since the existence of this nation, our general government, pursuing the course alike of policy and benevolence, have acknowledged

---

[1] Chiefs.

these people as free and independent nations, and has protected them in the quiet possession of their lands. In repeated treaties with the Indians, the United States, by the hands of the most distinguished statesmen, after purchasing the greater part of their best lands, have *promised* them "*to continue the guarantee of the remainder of their country* FOR EVER." And so strictly has government guarded the Indian's right to his lands, that even to go on to their boundaries to survey the land, subjects to heavy fines and imprisonment.

Our government also, with parental care, has persuaded the Indians to forsake their savage life, and to adopt the habits and pursuits of civilized nations, while the charities of Christians and the labours of missionaries have sent to them the blessings of the gospel to purify and enlighten. The laws and regular forms of a civilized government are instituted; their simple and beautiful language, by the remarkable ingenuity of one of their race, has become a written language with its own peculiar alphabet, and, by the printing press, is sending forth among these people the principles of knowledge, and liberty, and religion. Their fields are beginning to smile with the labours of the husbandman; their villages are busy with the toils of the mechanic and the artisan; schools are rising in their hamlets, and the temple of the living God is seen among their forests.

Nor are we to think of these people only as naked and wandering savages. The various grades of intellect and refinement exist among them as among us; and those who visit their chieftains and families of the higher class, speak with wonder and admiration of their dignified propriety, nobleness of appearance, and refined characteristics as often exhibited in both sexes. Among them are men fitted by native talents to shine among the statesmen of any land, and who have received no inferior degree of cultivation. Among them, also, are those who, by honest industry, have assembled around them most of the comforts and many of the elegancies of life.

But the lands of this people are *claimed* to be embraced within the limits of some of our southern states, and as they are fertile and valuable, they are demanded by the whites as their own possessions, and efforts are making to dispossess the Indians of their native soil. And such is the singular state of concurring circumstances, that it has become almost a certainty that these people are to have their lands torn from them, and to be driven into western wilds and to final annihilation, unless the feelings of a humane and Christian nation shall be aroused to prevent the unhallowed sacrifice.

Unless our general government interfere to protect these nations, as by solemn and oft-repeated treaties they are bound to do, nothing can save them. The states which surround them are taking such measures as will speedily drive them from their country, and cause their final extinction. . . .

Have not then the females of this country some duties devolving upon them in relation to this helpless race? — They are protected from the blinding influence of party spirit, and the asperities of political violence. They have nothing to do with any struggle for power, nor any right to dictate the decisions of those that rule over them. — But they may *feel* for the distressed; they may stretch out the supplicating hand for them, and by their prayers strive to avert the calamities that are impending over them. It may be, that female petitioners can lawfully be heard, even by the highest rulers of our land. Why may we not approach and supplicate that we and our dearest friends may be saved from the awful curses denounced on all who oppress the poor and needy, by Him whose anger is to be dreaded more than the wrath of man; who can "blast us with the breath of his nostrils," and scatter our hopes like chaff before the storm. It may be this will be *forbidden*; yet still we remember the Jewish princess who, being sent to supplicate for a nation's life, was thus reproved for hesitating even when *death* stared her in the way: "If thou altogether hold thy peace at this time, then shall deliverance arise from another place; but thou and thy father's house shall be destroyed. And who knoweth whether thou art come to the kingdom for such a cause as this?"

To woman it is given to administer the sweet charities of life, and to *sway the empire of affection*; and to her it may also be said, "Who knoweth whether thou art come to the kingdom for such a cause as this?". . .

You who gather the youthful group around your fireside, and rejoice in their future hopes and joys, will you forget that the poor Indian loves his children too, and would as bitterly mourn over all their blasted hopes? And, while surrounded by such treasured blessings, ponder with dread and awe these fearful words of Him, who thus forbids the violence, and records the malediction of those, who either as individuals, or as nations, shall oppress the needy and helpless. . . .

This communication was written and sent abroad solely by the female hand. Let every woman who peruses it, exert that influence in society which falls within her lawful province, and endeavour by every suitable expedient to interest the feelings of her friends, relatives, and acquaintances, in behalf of this people, that are ready to perish. *A few weeks* must decide this interesting and important question, and after that time sympathy and regret will all be in vain.

December 1, 1829.

Lewis Cass Justifies Removal

*By the mid-1820s, Lewis Cass, governor of Michigan Territory between
1813 and 1831, had become widely regarded as one of the best informed,
most experienced, and highly thoughtful experts in the country on U.S.-
Indian policy and the histories and cultures of the tribes. As superintendent of Indian affairs, an office all territorial governors held, he was
certainly familiar with the details of U.S. relations with the Indians of
the Great Lakes. He had toured the region, visited many tribes in their
home countries, and arranged several treaties with them. He also was
reputed to be a hardheaded, tough, but fair negotiator who supported the
attempts of the government and the missionaries to "civilize" the Indians.
The policy of changing the cultures of the Indians, turning them into plow
farmers who produced surplus crops for sale in the marketplace, was the
only way, Cass and many others believed, that the Indians could survive.
If they remained "uncivilized," they would perish.*

*Cass made his reputation outside of government circles through a
series of essays published in national magazines. The* North American
Review, *one of the nation's leading literary journals, published several of
his essays. Written as extended reviews of books and articles about Indians, Cass used these essays to put forth his opinions about Indian policy
and U.S. relations with the tribes. His most significant essay appeared in
the January 1830 issue of the* North American Review *in the guise of a
commentary on the publication of several letters, addresses, and resolutions in support of removal. Cass's essay, fifty-nine pages in length, was
the first extended pro-removal document to appear in the popular press,
written by an expert, since the election of Andrew Jackson, the publication
of the "William Penn" essays, and the passage of Georgia's legislation to
extend its civil and criminal jurisdiction into the Cherokee Nation.*

*What does Cass think of the "civilization" policy now? To what does
he attribute its failure? Notice Cass's claims to expertise, his tone, his
range of arguments, and his use of evidence. What do his readers who
are not experts learn from him? How does he explain and justify Indian
removal? How does he deal with the reputation of the Cherokees as a
"civilized" people? And how does all of this lead him to interpret the
political and territorial rights of the Cherokees and all other tribes east of
the Mississippi?*

Francis Paul Prucha, Lewis Cass and American Indian Policy *(Detroit,
Mich.: Wayne State University Press, 1967), contains further information*

on Cass. A more recent biography is Willard Carl Klunder, Lewis Cass and the Politics of Moderation *(Kent, Ohio: Kent State University Press, 1996).*

17

LEWIS CASS

Removal of the Indians

January 1830

A barbarous people, depending for subsistence upon the scanty and precarious supplies furnished by the chase, cannot live in contact with a civilized community. As the cultivated border approaches the haunts of the animals, which are valuable for food or furs, they recede and seek shelter in less accessible situations. . . .

. . . From an early period, their rapid declension and ultimate extinction were foreseen and lamented, and various plans for their preservation and improvement were projected and pursued. Many of them were carefully taught at our seminaries of education, in the hope that principles of morality and habits of industry would be acquired, and that they might stimulate their countrymen by precept and example to a better course of life. Missionary stations were established among various tribes, where zealous and pious men devoted themselves with generous ardor to the task of instruction, as well in agriculture and the mechanic arts, as in the principles of morality and religion. . . . Unfortunately, they are monuments also of unsuccessful and unproductive efforts. What tribe has been civilized by all this expenditure of treasure, and labor, and care? . . .

The cause of this total failure cannot be attributed to the nature of the experiment, nor to the character, qualifications, or conduct, of those who have directed it. The process and the persons have varied, as experience suggested alterations in the one, and a spirit of generous self-devotion supplied the changes in the other. But there seems to be some insurmountable obstacle in the habits or temperament of the Indians, which has heretofore prevented, and yet prevents, the success of these labors. . . .

We have made the inquiry respecting the permanent advantage, which any of the tribes have derived from the attempts to civilize them, with a full knowledge of the favorable reports that have been circulated concerning the Cherokees. Limited as our intercourse with those Indians has been, we must necessarily draw our conclusions respecting them from facts which have been stated to us, and from the general resemblance they bear to the other cognate branches of the great aboriginal stock. . . .

That individuals among the Cherokees have acquired property, and with it more enlarged views and juster notions of the value of our institutions, and the unprofitableness of their own, we have little doubt. And we have as little doubt, that this change of opinion and condition is confined, in a great measure, to some of the *half-breeds* and their immediate connexions. These are not sufficiently numerous to affect our general proposition. . . .

. . . But, we believe, the great body of the people are in a state of helpless and hopeless poverty. With the same improvidence and habitual indolence, which mark the northern Indians, they have less game for subsistence, and less peltry for sale. We doubt whether there is, upon the face of the globe, a more wretched race than the Cherokees, as well as the other southern tribes, present. . . .

We are as unwilling to underrate, as we should be to overrate, the progress made by these Indians in civilization and improvement. We are well aware, that the constitution of the Cherokees, their press, and newspaper, and alphabet, their schools and police, have sent through all our borders the glad tidings, that the long night of aboriginal ignorance was ended, and that the day of knowledge had dawned. Would that it were so. None would rejoice more sincerely than we should. But this great cause can derive no aid from exaggerated representation; from promises never to be kept, and from expectations never to be realized. The truth must finally come, and it will come with a powerful reaction. We hope that our opinion upon this subject may be erroneous. But we have melancholy forebodings. That a few principal men, who can secure favorable cotton lands, and cultivate them with slaves, will be comfortable and satisfied, we may well believe. And so long as the large annuities received from the United States, are applied to the support of a newspaper and to other objects, more important to the rich than the poor, erroneous impressions upon these subjects may prevail. But to form just conceptions of the spirit and objects of these efforts, we must look at their practical operation upon the community. It is here, if the facts which have been stated to us are correct, and of which we have no doubt, that they will be found wanting.

The relative condition of the two races of men, who yet divide this portion of the continent between them, is a moral problem involved in much obscurity. The physical causes we have described, exasperated by the moral evils introduced by them, are sufficient to account for the diminution and deterioration of the Indians. But why were not these causes counteracted by the operation of other circumstances? As civilization shed her light upon them, why were they blind to its beams? Hungry or naked, why did they disregard, or regarding, why did they neglect, those arts by which food and clothing could be procured? Existing for two centuries in contact with a civilized people, they have resisted, and successfully too, every effort to meliorate their situation, or to introduce among them the most common arts of life. Their moral and their intellectual condition have been equally stationary. And in the whole circle of their existence, it would be difficult to point to a single advantage which they have derived from their acquaintance with the Europeans. . . .

There can be no doubt, and such are the views of the elementary writers upon the subject, that the Creator intended the earth should be reclaimed from a state of nature and cultivated; that the human race should spread over it, procuring from it the means of comfortable subsistence, and of increase and improvement. A tribe of wandering hunters, depending upon the chase for support, and deriving it from the forests, and rivers, and lakes, of an immense continent have a very imperfect possession of the country over which they roam. . . .

Our compacts with the Indians assume the form of solemn treaties, passing through the ordinary process of ratification. These are obligatory upon them and us, for all the purposes fairly inferable from them, and we trust they will never be violated. But because we have resorted to this method of adjusting some of the questions arising out of our intercourse with them, a speculative politician has no right to deduce from thence their claim to the attributes of sovereignty, with all its powers and duties. . . .

This question of jurisdiction over the Indian tribes is now, for the first time, seriously agitated. Heretofore, no one among them, or for them, has denied the obligation of any law passed to protect or restrain them. But new circumstances have intervened, and new pretensions are advanced. A government *de facto* has been organized within the limits of the state of Georgia, claiming legislative, executive, and judicial powers, and all the essential *attributes of sovereignty*, independent of that state. . . .

What has a Cherokee to fear from the operation of the laws of Georgia? If he has advanced in knowledge and improvement, as many sanguine persons believe and represent, he will find these laws more just, better administered, and far more equal in their operation, than the *regulations* which the chiefs have established and are enforcing. What Indian has ever been injured by the laws of any state? We ask the question without any fear of the answer. If these Indians are too ignorant and barbarous to submit to the state laws, or duly estimate their value, they are too ignorant and barbarous to establish and maintain a government which shall protect its own citizens, and preserve the necessary relations and intercourse with its neighbors. . . .

If the laws of the various states, founded essentially upon the English common law, modified by our peculiar circumstances, and administered in a spirit of fidelity and impartiality, which even in this land of violent political feuds, has left the judiciary without suspicion, excite the apprehensions of the Indians, and if they are anxious to escape from their operation and establish governments for themselves, ample provision has been made for their gratification. A region is open to them, where they and their descendants can be secured in the enjoyment of every privilege which they may be capable of estimating and enjoying. If they choose to remain where they now are, they will be protected in the possession of their land and other property, and be subject, as our citizens are, to the operation of just and wholesome laws.

Congress Acts

The Indian Removal Act, signed into law on May 28, 1830, by President Andrew Jackson, began its legislative history with Jackson's first State of the Union Address, delivered in December 1829. Each house of Congress referred the portion of the message dealing with Indian policy to its Committee on Indian Affairs. Both committees were chaired by Tennesseans — Hugh Lawson White in the Senate, John Bell in the House — and were dominated by southern Democrats. White's committee reported its bill to the Senate floor on February 22, 1830; Bell's committee followed suit two days later. The Senate's agenda permitted that body to complete debate on its version before the House could begin to work on its bill. Both were substantially the same, so Bell withdrew the version prepared by his committee and recommended that the House adopt the Senate bill. The House agreed, passed a slightly altered version of the Senate bill on

*May 26, and returned it to the Senate, which concurred two days later.
The president signed it immediately.*

*Many representatives and senators recalled that the debates in both
houses had been extremely bitter, highly partisan, emotionally supercharged, and exhausting. Senator Theodore Frelinghuysen of New Jersey,
a friend of Jeremiah Evarts, a strong supporter of Christian benevolence,
and a bitter anti-Jacksonian, led the attack in the upper house with a
six-hour speech that extended over three days. The thrust of his argument
was to uphold the sovereignty of the Cherokee Nation, condemn Georgia's
extension of jurisdiction and Jackson's refusal to protect the Cherokees
from Georgia law, charge that the entire scheme was a transparent attempt
to force the Cherokees and other tribes out of their lands, and predict terrible suffering for the Indian victims of the policy. Peleg Sprague (Maine)
and Asher Robbins (Rhode Island) joined with opposition speeches.
John Forsyth (Georgia) and Robert Adams (Mississippi), along with
chairman White, defended removal. Despairing of victory, opponents
also tried unsuccessfully to amend White's bill with language that would
force Jackson to protect the Cherokees from Georgia law until they were
removed. The final vote, clearly along party lines, was 28 to 19.*

*The same pattern of attack and defense occurred in the House, which
debated removal from May 13 to 26. Heavily influenced by the arguments and evidence presented in the "William Penn" essays, northern
anti-Jackson representatives did battle against southern, largely Georgia,
Democrats. But the party lines were not quite so strong in the House, and
some Democrats, particularly from Pennsylvania and the Ohio valley,
along with Tennessean Davy Crockett, voted in opposition. The final tally,
102 to 97, reflects how controversial the removal policy actually was.*

*Note carefully what the act did and did not provide. What was the pres-
ident authorized to do? How was removal to be arranged? How were
the rights of the tribes protected? Opponents of the bill claimed that it
would force the tribes to remove. Is there any evidence to support this
fear?*

This copy of the Indian Removal Act comes from United States Statutes at Large, *4: 411–12. The congressional debates over the removal bill
make fascinating reading. They can be found in Gales and Seaton's* Register of Debates, *vol. 6, pt. 2. A precursor of the* Congressional Record,
the Register *contains the record of debates in both houses of Congress.
Wilson Lumpkin, a representative from Georgia who sat on the House
Committee on Indian Affairs, probably did more than any other single
individual to achieve passage of the removal bill. Shortly after the bill was
signed into law, Lumpkin left Congress to serve two terms as governor of*

Georgia, where he worked with equal vigor to remove the Cherokees. He believed so strongly that this was the crowning achievement of his life that he titled his two-volume autobiography The Removal of the Cherokee Indians from Georgia *(New York: Dodd, Mead, 1907; reprint, New York: Augustus M. Kelley, 1971). The best analysis of the congressional debate on removal is in Ronald N. Satz,* American Indian Policy in the Jacksonian Era *(Lincoln: University of Nebraska Press, 1975), chaps. 1–2, and Francis Paul Prucha,* The Great Father: The United States Government and the American Indians *(Lincoln: University of Nebraska Press, 1984), vol. 1, chap. 7. See Fred S. Rolater, "The American Indian and the Origin of the Second Party System,"* Wisconsin Magazine of History *76 (1993): 180–203, for a fascinating discussion of the relation between Indian policy and party politics in the 1830s and 1840s.*

18

U.S. CONGRESS

Indian Removal Act

May 28, 1830

Chapter CXLVIII

An Act to provide for an exchange of lands with the Indians residing in any of the states or territories, and for their removal west of the river Mississippi.

Be it enacted by the Senate and House of Representatives of the United States of America, in Congress assembled, That it shall and may be lawful for the President of the United States to cause so much of any territory belonging to the United States, west of the river Mississippi, not included in any state or organized territory, and to which the Indian title has been extinguished, as he may judge necessary, to be divided into a suitable number of districts, for the reception of such tribes or nations of Indians as may choose to exchange the lands where they now reside, and remove there; and to cause each of said districts to be so described by natural or artificial marks, as to be easily distinguished from every other.

Sec. 2 *And be it further enacted,* That it shall and may be lawful for the President to exchange any or all of such districts, so to be laid off and described, with any tribe or nation of Indians now residing within the limits of any of the states or territories, and with which the United States have existing treaties, for the whole or any part or portion of the territory claimed and occupied by such tribe or nation, within the bounds of any one or more of the states or territories, where the land claimed and occupied by the Indians, is owned by the United States, or the United States are bound to the state within which it lies to extinguish the Indian claim thereto.

Sec. 3 *And be it further enacted*, That in the making of any such exchange or exchanges, it shall and may be lawful for the President solemnly to assure the tribe or nation with which the exchange is made, that the United States will forever secure and guaranty to them, and their heirs or successors, the country so exchanged with them; and if they prefer it, that the United States will cause a patent or grant to be made and executed to them for the same: *Provided always*, That such lands shall revert to the United States, if the Indians become extinct, or abandon the same.

Sec. 4 *And be it further enacted*, That if, upon any of the lands now occupied by the Indians, and to be exchanged for, there should be such improvements as add value to the land claimed by any individual or individuals of such tribes or nations, it shall and may be lawful for the President to cause such value to be ascertained by appraisement or otherwise, and to cause such ascertained value to be paid to the person or persons rightfully claiming such improvements. And upon the payment of such valuation, the improvements so valued and paid for, shall pass to the United States, and possession shall not afterwards be permitted to any of the same tribe.

Sec. 5 *And be it further enacted*, That upon the making of any such exchange as is contemplated by this act, it shall and may be lawful for the President to cause such aid and assistance to be furnished to the emigrants as may be necessary and proper to enable them to remove to, and settle in, the country for which they may have exchanged; and also, to give them such aid and assistance as may be necessary for their support and subsistence for the first year after their removal.

Sec. 6 *And be it further enacted*, That it shall and may be lawful for the President to cause such tribe or nation to be protected, at their new residence, against all interruption or disturbance from any other tribe or nation of Indians, or from any other person or persons whatever.

Sec. 7 *And be it further enacted*, That it shall and may be lawful for the President to have the same superintendence and care over any tribe or nation in the country to which they may remove, as contemplated by this act, that he is now authorized to have over them at their present places of residence: *Provided*, That nothing in this act contained shall be construed as authorizing or directing the violation of any existing treaty between the United States and any of the Indian tribes.

Sec. 8 *And be it further enacted*, That for the purpose of giving effect to the provisions of this act, the sum of five hundred thousand dollars is hereby appropriated, to be paid out of any money in the treasury, not otherwise appropriated.

Andrew Jackson Applauds the Removal Act

In his first annual message, delivered December 8, 1829, President Andrew Jackson outlined his Indian policy and called on Congress to enact legislation that would remove eastern Indians to the region west of the Mississippi. Jackson had a reputation, won during the Creek War of 1813–1814, as an Indian fighter, but this was not a blood and glory pronouncement. He was critical, however, of the policies of his predecessors. "Professing a desire to civilize and settle them, we have at the same time lost no opportunity to purchase their lands and thrust them further into the wilderness," he explained. Thus, the "civilization" policy, despite "lavish . . . expenditures," had largely been a failure, except in the South where the Cherokees "have lately attempted to erect an independent government." State legislation that subjected Indians to state laws induced the Cherokees to call on the United States for protection. Can the government, Jackson asked, "sustain these people in their pretensions?" The answer clearly was no. The Constitution expressly forbade the erection of one state within the borders of another without the consent of the latter. The Indians, therefore, had two choices: They could "emigrate beyond the Mississippi or submit to the laws of those States."

Jackson's address publicly clarified his recognition of the sovereign rights of the states over the Indian country within their borders. Previous administrations, even as they defended removal as the ideal policy solution to the growing "crisis in Indian affairs," had been unwilling to force the Indians to move. Indeed, the course of federal Indian policy since the 1790s had been the opposite as it sought to exclude and remove state involvement and interference and to emphasize the nation-to-nation relation between the United States and the tribes. Jackson's decision to actively support removal, therefore, was revolutionary, and political opponents seized on it as another demonstration of the president's regressive understanding of the nature of the federal union.

The selection printed here comes from Jackson's second State of the Union message, presented on December 6, 1830, after the passage of the Indian Removal Act. In it the president takes pride in the unfolding of his policy, extols its virtues, and predicts success. But the president still looks for vindication and is anxious for a speedy conclusion. Things will continue to go well, he assures his opponents, encouraging everyone to join in the humane task of convincing the tribes that so far have refused to retreat that for their own good they must do so now.

What are the benefits of removal that Jackson recounts? Are they important and valuable? Could they have been achieved in some other way? What is the tone of his expressions of sympathy for the Indians?

The preeminent scholar of the history of U.S.-Indian policy, Francis Paul Prucha, has argued in The Great Father *(Lincoln: University of Nebraska Press, 1984) that the chief characteristic of Jackson and everyone else involved in Indian policy was paternalism. The Indians did not know what was best for them, such people believed. Like children, they had to be guided. Someone had to show them, convince them, sometimes even force them to do and be what they should. Do you see examples of paternalism in Jackson's address?*

Jackson's presidential address comes from the third volume of James D. Richardson, comp., The Messages and Papers of the Presidents *(New York: Bureau of National Literature, 1897). Robert Remini's three-volume biography* Andrew Jackson *(New York: Harper and Row, 1977–1984) puts Indian policy in the context of Jackson's life and political program. See Remini's* Andrew Jackson and His Indian Wars *(New York: Viking, 2001) for a restatement of Remini's views on Andrew Jackson's Indian policy.*

19

ANDREW JACKSON

State of the Union Address
December 6, 1830

It gives me pleasure to announce to Congress that the benevolent policy of the Government, steadily pursued for nearly thirty years, in relation to the removal of the Indians beyond the white settlements is approaching to a happy consummation. . . .

Humanity has often wept over the fate of the aborigines of this country, and Philanthropy has been long busily employed in devising means to avert it, but its progress has never for a moment been arrested, and one by one have many powerful tribes disappeared from the earth. To follow to the tomb the last of his race and to tread on the graves of extinct nations excite melancholy reflections. But true philanthropy reconciles the mind to these vicissitudes as it does to the extinction of one generation to make room for another. In the monuments and fortresses of an unknown people, spread over the extensive regions of the West, we behold the memorials of a once powerful race, which was exterminated or has disappeared to make room for the existing savage tribes. Nor is there anything in this which, upon a comprehensive view of the general interests of the human race, is to be regretted. Philanthropy could not wish to see this continent restored to the condition in which it was found by our forefathers. What good man would prefer a country covered with forests and ranged by a few thousand savages to our extensive Republic, studded with cities, towns, and prosperous farms, embellished with all the improvements which art can devise or industry execute, occupied by more than 12,000,000 happy people, and filled with all the blessings of liberty, civilization, and religion?

The present policy of the Government is but a continuation of the same progressive change by a milder process. The tribes which occupied the countries now constituting the Eastern States were annihilated or have melted away to make room for the whites. The waves of population and civilization are rolling to the westward, and we now propose to acquire the countries occupied by the red men of the South and West by a fair exchange, and, at the expense of the United States, to send them to a land where their existence may be prolonged and perhaps made perpetual. Doubtless it will be painful to leave the graves of their fathers; but what do they more than our ancestors did or than our children are now doing? To better their condition in an unknown land our forefathers left all that was dear in earthly objects. Our children by thousands yearly leave the land of their birth to seek new homes in distant regions. Does Humanity weep at these painful separations from everything, animate and inanimate, with which the young heart has become entwined? Far from it. It is rather a source of joy that our country affords scope where our young population may range unconstrained in body or in mind, developing the power and faculties of man in their highest perfection. These remove hundreds and almost thousands of miles at their own expense, purchase the lands they occupy, and support themselves at their new homes from the moment of their arrival. Can it be cruel in this Government when, by events which it can not control, the Indian is made discontented in his ancient home to purchase his lands, to give him a new and extensive territory, to pay the expense of his removal, and support him a year in his new abode? How many thousands of our own people would gladly embrace the opportunity of removing to the West on such conditions! If the offers made to the Indians were extended to them, they would be hailed with gratitude and joy.

And is it supposed that the wandering savage has a stronger attachment to his home than the settled, civilized Christian? Is it more afflicting to him to leave the graves of his fathers than it is to our brothers and children? Rightly considered, the policy of the General Government toward the red man is not only liberal, but generous. He is unwilling to submit to the laws of the States and mingle with their population. To save him from this alternative, or perhaps utter annihilation, the General Government kindly offers him a new home, and proposes to pay the whole expense of his removal and settlement.

4

The Cherokee Debate

Although the majority consistently opposed land cession and removal, the Cherokees were never unanimous in their opposition. In the early nineteenth century, a group of self-serving chiefs succumbed to the temptations of the federal government and sold land. Their leader, Doublehead, incurred the full wrath of the Cherokees, and other chiefs, including Major Ridge, killed him for his behavior. In 1808–1810, the Nation divided over the removal issue, and for a time, the anti-removal forces deposed the principal chief, who favored removal. Ultimately, the Cherokees did cede territory, most who wanted to move west did so, and those who remained strengthened their national government. Again, in 1817–1819 the Cherokees debated land cession and removal. Under pressure from the federal government, the Cherokees surrendered more land, those who had promoted removal went west, and the remaining people established "articles of government" that clearly defined who had authority to cede land. These early removals had two important results. First, they siphoned off the individuals who supported land cession and western migration. The Cherokees who remained, therefore, became even more adamant in their refusal to negotiate removal, and little dissent from the official anti-removal position existed throughout the 1820s. Second, the people who first settled in western Arkansas and then moved in 1828 to northeastern Oklahoma established a distinct Cherokee society that numbered about four thousand by the 1830s. These Cherokees challenged the hegemony of the eastern Cherokees after the larger body of approximately sixteen thousand moved west in 1838–1839.

Women and Removal

In the public debates over removal, or indeed any political issue, the voices of Cherokee women were largely absent. Traditionally, men conducted foreign affairs while women attended to domestic ones. The increasing importance of war and trade in the eighteenth century had magnified this division and shifted political power to men. The adoption of Anglo-American political institutions, in which women did not participate, further excluded them from the political arena. Nevertheless, in the removal crisis of 1817–1819, Cherokee women made themselves heard on two occasions. In 1817 and 1818, women's councils presented petitions to the National Council, which was composed solely of men. Nancy Ward seems to have inspired and led these women's councils. Ward was a War Woman, a title traditionally awarded to women who distinguished themselves while accompanying war parties to cook food, carry water, and perform other gender-specific tasks. Ward had rallied the warriors after her husband's death in battle in 1755. She subsequently aided the patriot cause during the American Revolution and addressed the Hopewell treaty conference in 1785. Now the elderly Ward and other women turned their attention to land cession and removal. The impact of their petitions is difficult to determine. The Cherokees ceded land in 1817 and 1819, but they did not accept individual allotments, which the women had opposed, and after 1819 they ceded no more land until 1835.

How did the women refer to themselves in their petitions to the National Council? Do you think that a tradition of matrilineal kinship may have led the women to describe themselves in such terms? How did women feel about ceding land and moving west of the Mississippi? What reasons did they give for their position? How did they envision the Cherokee future? What did they think motivated the men who supported land cession and removal? Can you find an argument for Cherokee sovereignty in the first petition that supporters of the Cherokee cause later used?

In the second petition, the women also addressed the issue of allotment, that is, dividing Cherokee land into separate tracts and assigning (or allotting) those tracts to individuals. This would have been a dramatic departure from the Cherokee practice of holding land in common, which permitted any citizen to use unoccupied land but prevented an individual from selling the land he or she held. The federal government saw the allotment of land as a means to bypass Indian governments and enable either the United States or its citizens to purchase land from individual owners. Allotment became a feature of treaties with the Chickasaws, Choctaws, and Creeks and generally proved to be a disaster. Did the women support allotment? Can you think of any personal reasons that might have prompted them to oppose allotment?

The first petition can be found in the Presidential Papers Microfilm: Andrew Jackson (Washington, 1967, series 1, reel 22). The second *petition was enclosed in a letter from American Board missionaries to their headquarters in Boston. It is part of the Papers of the American Board of Commissioners for Foreign Missions, Houghton Library, Harvard University. The editors have altered punctuation to make the letters more readable.*

The third petition printed here is almost certainly from 1831 rather than 1821, the date attached to it. The letter was written in October and published in the Cherokee Phoenix *on November 12, 1831. A typographical error easily could have turned what should have been "1831" into "1821." In 1821, the Cherokees were not under any particular pressure from Georgia or the "general government" to remove; by 1831, they were indeed in a "deplorable situation." In any event, the third petition is quite different from the other two. How can you explain the differences? What did the petitioners believe was the proper role of women? How does their justification for petitioning the council compare with the reasoning of the women who wrote the earlier petitions? Do you see any similarities in the petitions?*

For more information about Cherokee women, see Theda Perdue, Cherokee Women: Gender and Culture Change, 1700–1835 *(Lincoln: University of Nebraska Press, 1998) and Carolyn Ross Johnston,* Cherokee Women in Crisis: The Trail of Tears, Civil War, and Allotment, 1838–1907 *(Tuscaloosa: University of Alabama Press, 2003), chap. 3.*

20

CHEROKEE WOMEN

Petition

May 2, 1817

The Cherokee ladys now being present at the meeting of the chiefs and warriors in council have thought it their duty as mothers to address their beloved chiefs and warriors now assembled.

Our beloved children and head men of the Cherokee Nation, we address you warriors in council. We have raised all of you on the land which we now have, which God gave us to inhabit and raise provisions. We know that our country has once been extensive, but by repeated sales has become circumscribed to a small track, and [we] never have thought it our duty to interfere in the disposition of it till now. If a father or mother was to sell all their lands which they had to depend on, which their children had to raise their living on, which would be indeed bad & to be removed to another country. We do not wish to go to an unknown country [to] which we have understood some of our children wish to go over the Mississippi, but this act of our children would be like destroying your mothers.

Your mothers, your sisters ask and beg of you not to part with any more of our land. We say ours. You are our descendants; take pity on our request. But keep it for our growing children, for it was the good will of our creator to place us here, and you know our father, the great president,[1] will not allow his white children to take our country away. Only keep your hands off of paper talks for its our own country. For [if] it was not, they would not ask you to put your hands to paper, for it would be impossible to remove us all. For as soon as one child is raised, we have others in our arms, for such is our situation & will consider our circumstance.

Therefore, children, don't part with any more of our lands but continue on it & enlarge your farms. Cultivate and raise corn & cotton and your mothers and sisters will make clothing for you which our father the president has recommended to us all. We don't charge any body for selling any lands, but we have heard such intentions of our children. But your talks become true at last; it was our desire to forwarn you all not to part with our lands.

Nancy Ward to her children: Warriors to take pity and listen to the talks of your sisters. Although I am very old yet cannot but pity the situation in which you will here of their minds. I have great many grand children which [I] wish them to do well on our land.

---

[1] James Monroe.

21

CHEROKEE WOMEN

Petition

June 30, 1818

Beloved Children,

We have called a meeting among ourselves to consult on the different points now before the council, relating to our national affairs. We have heard with painful feelings that the bounds of the land we now possess are to be drawn into very narrow limits. The land was given to us by the Great Spirit above as our common right, to raise our children upon, & to make support for our rising generations. We therefore humbly petition our beloved children, the head men & warriors, to hold out to the last in support of our common rights, as the Cherokee nation have been the first settlers of this land; we therefore claim the right of the soil.

We well remember that our country was formerly very extensive, but by repeated sales it has become circumscribed to the very narrow limits we have at present. Our Father the President advised us to become farmers, to manufacture our own clothes, & to have our children instructed. To this advice we have attended in every thing as far as we were able. Now the thought of being compelled to remove the other side of the Mississippi is dreadful to us, because it appears to us that we, by this removal, shall be brought to a savage state again, for we have, by the endeavor of our Father the President, become too much enlightened to throw aside the privileges of a civilized life.

We therefore unanimously join in our meeting to hold our country in common as hitherto.

Some of our children have become Christians. We have missionary schools among us. We have hard the gospel in our nation. We have become civilized & enlightened, & are in hopes that in a few years our nation will be prepared for instruction in other branches of sciences & arts, which are both useful & necessary in civilized society.

There are some white men among us who have been raised in this country from their youth, are connected with us by marriage, & have considerable families, who are very active in encouraging the emigration of our nation. These ought to be our truest friends but prove our worst enemies. They seem to be only concerned how to increase their riches, but do not care what becomes of our Nation, nor even of their own wives and children.

22

CHEROKEE WOMEN

Petition

October 17, 1821 [1831?]

To the Committee and Council,

We the females, residing in Salequoree and Pine Log, believing that the present difficulties and embarrassments under which this nation is placed demands a full expression of the mind of every individual, on the subject of emigrating to Arkansas, would take upon ourselves to address you. Although it is not common for our sex to take part in public measures, we nevertheless feel justified in expressing our sentiments on any subject where our interest is as much at stake as any other part of the community.

We believe the present plan of the General Government to effect our removal West of the Mississippi, and thus obtain our lands for the use of the State of Georgia, to be highly oppressive, cruel and unjust. And we sincerely hope there is no consideration which can induce our citizens to forsake the land of our fathers of which they have been in possession from time immemorial, and thus compel us, against our will, to undergo the toils and difficulties of removing with our helpless families hundreds of miles to unhealthy and unproductive country. We hope therefore the Committee and Council will take into deep consideration our deplorable situation, and do everything in their power to avert such a state of things. And we trust by a prudent course their transactions with the General Government will enlist in our behalf the sympathies of the good people of the United States.

Elias Boudinot's Editorials in the
Cherokee Phoenix

The Cherokees' national newspaper, the Cherokee Phoenix, *was a source of national pride and an important tool in their resistance to removal. In 1826, the National Council appropriated funds for the construction of a printing office in the Nation's capital, New Echota, the purchase of a press, and the casting of types in English and the Cherokee syllabary. The inaugural issue appeared in February 1828 with Elias Boudinot, a nephew of Major Ridge who was educated in mission schools, as editor. Subscribers included not only Cherokees but also citizens of the United States and even Europeans. The newspaper kept its readers informed about national and international events, and it published biblical passages and human interest stories. Laws passed by the Cherokee National Council, advertisements, and notices also appeared in its columns. Most important, the* Cherokee Phoenix *conveyed information to the Nation's citizens about the crisis confronting the Cherokees.*

As an official organ of the Cherokee Nation, the Cherokee Phoenix *presented the Nation's case against removal. The editor printed correspondence from the president and secretary of war, messages from Principal Chief John Ross, and editorials that explained the Cherokee position on removal. As a result, the newspaper became an important factor in uniting the Cherokee people against removal and in promoting sympathy among non-Cherokee readers. When Elias Boudinot began to change his views on removal in 1832, he wanted to open the columns of the* Phoenix *to a debate on the issue. The Council and the principal chief refused to permit open discussion, however, and Boudinot resigned. The paper continued publication under new editorship until 1834, when the federal government refused to pay annuities (annual payments for previously ceded land) into the Cherokee national treasury, and financial problems forced what the Cherokees hoped would be only a temporary suspension of publication. The members of the emerging pro-removal party and the state of Georgia understood the importance of the newspaper in maintaining Cherokee unity: In 1835, the Georgia Guard, accompanied by Boudinot's brother, seized the printing press.*

During the years Boudinot served as editor, he wrote a number of impassioned editorials in support of the Cherokee cause. The Cherokees faced pressure from both the United States and the states, particularly Georgia. The Cherokee capital, many mission schools, and most of the

*large plantations were on lands claimed by Georgia, and John Ridge,
Elias Boudinot, John Ross, and other prominent leaders lived there as
well. President Jackson and Secretary of War John Eaton made it very
clear in letters printed in the June 17, 1829, issue of the* Phoenix *that the
states had ultimate title to the land and that if Indians wanted to live on
land claimed by the states, they must obey state, rather than Cherokee,
law. The editorial from the June 17, 1829,* Phoenix, *reprinted here, com-
mented on a memorial by Chief Ross protesting the extension of Georgia
law over the Cherokees and on letters from Jackson and Eaton. What
irony did Boudinot see in the timing of efforts to remove the Cherokees?*

*On January 8, 1831, Boudinot wrote an editorial complaining about
Georgia's disregard of both Cherokee rights and federal judicial proceedings, in reference specifically to* Cherokee Nation v. Georgia. *Because
Georgia refused to cooperate with federal court proceedings, Boudinot
compared Georgia to South Carolina, which was involved in a controversy with the United States over high tariffs. South Carolina claimed
the right to nullify acts of Congress that were detrimental to the state,
and violence seemed likely until a compromise was reached. Is there
anything in this editorial, particularly in Boudinot's analysis of the
nullification crisis, that strikes you as prophetic?*

*The Georgia law that required white men to take oaths of allegiance
to the state, Boudinot believed, imperiled Cherokee "civilization." What
impact did the law have on the* Phoenix *(February 19, 1831, editorial)?
Why did Boudinot not merely hire a white man who had taken the oath?
The plight of the missionaries was particularly painful to Boudinot. He
lived near Samuel Austin Worcester, and they were working together on
the translation of the Bible into Cherokee. At the same time, he also was
sensitive to charges that Worcester was his ghost writer, and, in editorials
not reprinted here, he strongly defended his own ability and the paper's
integrity. Georgia viewed the missionaries, particularly Worcester, as
interlopers who garnered support for the Cherokees outside the Nation
and strengthened their resolve to resist removal. How did Boudinot view
them (November 12, 1831, editorial)? What kinds of activities in the
Nation were likely to end if the missionaries left?*

*Boudinot defended the progress of "civilization" in his editorials, and
the one he published on November 12, 1831, was particularly eloquent.
To whom did he attribute the introduction of "civilization"? How did "the
first Chief magistrate of the United States" explain differences between
Native peoples and Europeans? How had attitudes toward Indians
changed by the 1830s? What evidence did Boudinot cite to contradict
the view that "an Indian will still be an Indian"?*

Most issues of the Cherokee Phoenix *have survived and are avail-able on microfilm and online. For more information on Boudinot as well as a larger selection of his writings, see Theda Perdue, ed.,* Cherokee Editor: The Writings of Elias Boudinot *(Knoxville: University of Ten-nessee Press, 1983). The dated but standard biography is Ralph Henry Gabriel,* Elias Boudinot, Cherokee, and His America *(Norman: Univer-sity of Oklahoma Press, 1941). Also see Bernd Peyer,* The Tutor'd Mind: Indian Missionary Writers in Antebellum America *(Amherst: University of Massachusetts Press, 1997), chap. 5.*

23

ELIAS BOUDINOT

Editorials in the Cherokee Phoenix

1829, 1831

June 17, 1829

From the documents which we this day lay before our readers, there is not a doubt of the kind of policy, which the present administration of the General Government intends to pursue relative to the Indians. Pres-ident Jackson has, as a neighboring editor remarks, "recognized the doctrine contended for by Georgia in its full extent." It is to be regretted that we were not undeceived long ago, while we were hunters and in our savage state. It appears now from the communication of the Sec-retary of War to the Cherokee Delegation, that the illustrious Wash-ington, Jefferson, Madison and Monroe were only tantalizing us, when they encouraged us in the pursuit of agriculture and Government, and when they afforded us the protection of the United States, by which we have been preserved to this present time as a nation. Why were we not told long ago, that we could not be permitted to establish a government within the limits of any state? Then we could have borne disappoint-ment much easier than now. The pretext for Georgia to extend her juris-diction over the Cherokees has always existed. The Cherokees have always had a government of their own. Nothing, however, was said when we were governed by savage laws, when the abominable law of retaliation carried death in our midst, when it was a lawful act to shed the blood of a person charged with witchcraft, when a brother could kill a brother with impunity, or an innocent man suffer for an offending relative. At that time it might have been a matter of charity to have extended over us the mantle of Christian laws & regulations. But how happens it now, after being fostered by the U. States, and advised by great and good men to establish a government of regular law; when the aid and protection of the General Government have been pledged to us; when we, as dutiful "children" of the President, have followed his instructions and advice, and have established for ourselves a government of regular law; when everything looks so promising around us, that a storm is raised by the extension of tyrannical and unchristian laws, which threatens to blast all our rising hopes and expectations?

There is, as would naturally be supposed, a great rejoicing in Georgia. It is a time of "important news"—"gratifying intelligence"—"The Cherokee lands are to be obtained speedily." It is even reported that the Cherokees have come to the conclusion to sell, and move off to the west of the Mississippi—not so fast. We are yet at our homes, at our peaceful firesides, (except those contiguous to Sandtown, Carroll, &c.) attending to our farms and useful occupations.

We had concluded to give our readers fully our thoughts on the subject, which we, in the above remarks, have merely introduced, but upon reflection & remembering our promise, that we will be moderate, we have suppressed ourselves, and have withheld what we had intended should occupy our editorial column. We do not wish, by any means, unnecessarily to excite the minds of the Cherokees. To our home readers we submit the subject without any special comment. They will judge for themselves. To our distant readers, who may wish to know how we feel under present circumstances, we recommend the memorial, the leading article in our present number. We believe it justly contains the views of the nation.

January 8, 1831

The Georgians have again made another warlike irruption into the nation, of which the following particulars may be relied upon as substantially correct.

A company of twenty five armed men from Carrol County, under the command of one Major Bogus, came into the neighborhood of Hightower, about two weeks since, for the purpose of arresting a number of Cherokees. On their way to Beanstick's they came across two lads, utterly unknown to them. On seeing such an armed force making towards them, the lads fled towards the river, and plunged into the water. Some of the Company pursued them to the bank of the river, and fired at them as they were swimming, and, it is said, came very near shooting one of them. They then went to Beanstick's and arrested his son Joseph. Here they wheeled about, and after parading about the neighborhood with characteristic bravery, marched towards Georgia. They soon discovered that they had mistaken their prisoner Joseph, for one Moses Beanstick, for whom it seems they had a warrant. But it made not a cent's difference with them, for they took him on into Carrol. He had not returned on last monday.

Our feelings are not in a proper state to allow us to make comments upon such proceedings. Will the Congress of the United States permit its citizens to invade us in a warlike manner in time of peace?

[January 8, 1831 — Second Editorial]

During last summer, a Cherokee, by the name of George Tassel, was arrested within the limits of this nation by the Sheriff of Hall County, for murder committed upon the body of another Cherokee, likewise within the limits of the nation. Tassel was taken over the line, and committed to jail. At the last term of Superior Court of Hall County, he was brought out for trial, but the Judge postponed the trial until a convention of Judges at Milledgeville should pronounce upon the constitutionality of the act extending the jurisdiction of the State over the Cherokees. As was to be expected, the convention decided in favor of the jurisdiction of the State. Judge Clayton therefore called a court for the purpose of trying Tassel, who was accordingly tried on the 22d of November, and found *guilty*. It appears that Judge Clayton refused to grant an appeal by a writ of error, to the Supreme Court of the United States, and even refused to certify that Tassel was tried. Tassel was therefore sentenced to be hung on the 24th of last month, on which day he was executed, in defiance of a writ of error sanctioned by the Chief Justice of the United States, and served upon Governor Gilmer, on the 22d, two days previous to the execution. We invite the readers' attention to the following interesting information which we copy from the Milledgeville Recorder. The conduct of the Georgia Legislature is indeed surprising — one day they discountenance the proceedings of the nullifiers of South Carolina — at another, they even out-do the people of South Carolina, and authorize their Governor to hoist the flag of rebellion against the United States! If such proceedings are sanctioned by the majority of the people of the

U. States, the Union is but a tottering fabric, which will soon fall and crumble into atoms.

February 19, 1831

This week we present to our readers but half a sheet—the reason is, one of our printers has left us; and we expect another (who is a white man) to quit us very soon, either to be dragged to the Georgia penitentiary for a term not less than four years, or for his personal safety, to leave the nation, and us to shift for ourselves as well as we can. And, our friends will please to remember, we cannot invite another white printer to our assistance without subjecting him to the same punishment; and to have in our employ one who has taken the oath to support the laws of Georgia which now oppress the Cherokees, is utterly out of the question. Thus is the liberty of the press guarantied by the Constitution of Georgia.

But we will not give up the ship while it is afloat. We have intelligent youths in the nation, and we hope before long to make up our loss. In the mean time our patrons will bear with us & have patience—let them bear in mind that we are in the woods, and, as it is said by some, in a savage country, where printers are not plenty, and a substitute not easily obtained when one of our hands leave us or become indisposed—our paper is therefore easily deranged. Our readers will please not expect to receive the Phoenix very regularly for a while. We shall do the best we can.

We have already noticed the late law of Georgia, making a high misdemeanor, punishable with four years imprisonment at hard labour in the penitentiary, for any white man to reside, after the 1st of March, *within the limits of the Cherokee nation,* (so the copy of the laws we received reads—let the people of Alabama, Tennessee and North Carolina look out—the Georgia legislature is carrying its sovereignty too far,) unless he takes the oath of allegiance, and obtains from the Governor's agent a permit to continue his residence *until further orders.* We cannot help alluding again to that law as being extremely unjust, without saying any thing of its oppressive tendency, both to the whites and Cherokees. It is certainly oppressive on the whites, even admitting that the state of Georgia has an undoubted jurisdiction over the Cherokee territory. Why is it that it is required of *them* to take the oath, when by the extension of that jurisdiction, they were admitted as citizens of the state? Is such requirement made of other citizens? Do the constitution and the laws recognize such a distinction? But what becomes of the liberty of conscience in this case?—Here a white man cannot enjoy that liberty without going to the penitentiary.

What are the effects of this law on the Cherokees? Disastrous. Just such effects as were intended the law should produce. The design appears to be to bring them back to their old station—carry them back twenty years hence. Deprive them of all their means of improvement, and remove all the whites, and it is thought by some, the great obstacle is taken out of the way, and there will be no difficulty to bring the Cherokees to terms. If this is not the *design* it may possibly be the *tendency* of the law. Now let the reader just consider. If we introduce a minister of the Gospel to preach to us the way of life and salvation, here is a law of Georgia, a Christian law too it is said, ready to seize him and send him to the Penitentiary, in violation of the constitution of the state itself. [See Constitution of Georgia, Art. 4—Sec. 10.] If we bring in a white man to teach our children, he is also arrested and suffers a similar punishment. If we wish a decent house built, and invite a carpenter into the nation to do the work, here is a law which forces him from our employ and soon numbers him with culprits. If we introduce a Blacksmith, or any other mechanic, it is the same. Is it not natural to suppose that the tendency of such a law on the Cherokees would be disastrous? It forces from them the very means of their improvement in religion and morals, and in the arts of civilized life.

November 12, 1831

It has been customary to charge the failure of attempts heretofore made to civilize and christianize the aborigines to the Indians themselves. Whence originated the common saying, "An Indian will still be an Indian."—Do what you will, he cannot be civilized—you cannot reclaim him from his wild habits—you may as well expect to change the spots of the Leopard as to effect any substantial renovation in his character—he is as the wild Turkey, which at "night-fall seeks the tallest forest tree for his roosting place." Such assertions, although inconsistent with the general course of providence and the history of nations, have nevertheless been believed and acted upon by many well meaning persons. Such persons do not sufficiently consider that causes, altogether different from those they have been in the habit of assigning, may have operated to frustrate the benevolent efforts made to reclaim the Indian. They do not, perhaps, think that as God has, of one blood, created all the nations of the earth, their circumstances, in a state of nature, must be somewhat the same, and therefore, in the history of mankind, we have no example upon which we can build the assertion, that it is impossible to civilize and christianize the Indian. On the contrary we have instances of nations, originally as ignorant and barbarous as the American natives, having risen from their degraded state to a high pitch of refinement—from the worst kind of paganism to the knowledge of the true God.

We have on more than one occasion remarked upon the difficulties which lie in the way of civilizing the Indians. Those difficulties have been fully developed in the history of the Cherokees within the last two years. They are such as no one can now mistake—their nature is fully revealed and the source from whence they rise can no longer be a matter of doubt. They are not to be found in the "nature" of the Indians, which a man in high authority once said was as difficult to change as the Leopard his spots. It is not because they are, of all others, the most degraded and ignorant that they have not been brought to enjoy the blessings of a civilized life.—But it is because they have to contend with obstacles as numerous as they are peculiar.

With a commendable zeal the first Chief magistrate of the United States undertook to bring the Cherokees into the pale of civilization, by establishing friendly relations with them by treaties, and introducing the mechanic arts among them. He was indeed a "father" to them—They regarded him as such—They placed confidence in what he said, and well they might, for he was true to his promises. Of course the foundation for the improvement which the Cherokees have since made was laid under the patronage of that illustrious man. His successors followed his example and treated their "red children" as human beings, capable of improvement, and possessing rights derived from the source of all good, and guarantied by compacts as solemn as a great Republic could make. The attempts of those good men were attended with success, because they believed those attempts were feasible and acted accordingly.

Upon the same principle have acted those benevolent associations who have taken such a deep interest in the welfare of the Indians, and who may have expended so much time and money in extending the benign influence of religion. Those associations went hand in hand with the Government—it was a work of co-operation. God blessed their efforts. The Cherokees have been reclaimed from their wild habits—Instead of hunters they have become the cultivators of the soil—Instead of wild and ferocious savages, thirsting for blood, they have become the mild "citizens," the friends and brothers of the white man—Instead of the superstitious heathens, many of them have become the worshippers of the true God. Well would it have been if the cheering fruits of those labors had been fostered and encouraged by an enlightened community! But alas! no sooner was it made manifest that the Cherokees were becoming strongly attached to the ways and usages of civilized life, than was aroused the opposition of those from whom better things ought to have been expected. No sooner was it known that they had learned the proper use of the earth, and that they were now less likely to dispose of their lands for a mess of pottage, than they came in conflict with the cupidity and self-interest of those who ought to have been their benefactors—Then commenced a series of obstacles hard to overcome, and difficulties intended as a stumbling block, and unthought of before. The "Great Father" of the "red man" has lent his influence to encourage those difficulties. The *guardian* has deprived his *wards* of their rights—The sacred obligations of treaties and laws have been disregarded—The promises of Washington and Jefferson have not been fulfilled. The policy of the United States on Indian affairs has taken a different direction, for no other reason than that the Cherokees have so far become civilized as to appreciate a regular form of Government. They are now deprived of rights they once enjoyed—A neighboring power is now permitted to extend its withering hand over them—Their own laws, intended to regulate their society, to encourage virtue and to suppress vice, must now be abolished, and civilized acts, passed for the purpose of expelling them, must be substituted.—Their intelligent citizens who have been instructed through the means employed by former administrations, and through the efforts of benevolent societies, must be abused and insulted, represented as avaricious, feeding upon the poverty of the common Indians—the hostility of all those who want the Indian lands must be directed against them. That the Cherokees may be kept in ignorance, teachers who had settled among them by the approbation of the Government, for the best of all purposes, have been compelled to leave them by reason of laws unbecoming any civilized nation—Ministers of the Gospel, who might have, at this day of trial, administered to them the consolations of Religion, have been arrested, chained, dragged away before their eyes, tried as felons, and finally immured in prison with thieves and robbers.

Is not here an array of *difficulties?*—The truth is, while a portion of the community have been, in the most laudable manner, engaged in using efforts to civilize and christianize the Indian, another portion of the same community have been busy in counteracting those efforts. Cupidity and self-interest are at the bottom of all these difficulties—A desire *to possess* the Indian land is paramount to a desire to see him *established* on the soil as a *civilized* man.

The Treaty of New Echota

When the Supreme Court ordered the release of the imprisoned missionaries, the Cherokees were jubilant. Soon, however, their joy turned to dismay. State officials simply ignored the Supreme Court ruling, and President Jackson declined to force the state to comply. At this point, Elias Boudinot and John Ridge, along with several other Cherokee leaders, began to doubt whether the Cherokees would ever receive justice. Invaded by Georgians, powerless to resist, and pressured by both federal and state authorities, the Cherokees seemed to have no alternative to negotiating removal. Those who despaired of remaining in the East and advocated negotiation became known as the Treaty Party. They attracted relatively few followers since the vast majority of Cherokees continued to place their faith in John Ross's leadership and their own sense of righteousness.

The breach between those who favored negotiation and those who refused to even consider removal widened. In June 1834, Treaty Party members, led by Ross's own brother Andrew, signed a removal treaty, but the Senate refused to ratify the clearly fraudulent document. Each side sent delegations to Washington, but the Treaty Party, now led by Ridge and Boudinot, found the warmer reception. Forced into negotiating, Ross agreed to take a proposed treaty to the annual Council meeting in October 1835, but he made only vague references to a financial settlement offered by the U.S. Senate. The Council rejected the Senate's offer and then appointed a delegation of treaty and antitreaty men to go to Washington and work out a mutually acceptable agreement. Boudinot soon resigned from the delegation, but Ridge went to Washington with Ross.

In the meantime, U.S. treaty commissioner John F. Schermerhorn called for a conference at New Echota in December 1835. John Ross and the Cherokee Council did not attend. Out of a total population of approximately sixteen thousand, just over two hundred Cherokees met there and ratified a removal treaty by a vote of seventy-five to seven. Although Ridge was not in attendance, he later attached his signature to the document his father,

Major Ridge, and cousin, Elias Boudinot, had already signed. Despite Cherokee protests, the U.S. Senate ratified the Treaty of New Echota in the spring of 1836, and the government prepared to enforce its provisions.

What did the Cherokees receive in exchange for their territory? What guarantees were made to them? How long did they have to prepare for the journey west? What responsibility did the United States have for their move? Has Congress acted on Article 7? Compare the description of the Cherokees in Article 7 to the descriptions of Cass and Jackson.

An excerpt of the Treaty of New Echota is printed here. If you would like to read the entire text, you can find it in Charles J. Kappler, ed., Indian Affairs: Laws and Treaties, 5 vols. (Washington, D.C.: Government Printing Office, 1904–1941). Colin G. Calloway addresses the treaty in Chapter 4 of Pen and Ink Witchcraft (New York: Oxford University Press, 2013).

24

Treaty with the Cherokees

1835

Whereas the Cherokees are anxious to make some arrangements with the Government of the United States whereby the difficulties they have experienced by a residence within the settled parts of the United States under the jurisdication and laws of the State Governments may be terminated and adjusted; and with a view to reuniting their people in one body and securing a permanent home for themselves and their posterity in the country selected by their forefathers without the territorial limits of the State sovereignties, and where they can establish and enjoy a government of their choice and perpetuate such a state of society as may be most consonant with their views, habits and condition; and as may tend to their individual comfort and their advancement in civilization. . . .

And whereas the Cherokee people, at their last October council at Red Clay, fully authorized and empowered a delegation or committee of twenty persons of their nation to enter into and conclude a treaty with the United States commissioner then present, *at that place or elsewhere* and as the people had good reason to believe that a treaty would then and there be made or at a subsequent council at New Echota which the commissioners it was well known and understood, were authorized and instructed to convene for said purpose; and since the said delegation have gone on to Washington city, with a view to close negotiations there, as stated by them notwithstanding they were officially informed by the United States commissioner that they would not be received by the President of the United States; and that the Government would transact no business of this nature with them, and that if a treaty was made it must be done here in the nation, where the delegation at Washington last winter *urged that it should be done for the purpose of promoting peace and harmony among the people*; and since these facts have also been corroborated to us by a communication recently received by the commissioner from the Government of the United States and read and explained to the people in open council and therefore believing said delegation can effect nothing and since our difficulties are daily increasing and our situation is rendered more and more precarious uncertain and insecure in consequence of the legislation of the States; and seeing no effectual way of relief, but in accepting the liberal overtures of the United States. . . .

And whereas the said commissioners did appoint and notify a general council of the nation to convene at New Echota on the 21st day of December 1835; and informed them that the commissioners would be prepared to make a treaty with the Cherokee people who should assemble there and those who did not come they should conclude gave their assent and sanction to whatever should be transacted at this council and the people having met in council according to said notice.

Therefore the following articles of a treaty are agreed upon and concluded between William Carroll and John F. Schermerhorn commissioners on the part of the United States and the chiefs and head men and people of the Cherokee nation in general council assembled this 29th day of Decr 1835.

Article 1

The Cherokee nation hereby cede relinquish and convey to the United States all the lands owned claimed or possessed by them east of the Mississippi river, and hereby release all their claims upon the United States for spoliations of every kind for and in consideration of the sum of five millions of dollars to be expended paid and invested in the manner stipulated and agreed upon in the following articles. But as a question has arisen between the commissioners and the Cherokees whether the Senate in their resolution by which they advised "that a sum not exceeding five millions of dollars be paid to the Cherokee Indians for all their lands and possessions east of the Mississippi river" have included and made any allowance or consideration for claims for spoliations it is therefore agreed on the part of the United States that this question shall be again submitted to the Senate for their consideration and decision and if no allowance was made for spoliations that then an additional sum of three hundred thousand dollars be allowed for the same. . . .

Article 5

The United States hereby covenant and agree that the lands ceded to the Cherokee nation in the forgoing article shall, in no future time without their consent, be included within the territorial limits or jurisdiction of any State or Territory. But they shall secure to the Cherokee nation the right by their national councils to make and carry into effect all such laws as they may deem necessary for the government and protection of the persons and property within their own country belonging to their people or such persons as have connected themselves with them: provided always that they shall not be inconsistent with the constitution of the United States and such acts of Congress as have been or may be passed regulating trade and intercourse with the Indians; and also, that they shall not be considered as extending to such citizens and army of the United States as may travel or reside in the Indian country by permission according to the laws and regulations established by the Government of the same. . . .

Article 7

The Cherokee nation having already made great progress in civilization and deeming it important that every proper and laudable inducement should be offered to their people to improve their condition as well as to guard and secure in the most effectual manner the rights guarantied to them in this treaty, and with a view to illustrate the liberal and enlarged policy of the Government of the United States towards the Indians in their removal beyond the territorial limits of the States, it is stipulated that they shall be entitled to a delegate in the House of Representatives of the United States whenever Congress shall make provision for the same.

Article 8

The United States also agree and stipulate to remove the Cherokees to their new homes and to subsist them one year after their arrival there and that a sufficient number of steamboats and baggage-wagons shall be furnished to remove them comfortably, and so as not to endanger their health, and that a physician well supplied with medicines shall accompany each detachment of emigrants removed by the Government. Such persons and families as in the opinion of the emigrating agent are capable of subsisting and removing themselves shall be permitted to do so; and they shall be allowed in full for all claims for the same twenty dollars for each member of their family; and in lieu of their one year's rations they shall be paid the sum of thirty-three dollars and thirty-three cents if they prefer it.

Such Cherokees also as reside at present out of the nation and shall remove with them in two years west of the Mississippi shall be entitled to allowance for removal and subsistence as above provided.

Article 9

The United States agree to appoint suitable agents who shall make a just and fair valuation of all such improvements now in the possession of the Cherokees as add any value to the lands; and also of the ferries owned by them, according to their net income; and such improvements and ferries from which they have been dispossessed in a lawless manner or under any existing laws of the State where the same may be situated.

The just debts of the Indians shall be paid out of any monies due them for their improvements and claims; and they shall also be furnished at the discretion of the President of the United States with a sufficient sum to enable them to obtain the necessary means to remove themselves to their new homes, and the balance of their dues shall be paid them at the Cherokee agency west of the Mississippi. The missionary establishments shall also be valued and appraised in a like manner and the amount of them paid over by the United States to the treasurers of the respective missionary societies by whom they have been established and improved in order to enable them to erect such buildings and make such improvements among the Cherokees west of the Mississippi as they may deem necessary for their benefit. Such teachers at present among the Cherokees as this council shall select and designate shall be removed west of the Mississippi with the Cherokee nation and on the same terms allowed to them.

Article 10

The President of the United States shall invest in some safe and most productive public stocks of the country for the benefit of the whole Cherokee nation who have removed or shall remove to the lands assigned by this treaty to the Cherokee nation west of the Mississippi the following sums as a permanent fund for the purposes hereinafter specified and pay over the net income of the same annually to such person or persons as shall be authorized or appointed by the Cherokee nation to receive the same and their receipt shall be a full discharge for the amount paid to them viz: the sum of two hundred thousand dollars in addition to the present annuities of the nation to constitute a general fund the interest of which shall be applied annually by the council of the nation to such purposes as they may deem best for the general interest of their people. The sum of fifty thousand dollars to constitute an orphans' fund the annual income of which shall be expended towards the support and education of such orphan children as are destitute of the means of subsistence. The sum of one hundred and fifty thousand dollars in addition to the present school fund of the nation shall constitute a permanent school fund, the interest of which shall be applied annually by the council of the nation for the support of common schools and such a literary institution of a higher order as may be established in the Indian country. And in order to secure as far as possible the true and beneficial application of the orphans' and school fund the council of the Cherokee nation when required by the President of the United States shall make a report of the application of those funds and he shall at all times have the right if the funds have been misapplied to correct any abuses of them and direct the manner of their application for the purposes for which they were intended. The council of the nation may by giving two years' notice of their intention withdraw their funds by and with the consent of the President and Senate of the United States, and invest them in such manner as they may deem most proper for their interest. The United States also agree and stipulate to pay the just debts and claims against the Cherokee nation held by the citizens of the same and also the just claims of citizens of the United States for services rendered to the nation and the sum of sixty thousand dollars is appropriated for this purpose but no claims against individual persons of the nation shall be allowed and paid by the nation. The sum of three hundred thousand dollars is hereby set apart to pay and liquidate the just claims of the Cherokees upon the United States for spoliations of every kind, that have not been already satisfied under former treaties. . . .

Article 16

It is hereby stipulated and agreed by the Cherokees that they shall remove to their new homes within two years from the ratification of this treaty and that during such time the United States shall protect and defend them in their possessions and property and free use and occupation of the same and such persons as have been dispossessed of their improvements and houses; and for which no grant has actually issued previously to the enactment of the law of the State of Georgia, of December 1835 to regulate Indian occupancy shall be again put in possession and placed in the same situation and condition, in reference to the laws of the State of Georgia, as the Indians that have not been dispossessed; and if this is not done, and the people are left unprotected, then the United States shall pay the several Cherokees for their losses and damages sustained by them in consequence thereof. And it is also stipulated and agreed that the public buildings and improvements on which they are situated at New Echota for which no grant has been actually made previous to the passage of the above recited act if not occupied by the Cherokee people shall be reserved for the public and free use of the United States and the Cherokee Indians for the purpose of settling and closing all the Indian business arising under this treaty between the commissioners of claims and the Indians. . . .

Article 19

This treaty after the same shall be ratified by the President and Senate of the United States shall be obligatory on the contracting parties. . . .

In testimony whereof, the commissioners and the chiefs, head men, and people whose names are hereunto annexed, being duly authorized by the people in general council assembled, have affixed their hands and seals for themselves, and in behalf of the Cherokee nation.

I have examined the foregoing treaty, and although not present when it was made, I approve its provisions generally, and therefore sign it.

Wm. Carroll,
J. F. Schermerhorn

Major Ridge, his x mark,	[L.S.]	Te-gah-e-ske, his x mark,	[L.S.]
James Foster, his x mark,	[L.S.]	Robert Rogers,	[L.S.]
Tesa-ta-esky, his x mark,	[L.S.]	John Gunter,	[L.S.]
Charles Moore, his x mark,	[L.S.]	John A. Bell,	[L.S.]
George Chambers, his x mark,	[L.S.]	Charles F. Foreman,	[L.S.]
Tah-yeske, his x mark,	[L.S.]	William Rogers,	[L.S.]
Archilla Smith, his x mark,	[L.S.]	George W. Adair,	[L.S.]
Andrew Ross,	[L.S.]	Elias Boudinot,	[L.S.]
William Lassley,	[L.S.]	James Starr, his x mark,	[L.S.]
Cae-te-hee, his x mark,	[L.S.]	Jesse Half-breed, his x mark,	[L.S.]

Signed and sealed in presence of—

Western B. Thomas, secretary.
Ben. F. Currey, special agent.
M. Wolfe Batman, first lieutenant, sixth
    U.S. Infantry, disbursing agent.
Jon. L. Hooper, lieutenant,
    fourth Infantry.

C. M. Hitchcock, M.D., assistant
    surgeon, U. S. A.
G. W. Currey,
Wm. H. Underwood,
Cornelius D. Terhune,
John W. H. Underwood.

The Opposition Continues

*The signing of a removal treaty in December 1835 and its ratification by
the Senate in the spring of 1836 did not end opposition to removal. John
Ross continued his efforts to have the treaty abrogated. Simultaneously
and in apparent contradiction to his resistance to removal, he lobbied to
have the payment for lands in the East increased and the title to a western territory guaranteed. He suggested alternatives to removal, including
the extension of U.S. citizenship to Cherokees remaining in the East and
their acceptance of fair state laws. Such a measure would have ended
the Cherokee Nation and his own political career. He even explored the
possibility of emigration to Mexico, where the Cherokees would at last be
beyond the reach of the United States. Ross worried that removal under
the Treaty of New Echota would not be the Cherokees' last. Indeed, in
1828 Cherokees who had earlier moved west had to give up their land in
what became Arkansas and move even farther west.*

*Most Cherokees continued to support Ross even when his position was
not clear. The public statements of the vast majority of Cherokees left
little doubt where they stood. Councils rejected negotiation, and fifteen
thousand Cherokees protested the Treaty of New Echota in petitions to
the U.S. Senate. Ross insisted that he merely represented their views. The
Treaty Party, according to Ross, had behaved unethically, illegally, and
undemocratically. They had subverted, Ross believed, the incontrovertible
will of the people.*

*Because the president and the Congress recognized the Treaty Party
and the Treaty of New Echota as legitimate, Ross felt compelled to go on
the offensive. Ross relied on the pen of his friend John Howard Payne,
a journalist who had been arrested along with the chief by the Georgia
Guard, and sympathetic newspapers. With Payne's advice, in 1836 Ross
published a pamphlet,* Letter from John Ross . . . in Answer to Inquiries from a Friend Regarding the Cherokee Affairs with the United
States. *Excerpts from his pamphlet appeared, with supporting editorial*

comment, in the widely read Niles Weekly Register *and in other periodicals. Journalism in the antebellum period rarely measured up to modern standards of impartiality; indeed, most newspapers were openly partisan. Consequently, Ross managed to get fairly good coverage for his position in the anti-Jackson Whig press.*

How good a deal did Ross believe the Cherokees got in the Treaty of New Echota? What were his specific objections to the terms of the treaty? Did Ross believe that the signatures of any group of Cherokees—authorized or unauthorized—could bind the Cherokees to the terms of a treaty? If not, how could a treaty be legitimately ratified? How did this compare to the United States' procedure for ratifying treaties? What do you think Ross meant when he demanded that Cherokees receive the "protection and privileges" of state law if they became citizens of the United States? How successfully do you think Ross believed Cherokees would assimilate into Anglo-American society if given the opportunity? What evidence did he give for Cherokee acculturation?

If you would like to know more about John Ross, who served the Cherokees as principal chief from 1828 to 1866, see Gary E. Moulton, John Ross, Cherokee Chief *(Athens: University of Georgia Press, 1991). Moulton also has edited Ross's letters and other papers, including the entire text from which this excerpt is taken, and they have been published as* The Papers of Chief John Ross, *2 vols. (Norman: University of Oklahoma Press, 1985).*

25

JOHN ROSS

*Letter in Answer
to Inquiries from a Friend*
July 2, 1836

I wish I could acquiesce in your impression, that a Treaty has been made, by which every difficulty between the Cherokees and the United States has been set at rest; but I must candidly say, that I know of no such Treaty. I do not mean to prophesy any similar troubles to those which have, in other cases, followed the failure to adjust disputed points with Indians; the Cherokees act on a principle preventing apprehensions of that nature—their principle is, "endure and forbear;" but I must distinctly declare to you that I believe, the document [Treaty of New Echota] signed by unauthorized individuals at Washington, will never be regarded by the Cherokee nation as a Treaty. The delegation appointed by the people to make a Treaty, have protested against that instrument "as deceptive to the world and a fraud upon the Cherokee people." You say you do *not* see my name appended to the paper in question, but that you regard the omission as a typographical mistake, because you *do* find my name among those who are mentioned in it as the future directors of Cherokee affairs.

I will answer these points separately: and, first,

My name is not, by mistake, omitted among the signers of the paper in question; and the reasons why it is not affixed to that paper, are the following:

Neither myself nor any other member of the regular delegation to Washington, can, without violating our most sacred engagements, ever recognize that paper as a Treaty, by assenting to its terms, or the mode of its execution. They are entirely inconsistent with the views of the Cherokee people. Three times have the Cherokee people formally and openly rejected conditions substantially the same as these. We were commissioned by the people, under express injunctions, not to bind the nation to any such conditions. The delegation representing the Cherokees, have, therefore, officially rejected these conditions themselves, and have regularly protested before the Senate and House of Representatives, against their ratification. The Cherokee people, in two protests, the one signed by twelve thousand seven hundred and fourteen persons, and the other by three thousand two hundred and fifty persons, spoke for themselves against the Treaty, even previous to its rejection by those whom they had selected to speak for them.

With your impressions concerning the advantages secured by the subtle instrument in question, you will, no doubt, wonder at this opposition. But it possesses not the advantages you and others imagine; and that is the reason why it has encountered, and ever will encounter opposition. You suppose we are to be removed through it from a home, by circumstances rendered disagreeable and even untenable, to be secured in a better home, where nothing can disturb or dispossess us. *Here is the great mystification.* We are not secured in the new home promised to us. We are exposed to precisely the same miseries, from which, if this measure is enforced, the United States' power professes to relieve us, but does so entirely by the exercise of that power, against our will.

If we really had the security you and others suppose we have, we would not thus complain. But mark the truth and judge for yourself.

... For example. Suppose it should suit the policy of the United States, hereafter, to pass a law organizing a territorial government upon the Cherokee lands, west? That law necessarily destroys the character of the Cherokee nation as a distinct community; the nation becomes legally extinct; the lands revert to the United States, and the Cherokee people are bound, by assenting to the conditions of the pretended Treaty, to acquiesce in this law providing a plausible pretext for their annihilation. And should they demur, what is the result? An article in the pretended Treaty expressly stipulates, that military posts, and military roads may, anywhere, and at any time, be established by the United States, in the new country, set apart for the Indians. Hence, any one who might complain of any act of the United States as unauthorized by the right construction of the pretended Treaty, would be as liable to ejectment for the purpose of creating a military post at the malcontent's abode in the Cherokee country west—as now he actually is, and long has been, under similar circumstances, in the Cherokee part of Georgia—and were vexations to become universal, as they have in Georgia, the region might, in the same manner, be filled with soldiers, and the existence of the Cherokee nation become at once extinguished by laws to which the people will be said themselves to have assented. That there is no disposition ever to interfere thus, is attempted to be proved by reference to an article of the pretended Treaty, excluding intruders and white men; but this very article is clogged with a worse than neutralizing condition—a condition pregnant with sources of future disquiet—a condition that it is not to prevent the introduction of useful farmers, mechanics, and teachers, under which denomination some future Executive of the United States may find it convenient, hereafter, to overwhelm the original population, and bring about the Territorial Government, by which the Cherokees will be regarded as legally extinguished, and the country of their exile as *reverting* to its real proprietor, the United States. Thus will the favourite theory, which has been ascribed to the President [Andrew Jackson], be fully realized. This policy will *legislate the Indians off the land*!

That all these things are possible, is proved by the present posture of affairs in the region of our birth, our sacred inheritance from our fathers. It is but a few years, since the apprehension of scenes like those from which the United States acknowledges her incompetency to protect us, even under the pledge of Treaties, would have been regarded as a morbid dream. But a State has already been created on the boundary of the retreat set apart for the exile of the Indians—the State of Arkansas; another State, and an independent one—a new republic, made up of many of the old foes of the Indians—Texas, is rising on another boundary; and who shall say how soon these, and other new bordering states, may become as uneasy from the Indian neighbourhood, as the old ones are now? It was at one time thought that the United States never could declare she was unable to keep the Treaties of former days. Is it less possible that she may hereafter experience the same difficulty in keeping those of the days in which we live? especially, as in the present instance, she may be called upon, not only to defend those Treaties from violation by her own citizens, but by the people, though of the same origin, belonging to a new, a warlike, an independent republic. . . .

I must here beg leave to observe that I have never yet been placed in a position which could render *my* individual decision conclusive upon any matters of this nature, nor could I ever wish for such responsibility. The Cherokee people are not "my people;" I am only one of their agents and their elected chief: It is I who serve under them, not they under me. At the time of the transaction to which you allude, the delegation, of which I was a member, had ample powers to make a treaty for a partial cession of the country, with security in the residue; but we had no authority for the extension of our discretionary power to any treaty for an entire sale of the country; such a suggestion was not contemplated by the people and it would consequently be impossible for us to decide upon such, without a reference to those who sent us. I myself was only one among many. I could not, by my single act, bind even my associates to any promise of an entire sale, nor of course to any *award*, even had such an *award* been made, for the amount to be paid for an entire sale; I could only, with them, submit such an offer, if made, to the people. . . .

In conclusion I would observe, that I still strongly hope we shall find ultimate justice from the good sense of the administration and of the people of the United States. I will not even yet believe that either the one or the other would wrong us with their eyes open. I am persuaded they have erred only in ignorance, and an ignorance forced upon them by the misrepresentation and artifices of the interested. . . . The Cherokees, under any circumstances, have no weapon to use but argument. If that should fail, they must submit, when their time shall come, in silence, but honest argument they cannot think will be forever used in vain. The Cherokee people will always hold themselves ready to respect a *real* treaty and bound to sustain any treaty which they can feel that they are bound to respect. But they are certain not to consider the attempt of a very few persons to sell the country for themselves, as obligatory upon them, and I and all my associates in the regular delegation, still look confidently to the effect of a sense of justice upon the American community, in producing a real settlement of this question, upon equitable terms and with competent authorities. But, on one point, you may be perfectly at rest. Deeply as our people feel, I cannot suppose they will ever be goaded by those feelings to any acts of violence. No, sir. They have been too long inured to suffering without resistance, and they still look to the sympathies and not to the fears, of those who have them in their power. In certain recent discussions in the representative hall at Washington, our enemies made it an objection against me and against others, that we were not Indians, but had *the principles of white men*, and were consequently unworthy of a hearing in the Indian cause. I will own that it has been my pride, as Principal Chief of the Cherokees, to implant in the bosoms of the people, and to cherish in my own, *the principles* of white men! It is to this fact that our white neighbours must ascribe their safety under the smart of the wrongs we have suffered from them. It is in this they may confide for our continued patience. But when I speak of *the principles of white men*, I speak not of such principles as actuate those who talk thus to us, but of those mighty principles to which the United States owes her greatness and her liberty. To principles like these even yet we turn with confidence for redemption from our miseries. When Congress shall be less overwhelmed with business, no doubt, in some way, the matter may be brought to a reconsideration, and when the representatives of the American people have leisure to see how little it will cost them to be just, we are confident they will be true to themselves, in acting with good faith towards us. Be certain that while the Cherokees are endeavouring to obtain a more friendly consideration from the United States, they will not forget to show by their circumspection how well they merit it; and though no doubt there are many who will represent them otherwise, for injurious purposes, I can assure you that the white people have nothing to apprehend, even from our sense of contumely and unfairness, unless it be through the perverse and the treacherous manoeuvres of such agents as they themselves may keep among us.

The Treaty Party's Defense

The Treaty Party smarted from the published attacks on it and struck back. The primary public defender of the Treaty of New Echota was Elias Boudinot, who had served as editor of the Cherokee Phoenix *until 1832. His vituperative personal attack on Ross makes modern criticism of chief executives seem tame by comparison, but Boudinot felt that the Ross partisans had besmirched his good name and he struck back in defense of his honor. Boudinot had a long career of service to the Nation, as did his uncle Major Ridge and his cousin John Ridge. The elder Ridge had been a member of the Lighthorse Guard (the Cherokee police force), treaty commissioner, delegate to Washington, ambassador to the Creek Indians, member and speaker of the Council, and co-chief with Ross in 1827–1828. His son John had served as clerk of the Council, member and president of the Committee (the upper house in the Cherokee's bicameral legislature), and member of several delegations to Washington. Like Ross, the Ridges had deep roots in the Cherokee Nation and struggled to decide on the best course for their people. The absolute intransigence of Georgia, exhibited by the state's refusal to acknowledge the Supreme Court's decision and the legislature's increasingly oppressive measures, led them to decide that removal was unavoidable. The Cherokees as a people could survive only if they gave up the land. The true patriot, they believed, could not countenance their further suffering. The problem was convincing other Cherokees that removal was the only viable course left.*

The absence of elections meant that little opportunity existed to hold a national referendum on removal generally or the Treaty of New Echota specifically. State laws had prohibited the Cherokee government from operating according to its constitution of 1827. Because elections could not be held, the Council extended the terms of officeholders through the duration of the crisis with Georgia. An election would have enabled candidates on either side of the issue to debate the merits of their respective positions. Without elections, no real forum existed. The Cherokee Phoenix *had ceased publication in 1834, but as an official organ of the government, its columns had always been closed to debate. Other newspapers circulated in the Nation, but little Cherokee debate over removal took place in public. Consequently, the Cherokees were somewhat limited in the information available to them. Furthermore, Boudinot, a New England–educated intellectual, had serious misgivings about the ability of the majority of Cherokees to make a rational decision. His arrogance and condescension as well as his harsh comments about Ross, however, should not obscure his arguments in favor of negotiating a removal treaty.*

What did Boudinot believe the outcome of a national Cherokee debate would have been? According to the previous document, A Letter from John Ross, *what would the result have been? Who cited the best evidence? In what ways, both public and private, did Boudinot believe that Ross had abused his authority? How did Boudinot's depiction of the Cherokees compare with that of Ross (Document 25)? How did it compare with that of Cass (Document 17)?*

Boudinot published his pamphlet in Athens, Georgia, in 1837 as Letters and Other Papers Relating to Cherokee Affairs: Being a Reply to Sundry Publications Authorized by John Ross. *In 1838 Wilson Lumpkin, a senator from 1837 to 1841, submitted it for publication as Senate Document 121, 25th Cong., 2nd sess.*

26

ELIAS BOUDINOT

Letters and Other Papers Relating to Cherokee Affairs: Being a Reply to Sundry Publications Authorized by John Ross

1837

What is termed the "Cherokee question" may be considered in two points of view: the controversy with the States and the General Government, and the controversy among the Cherokees themselves. The first has been agitated in so many ways, and before so many tribunals, that it is needless, for any good purpose, to remark upon it at this place. The latter is founded upon the question of a remedy, to extricate the Cherokees from their difficulties, in consequence of their conflict with the States. Upon this point, less has been said or known before the public but it has not been the less interesting to the Cherokees. It is here where different views and different feelings have been excited.

"What is to be done?" was a natural inquiry, after we found that all our efforts to obtain redress from the General Government, *on the land of our fathers*, had been of no avail. The first rupture among ourselves was the moment we presumed to answer that question. To a portion of the Cherokee people it early became evident that the interest of their countrymen and the happiness of their posterity, depended upon an entire change of policy. Instead of contending uselessly against superior power, the only course left, was, to yield to circumstances over which they had no control.

In all difficulties of this kind, between the United States and the Cherokees, the only mode of settling them has been by treaties; consequently, when a portion of our people became convinced that no other measures would avail, they became the *advocates of a treaty*, as the only means to extricate the Cherokees from their perplexities; hence they were called *the treaty party*. Those who maintained the old policy, were known as the *anti-treaty party*. At the head of the latter has been Mr. John Ross. . . .

We charge Mr. Ross with having deluded them with expectations incompatible with and injurious to, their interest. He has prevented the discussion of this interesting matter, by systematic measures, at a time when discussion was of the most vital importance. By that means the people have been kept ignorant of their true condition. They have been taught to feel and expect what *could not* be realized, and what Mr. Ross himself must have known *would not* be realized. This great delusion has lasted to this day. Now, in view of such a state of things, we cannot conceive of the acts of a *minority* to be so reprehensible or unjust as are represented by Mr. Ross. If one hundred persons are ignorant of their true situation, and are so completely blinded as not to see the destruction that awaits them, we can see strong reasons to justify the action of a minority of fifty persons to do what the majority *would do* if they understood their condition—to save a *nation* from political thraldom and moral degradation. It is not intended to discuss the question here, but simply to show that a great deal may be said on both sides; besides, the reader will recollect that it is in reference to an Indian community, and to very extraordinary circumstances. . . .

According to a provision of the Cherokee constitution, the office of the principal chief and the members of the council are to be filled, the latter by election of the people, for two years, and the former by the general council, for four years. The last election held was in the month of August, of 1830, and the next was to have been held in 1832. In the same year, in the month of October, came the election, by the council, for the principal chief. On account of a law of the State of Georgia, there was no election held in August, 1832; and, consequently, the members of the council, who were, according to the constitution, to elect the principal chief in the month of October following, were not elected. In this state of things, the members of the council, whose term of service was about to expire, took the following measures, at a called council, held, I think, in the month of August. I will be short. They passed a resolution appointing twenty-four men, selected (by the council) from the Cherokee people then on the ground, the aggregate number of which did not *exceed* two hundred. These twenty-four men were required to meet, as the resolution expressed it, in *convention*. I claim to know something of this matter, because I was a member of the *convention*. Two propositions were introduced: 1. That the Cherokee Government should be continued, *as it was*, for two years. This was my proposition. 2. That the Cherokee Government should be continued, as it was, *while our difficulties lasted*. The latter prevailed, and it was sent to the council as the *advice* of the *convention,* which the council very gravely *accepted*, and referred to the people *on the ground* for their confirmation. The members of the council, the chiefs, and all, accordingly retained their seats after the expiration of their term of office prescribed in the constitution, and have retained them ever since. . . .

Again, it is a "fraud upon the world" to say that "upwards of fifteen thousand Cherokees have protested against the treaty, solemnly declaring they will never acquiesce," and to produce before the world a paper containing that number of signatures. Let us see how this matter is. I will quote another sentence. "The Cherokee people, in two protests, the one signed by twelve thousand seven hundred and fourteen persons, and the other by three thousand two hundred and fifty persons, spoke for themselves against the treaty." In order to illustrate these, I take another from your memorial. "The Cherokee population has recently been reported by the War Department to be 18,000." Of these 18,000, there are upwards of 1,000 blacks, who, you will not allege, have been among the signers. Of the remaining sixteen or seventeen thousand, (for I have not the census before me,) upwards of 1,000, at the lowest estimate, had been registered for removal, none of whom, it is likely, would have signed any protest. Here are then about 15,000, probably less, to do what? To "*protest*," "SOLEMNLY DECLARE," to "sign," to SPEAK FOR THEMSELVES against the treaty! I must confess my impotency to unravel such a mystery as this. A *population* of 15,000 furnish 15,000 who are able and competent *to declare* and *to speak for themselves*! I suppose, however, we are required to believe it implicitly. This must indeed be a wise and precocious nation. Well may you say, "that owing to the intelligence of the Cherokee people, they have a correct knowledge of their own rights." . . .

To be sure, from your account of the condition and circumstances of the Cherokees, the public may form an idea different from what my remarks may seem to convey. When applied to a portion of our people, confined mostly to whites intermarried among us, and the descendants of whites, your account is probably correct, divesting it of all the exaggeration with which you have encircled it; but look at the mass, look at the entire population as it now is, and say, can you see any indication of a progressing improvement, anything that can encourage a philanthropist? You know that it is almost a dreary waste. I care not if I am accounted a slanderer of my country's reputation; every observing man in this nation knows that I speak the words of truth and soberness. In the light that I consider my countrymen, not as mere animals, and to judge of their happiness by their condition as such, which, to be sure, is bad enough, but as moral beings, to be affected for better or for worse by moral circumstances, I say their condition is wretched. . . .

If the dark picture which I have here drawn is a true one, and no candid person will say it is an exaggerated one, can we see a brighter prospect ahead? In another country, and under other circumstances, there is a *better* prospect. Removal, then, is the only remedy, the only *practicable* remedy. By it there *may be* finally a renovation; our people *may* rise from their very ashes, to become prosperous and happy, and a credit to our race. Such has been and is now my opinion, and under such a settled opinion I have acted in all this affair. My language has been; "fly for your lives;" it is now the same. I would say to my countrymen, you among the rest, fly from the moral pestilence that will finally destroy our nation.

What is the prospect in reference to *your* plan of relief, if you are understood at all to have any plan? It is dark and gloomy beyond description. Subject the Cherokees to the laws of the States in their present condition? It matters not how favorable those laws may be, instead of remedying the evil you would only rivet the chains and fasten the manacles of their servitude and degradation. The final destiny of our race, under such circumstances, is too revolting to think of. Its course *must* be downward, until it finally becomes extinct or is merged in another race, more ignoble and more detested. Take my word for it, it is the sure consummation, if you succeed in preventing the removal of your people. The time will come when there will be only here and there those who can be called upon to sign a protest, or to vote against a treaty for their removal; when the few remnants of our once happy and improving nation will be viewed by posterity with curious and gazing interest, as relics of a brave and noble race. Are our people destined to such a catastrophe? Are we to run the race of all our brethren who have gone before us, and of whom hardly any thing is known but their name, and, perhaps, only here and there a solitary being, waking, "as a ghost over the ashes of his fathers," to remind a stranger that such a race *once* existed? May God preserve us from such a destiny.

5

The Trail of Tears

Removal did not begin with the Treaty of New Echota. Cherokees had moved west in large numbers between 1808 and 1810 and between 1817 and 1819. United States agents continued to encourage individual Cherokees to move, and the treaty negotiated with Arkansas Cherokees in 1828 included a provision for the relocation of eastern Cherokees to their new western territory. Pressure to go west increased dramatically in the 1830s, but relatively few Cherokees accepted inducements to move beyond the Mississippi. Under the terms of the Treaty of New Echota, the Cherokees had two years to move to their new home in the West. Confident that John Ross would prevail, most Cherokees resisted enrollment and made no preparation for leaving their homes and farms.

As the deadline approached in the spring of 1838, only about two thousand Cherokees had moved west. The United States ordered troops to round up the remaining Cherokees and imprison them in stockades in preparation for their forced removal. By mid-June, the soldiers had captured most of the Cherokees. Nearly three thousand divided into three detachments began their march west, but the grueling journey in the middle of a hot, dry summer claimed many lives. The commanding officer, General Winfield Scott, first agreed to allow the rest of the Cherokees to wait until fall to move west and then granted permission for the Cherokees to conduct their own removal. John Ross placed his brother Lewis Ross, a prominent merchant, in charge of provisioning the Cherokees and named conductors to organize detachments. The logistics proved challenging. The Rosses had to plan routes; provide transportation, tolls for roads and ferries, and blankets and clothing; and secure food and forage along the way. On August 23, the first of thirteen detachments under the direction of John Ross left the Cherokee homeland in the East and arrived in the western Cherokee Nation on January 17, 1839. The final detachments arrived in late March. The total number of lives claimed by Cherokee removal is difficult to determine because many Cherokees died in the stockades before ever setting out on the

Trail of Tears, but most scholars think that the death toll was at least four thousand, and some suggest that the population loss may have been as high as eight thousand.

The standard work on the removal of southern Indians is Grant Foreman, *Indian Removal: The Emigration of the Five Civilized Tribes of Indians* (Norman: University of Oklahoma Press, 1932). Among the useful essays in William L. Anderson, ed., *Cherokee Removal: Before and After* (Athens: University of Georgia Press, 1991), is Russell Thornton, "The Demography of the Trail of Tears Period: A New Estimate of Cherokee Population Losses," 75–95.

Enrollment

The treaty that Arkansas Cherokees negotiated with the United States in 1828 provided transportation and subsistence, as well as payment for improvements, for Cherokees in the East who wanted to move west. The Cherokee Nation officially opposed this policy and enacted legislation in 1829 that revoked the citizenship of Cherokees who enrolled for removal. This official sanction plus private bullying discouraged most Cherokees who might have been inclined to go west from doing so. The slow pace of removal infuriated Georgians. In 1831, President Jackson appointed Benjamin F. Currey, a Tennessean, as the chief enrolling agent for Georgia. Currey was committed to the Indian policy of the U.S. government, which he interpreted as making "the situation of the Indians so miserable as to drive them into a treaty, or an abandonment of their country." The Cherokees protested to Congress about Currey's tactics in "Memorial of Protest of the Cherokee Nation, June 22, 1836," document no. 286, U.S. House of Representatives, 24th Cong., 1st sess., which cites specific abuses of his authority as enrolling agent. (Another excerpt from this document can be found on pp. 85–89.)

What tactics did Currey use to enroll Cherokees? Was there any check on his behavior? How did traditional Cherokee kinship and property law penalize husbands who refused to join their wives in enrolling? To what extent did Currey recognize the separate legal existence of married Cherokee men and women?

27

Memorial of Protest of the Cherokee Nation
June 22, 1836

Wahka and his wife were natives of, and residents in, the Cherokee nation east of the Mississippi. The agents of the United States prevailed upon the wife to enrol for emigration, against the remonstrances of the husband, and they afterwards, by force, separated her from her husband, and took her and the children to Arkansas, leaving the husband and father behind, because he would not enrol. The improvements upon which he resided, were valued in the name of the wife, and he turned out of possession.

Atalah Anosta was prevailed upon to enrol when drunk, contrary to the wish and will of his wife and children; when the time arrived for him to leave for Arkansas, he absconded. A guard was sent after him by B. F. Currey, which arrested the woman and children, and brought them to the agency about dark, in a cold rain, shivering and hungry. They were detained under guard all night, and part of the next day, and until the woman agreed to enrol her name as an emigrant. The husband then came in, and he and his wife and their children were put on board a boat and taken to Arkansas. There they soon lost two or three of their children, and then returned on foot to the Cherokee nation east of the Mississippi.

Sconatachee, when drunk, was enrolled by Benjamin F. Currey; when the emigrants were collecting, he did not appear, and Currey and John Miller, the interpreter, went after him. Currey drew a pistol, and attempted to drive the old man to the agency, who presented his gun and refused to go. Currey and Miller returned without him. He made the facts known to Hugh Montgomery, the Cherokee agent, who gave him a certificate that he should not be forced away against his will. So the matter rested till the emigrants were collected the next year, and then Currey sent a wagon and guard for him. He was arrested, tied, and hauled to the agency, leaving some of his children behind in the woods, where they had fled on the approach of the guard. Richard Cheek enrolled for emigration, but before the time of departure, he hired to work on the Tuscumbia rail-road, in Alabama. When the emigrants started, Currey had Cheek's wife taken, put on board a boat, and started to Arkansas. She was even denied the privilege of visiting her husband as she descended the river. He was left behind, and never saw her more. She died on the way.

Such outrages, and violations of treaty stipulations, have been the subject of complaint to the Government of the United States, on the part of the Cherokees, for years past; and the delegation are not surprised, that the American people are not now startled at those wrongs, so long continued, for by habit men are brought to look with indifference upon death itself. If the Government of the United States have determined to take the Cherokee lands without their consent, the power is with them; and the American people can "reap the field that is not their own, and gather the vintage of his vineyard whom by violence they have oppressed."

Forced Removal

Evan Jones, a Baptist missionary who worked among the Cherokees in North Carolina, accompanied his congregation to the stockades and on the westward trek. Jones, like Worcester and other missionaries, did much to publicize the Cherokee cause and garner support among evangelical Protestants in the North. Their courage in defying both state and federal authorities and their willingness to share the Cherokees' suffering gained such missionaries considerable trust and admiration. Jones, who came to the most conservative part of the Cherokee Nation in 1822, also had developed a tolerance and even appreciation for traditional Cherokee cul-ture that was rare among missionaries. Clearly John Ross had confidence in him, for he acted as the principal chief's secretary during the summer of 1838. When the time came to go west, Ross named Jones as assistant conductor of a detachment, and he became one of only three white mis-sionaries who actually accompanied the Cherokees on the Trail of Tears. His detachment of 1,250 people left in October, and the journey took three and a half months. Seventy-one people died en route, and five babies were born before they arrived in their new homeland.

Jones's feelings about the Cherokees are clear in letters he sent to the Baptist Missionary Magazine, *which reprinted excerpts in its issues of September 1838 and April 1839. If you would like to know more about Evan Jones and his son John, see William G. McLoughlin's superb book,* Champions of the Cherokees: Evan and John B. Jones *(Princeton, N.J.: Princeton University Press, 1990).*

How did Jones regard the Cherokees? What was his opinion of white Georgians? How did the Cherokees spend their time in the stockade? What were conditions on the removal west?

28

EVAN JONES

Letters

May–December 1838

May 21

Our minds have, of late, been in a state of intense anxiety and agitation. The 24th of May is rapidly approaching. The major-general has arrived, and issued his summons, declaring that every man, woman and child of the Cherokees must be on their way to the west before another moon shall pass. The troops, by thousands, are assembling around the devoted victims. The Cherokees, in the mean time, apprized of all that is doing, wait the result of these terrific preparations; with feelings not to be described. Wednesday, the 16th inst.,[1] was appointed as a day of solemn prayer.

Camp Hetzel, Near Cleveland, June 16

The Cherokees are nearly all prisoners. They have been dragged from their houses, and encamped at the forts and military posts, all over the nation. In Georgia, especially, multitudes were allowed no time to take any thing with them, except the clothes they had on. Well-furnished houses were left a prey to plunderers, who, like hungry wolves, follow in the train of the captors. These wretches rifle the houses, and strip the helpless, unoffending owners of all they have on earth. Females, who have been habituated to comforts and comparative affluence, are driven on foot before the bayonets of brutal men. Their feelings are mortified by vulgar and profane vociferations. It is a painful sight. The property of many has been taken, and sold before their eyes for almost nothing—the

---

[1]"Instant": the current month.

sellers and buyers, in many cases, being combined to cheat the poor Indians. These things are done at the instant of arrest and consternation; the soldiers standing by, with their arms in hand, impatient to go on with their work, could give little time to transact business. The poor captive, in a state of distressing agitation, his weeping wife almost frantic with terror, surrounded by a group of crying, terrified children, without a friend to speak a consoling word, is in a poor condition to make a good disposition of his property and is in most cases stripped of the whole, at one blow. Many of the Cherokees, who, a few days ago, were in comfortable circumstances, are now victims of abject poverty. Some, who have been allowed to return home, under passport, to inquire after their property, have found their cattle, horses, swine, farming-tools, and house-furniture all gone. And this is not a description of extreme cases. It is altogether a faint representation of the work which has been perpetrated on the unoffending, unarmed and unresisting Cherokees.

Our brother Bushyhead and his family, Rev. Stephen Foreman, native missionary of the American Board, the speaker of the national council, and several men of character and respectability, with their families, are here prisoners.

It is due to justice to say, that, at this station, (and I learn the same is true of some others,) the officer in command treats his prisoners with great respect and indulgence. But fault rests somewhere. They are prisoners, without a crime to justify the fact.

These *savages*, prisoners of *Christians*, are now all hands busy, some cutting and some carrying posts, and plates, and rafters—some digging holes for posts, and some preparing seats, for a temporary place for preaching tomorrow. There will also be preaching at another camp, eight miles distant. We have not heard from our brethren in the mountains since their capture. I have no doubt, however, but the grace of God will be sufficient for them, and that their confidence is reposed in the God of their salvation. My last accounts from them were truly cheering. In a few days they expected the victorious army, to sweep them into their forts, but they were going on steadily in their labors of love to dying sinners. Brother O-ga-na-ya wrote me, May 27, that seven, (four males and three females,) were baptized at Taquohee on that day. He says, "If it shall be peace, we intend to meet at this place on the second Saturday. We are in great trouble. It is said, that on Monday next we are to be arrested, and I suppose it to be true. Many are greatly terrified."

The principal Cherokees have sent a petition to Gen. Scott, begging most earnestly that they may not be sent off to the west till the sickly season is over. They have not received any answer yet. The agent is shipping them by multitudes from Ross's Landing. Nine hundred in one detachment, and seven hundred in another, were driven into boats, and it will be a miracle of mercy if one-fourth escape the exposure to that sickly climate. They were exceedingly depressed, and almost in despair.

July 10

The work of war in time of peace, is commenced in the Georgia part of the Cherokee nation, and is carried on, in most cases, in the most unfeeling and brutal manner; no regard being paid to the orders of the commanding General, in regard to humane treatment of the Indians. I have heard of only one officer in Georgia, (I hope there are more,) who manifests any thing like humanity, in his treatment of this persecuted people. . . .

The work of capturing being completed, and about 3,000 sent off, the General has agreed to suspend the further transportation of the captives till the first of September. This arrangement, though but a small favor, diffused universal joy through the camps of the prisoners. . . .

July 11

Brethren Wickliffe and O-ga-na-ya, and a great number of members of the church at Valley Towns, fell into Fort Butler, seven miles from the mission. They never relaxed their evangelical labors, but preached constantly in the fort. They held church meetings, received ten members, and on Sabbath, June 17, by permission of the officer in command, went down to the river and baptized them, (five males and five females.) They were guarded to the river and back. Some whites present, affirm it to have been the most solemn and impressive religious service they ever witnessed.

I have omitted till now to say that as soon as General Scott agreed to suspend the transportation of the prisoners till autumn, I accompanied brother Bushyhead, who, by permission of the General, carried a message from the chiefs to those Cherokees who had evaded the troops by flight to the mountains. We had no difficulty in finding them. They all agreed to come in, on our advice, and surrender themselves to the forces of the United States; though, with the whole nation, they are still as strenuously opposed to the treaty as ever. Their submission, therefore, is not to be viewed as an acquiescence in the principles or the terms of the treaty; but merely as yielding to the physical force of the U. States.

On our way, we met a detachment of 1,300 prisoners. As I took some of them by the hand, the tears gushed from their eyes. Their hearts, however, were cheered to see us, and to hear a word of consolation. Many members of the church were among them. At Fort Butler, we found a company of 300, just arrived from the mountains, on their way to the general depot, at the Agency. Several of our members were among these also. I believe the Christians, the salt of the earth, are pretty generally distributed among the several detachments of prisoners, and these Christians maintain among themselves the stated worship of God, in the sight of their pagan brethren, and of the white heathens who guard them.

We had a very laborious journey through the mountains, which we extended to the Cherokee settlement in North Carolina. Here we had several meetings with whites and Indians, and on Sabbath, the 1st inst., had the pleasure to baptize, on profession of their faith, three Cherokee females, who had previously been examined and approved.

December 30

We have now been on our road to Arkansas seventy-five days, and have travelled five hundred and twenty-nine miles. We are still nearly three hundred miles short of our destination. We have been greatly favored by the kind providence of our heavenly Father. We have as yet met with no serious accident, and have been detained only two days by bad weather. It has, however, been exceedingly cold for some time past, which renders the condition of those who are but thinly clad, very uncomfortable. In order, however, to counteract the effects of the severity of the weather in some degree, we have, since the cold set in so severely, sent on a company every morning, to make fires along the road, at short intervals. This we have found a great alleviation to the sufferings of the people. . . .

The members of the church, generally, maintain consistency of conduct, and many of them are very useful. Our native preachers are assiduous in their labors, seizing all favorable opportunities to cherish a devotional spirit among the brethren. Their influence is very salutary.

I am afraid that, with all the care that can be exercised with the various detachments, there will be an immense amount of suffering, and loss of life attending the removal. Great numbers of the old, the young, and the infirm, will inevitably be sacrificed. And the fact that the removal is effected by coercion, makes it the more galling to the feelings of the survivers.

Waiting to Cross the Mississippi

Of the many physical obstacles facing the Cherokees as they moved west, perhaps the most daunting was the Mississippi River. Chunks of ice made crossing the great river extremely dangerous, and Cherokee detachments camped on the east bank to await a thaw. The cold, damp weather made the delay almost unbearable, as the following letter from George Hicks, the leader of a detachment, demonstrates. Marshall of one of the eight Cherokee districts, Hicks had attended the Moravian mission school and had become a church member. Unlike John Ridge and Elias Boudinot, who also attended the Moravian school, George Hicks continued to oppose removal, and his continuing commitment to his Moravian faith and to the missionaries, along with the friendship of other Cherokee leaders, helped assuage suspicions about the Moravians, who opposed removal but remained silent publicly. Three Moravian missionaries originally planned to travel with Hicks to the West, but delays in his departure prompted them to go on ahead. His detachment, the last of the thirteen to leave the East, departed on November 4, 1838, with 1,118 people, and they arrived in the new Cherokee Nation in the West on March 5, 1838, with 1,039.

Hicks addressed his letter to Reverend William Van Vleck, a Moravian bishop and minister in Salem, North Carolina, and the original is in the Moravian Archives in Winston-Salem, North Carolina. Research rarely takes place in a vacuum: Scholars with similar interests usually share ideas and sources. This letter appears in this book as a result of that process. Our friend Anna Smith discovered the letter while pursuing her own research project and shared it with us. C. Daniel Crews, archivist at the Moravian Archives, kindly permitted us to publish it. The editors have standardized punctuation and spelling.

29

GEORGE HICKS

Letter from the Trail of Tears
January 13, 1839

JOHNSON CTY ILLINOIS 13TH JANY. 1839

My Dear Friend & Brother,

Having a few leisure moments to spare & thinking you would like to hear from us, I cannot more agreeably imploy a few moments than in addressing you a few lines. We left the Cherokee Nation East, the land of our nativity, on the first day of last November & took up the line of our March for the far West & through the Mercies of an all Wise Providence, who is ever ready to assist the oppressed & whose ear is ever open to their cries, have arrived thus far on our Journey West. The fall & Winter has been very cold & we have necessarily Suffered a great [deal] from exposure, from cold & from fatigue. Our people, a great many of them were very poor & very destitute of clothing & of the means of rendering themselves comfortable. We done all in our power to remedy their destitute situation & contributed very much to their comfort by supplying them, so far as we could, with clothing Blankets & shoes, but still we have Suffered a great deal with sickness & have lost since the 21st of October last about 35, a great proportion of them were aged & children. Our numbers are probably over 1100 & so large a train to see to, to attend to their wants & to watch over required a great deal of care & industry & caused a great anxiety of mind & so much responsibility added to the fatigue of travelling brought upon me a spell of sickness from which I thought I should not recover, but through the the mercies of an all wise providence, I have in a good degree recovered my health. We are now lying within about 20 miles of the Mississippi river which we could not cross on account of Ice. We have been lying by about two weeks & have not been travelling on account of their [*sic*] being ahead of us two detachments of Cherokees who must cross before we can cross. The Mississippi has been full of large quantities of floating Ice, which at times rendered it impassable, but they still keep crossing & I am in hopes we will get over in one or two weeks. We will start in the Morning again on our Journey West. The roads are in very bad Order as the ground was frozen very deep & there has been for the last ten days a general thaw, not even any frost, together with a good deal of wet which probably will make them almost impassable, but we must necessarily calculate on suffering a great deal from hardships & exposure before we yet reach our homes in the far West. We look to the Almighty for strength & protection to enable us to reach the place of destination— As yet we are hardly half way—& to look forward to the Termination of Journey & our toils we can not as yet—But hope for the best.

I Shall never so long as memory remains forget the kind friends, Brethren in Christ, which I met in last August in your country. The recollection of the happiness I felt among them & of their kindness & hospitality affords to me a pleasing reflection & shows the happiness a christian community can enjoy with one another when all are united in the bonds of brotherly love and affection. I solicit from you & from my dear friends and Brothers in Christ an Interest in your prayers at a throne of grace for continuance of Divine favor & for protection. My family are all in the enjoyment of as good health as we could expect. I should be Extremely happy when leisure offers to hear from you & my Christian friends when we arrive West.

& Believe me I ever Remain
Your friend & Brother in christ

Respectfully
George Hicks

Rev. Wm. Van Vleck

The Aftermath

Arriving in the West in the spring of 1839, the Cherokees faced a new set of challenges. The Old Settlers, who had removed prior to the Treaty of New Echota, expected the more numerous newcomers to live under their government, and members of the despised Treaty Party sought a major role in any new government. Early efforts at reconciliation failed when a number of newcomers, distraught over the treaty and removal, killed the three leaders of the Treaty Party: Major Ridge, John Ridge, and Elias Boudinot. The unknown assailants probably saw themselves as executioners of an ancient Cherokee law, cited by John Ridge in 1826 and committed to writing in 1829, that made land cession a capital crime. The friends and families of the slain men swore vengeance on John Ross, who insisted that he knew nothing about plans to kill Treaty Party men. A period of intermittent hostilities followed until all sides agreed on a tenuous peace in 1846.

Newspapers throughout the country reported the deaths, but descriptions of the dead men and the cause they had espoused varied. The two selections that follow reflect different views of the situation in the Cherokee Nation and the characters of the deceased. Newspapers at the time were openly and unabashedly partisan, and they borrowed heavily from each other. These selections are representative of what most Americans, depending on their political views, read about the event. The first originally appeared in the St. Louis Republican *but was reprinted widely, including by the* Weekly Standard *in Raleigh, North Carolina. The second selection appeared in the* Evangelist, *a Presbyterian newspaper edited in New York, before being reprinted in the* Liberator, *published in Boston. A number of digitized newspaper collections exist.*

What is the opinion that each article expresses of the Ridges? How can you explain any differences? What position do you think these newspapers took on the removal issue?

30

The Cherokee War

August 21, 1839

The following letter, published in the St. Louis Republican, furnishes the most particular account we have yet seen of the causes of the present hostilities among the Cherokees who are settled in their new homes, west of the Mississippi.

NEWTON COUNTY, (MISSOURI) June 29.
Messrs. Editors: A bloody tragedy has just been acted near the State line, in the Cherokee nation, which for brutality, almost beggars description, and which I give you such an account of as I have been able to learn.

On the 22d inst. about forty half and full blooded Cherokee Indians came to the house of John Ridge, esq. a distinguished Cherokee, and just about daylight entered the chamber of Mr. Ridge, unperceived by any of the family, and bursted a cap at his head, which awoke him, who then saw and felt his impending fate no doubt, and called on his assailants for mercy—Finding the instrument of death which they had presented, failed in its fatal purpose, they took him out of his bed from beside his wife, carried him into the yard, and there butchered him in a most savage, brutal manner, by stabbing him in the body some twenty-seven times. They then threw him up in the air as far as they could, and when his dying body reached the ground, each one stamped upon the body as they marched over it by single file, until the last man of them had accomplished his fiendish purpose. This tragedy was executed in the presence of his wife, children, and servants. The shock to Mrs. Ridge was more than she could bear, and she was seized with spasms which threatened her life.

The party, after killing Mr. John Ridge, took up the line of march in pursuit of major Ridge, the father of John Ridge, who had the day before started with his servant, to visit some friends in Van Buren, Arkansas. Report reaches us that the party overtook major Ridge in the evening of the 22d, and killed him on his horse, by shooting him. This report is doubtless true. It is also reported that the well known Elias Boudenot and Col. Bell and six other principal men of the Ridge party, have shared the same fate of the unfortunate John Ridge and his father. I entertain some doubts as to the deaths of those last mentioned persons—but it is altogether probable. . . .

The cause which led to this melancholy event, has grown out of the dissatisfaction of perhaps a majority of the old Cherokee nation, in opposition to the treaty familiarly called the "Ridge Treaty," and those other persons said to be killed are some of the most prominent men, who, with the Ridges and others, concluded the treaty with Mr. Schermerhorn and Gov. Carroll, a few years since, the history of which is well known to your readers.

The recent congregating of the whole nation, has enkindled afresh these old feuds, and they have now consummated the threats of killing Ridge, for some time past made.

The friends of major Ridge, and his son John Ridge have, as I am informed, sworn eternal vengeance against some of the head men of the nation of the other party. Where these tragedies will end, time alone can unfold and determine. John Ridge was a gentleman of a highly cultivated mind, having received a liberal education at one of the colleges in Connecticut, where he married a most respectable lady, a Miss Northrop of that State. Major Ridge and his son were both considered wealthy and were extensively engaged in mercantile business.

Major Ridge was formerly one of the principal chiefs of his nation, and commanded a battalion of his countrymen under Gen. Jackson, against the Creeks during the last war; and although unlettered was altogether a man of strong and discriminating mind. His intercourse with the intelligent and wealthy gave him the appearance of a wealthy southerner. He was kind, hospitable—was about sixty-five years of age.

John Ridge was about 37 years of age—he left a wife and six children. The death of the two Ridges will long be regretted by their friends and acquaintances.

31

John Ridge
August 2, 1839

The newspapers announce the assassination of John Ridge, and Major Ridge, his father. Both these individuals were extensively known. Ridge senior, called in his own nation and elsewhere Major Ridge, was a distinguished chief in the Cherokee nation; has frequently visited Washington, and was a man of uncommon ability and influence. His son John was educated at the Cornwall School in Connecticut, where he married a respectable white lady. She accompanied him back to his tribe, and is now, with her children, west of the Mississippi, at the late residence of her husband, Honey Creek, near the corner of Arkansas and Missouri.

John Ridge was about 38 years of age; was formerly a practicing attoney [*sic*] among the Cherokees; and at one time, president of the Senate of that nation. In the year 1832, he and Elias Boudinot, both Cherokees, visited this city, Boston &c. and addressed several meetings on behalf of their nation. Those who saw and heard Mr. Ridge, will remember his gentlemanly bearing and stirring eloquence. At a subsequent period, Messrs. Ridge, father and son, were induced to cease their opposition to the removal of the Cherokees west of the Mississippi, and to become the warm advocates of that measure. Mr. Ross, and the party among the nation who opposed the removal, accused Major Ridge and his son of having been bribed to forsake what they considered the true interests of their people. And the sudden and ample means possessed by Messrs. Ridge seemed to evince that if not bribed, they had partaken largely of the "loaves and fishes," so bountifully scattered by our government to make the Cherokees willing to remove.

Since the emigration of the Cherokees to the west of the "Father of Waters," John Ridge has been engaged in trade, and has visited this city two or three times, where he has purchased goods largely. His last visit was in May, when he paid for the principle part of his purchases in post notes of the United States Bank. He was accompanied by two young gentleman of the Cherokee nation, who were also engaged in trade.

Both Major Ridge and his son were slaveholders: John Ridge outvied many of fairer complexion in his prejudice against skin of the African dye; and made himself somewhat ridiculous at the collation given on board the Great Western, at the first arrival of that steamer in this port, by some remarks he made in allusion to people of color, although his speech on that occasion was considered in other respects a specimen of eloquence. He was fond of distinction, wealth, and power—was pleased with rich apparel and ornaments—was jealous of his supposed rights; but was enterprising, possessed rare abilities, and seemed to be an affectionate husband and father.

Rebuilding the Cherokee Nation

In 1841, Ethan Allen Hitchcock traveled west to investigate charges of corruption in the removal of the southern Indians. In addition to writing a scathing report on the government's Indian policy, which was suppressed, he kept a diary of his travels. He visited many Cherokee homes and dined at Cherokee tables. What he saw in the Cherokee Nation was a people rebuilding. Only two years after their arrival, the Cherokees were tilling fields, sending their children to school, and attending Council meetings. Although there was political turmoil and considerable violence, the lives of most Cherokees seemed to be returning to normal. Certainly suffering continued, but the Cherokees seemed determined to put removal behind them and look to the future. How does this account of the Cherokees compare with that written by John Ridge in 1828? (See Document 3.)

The following selection is from Grant Foreman, ed., A Traveler in Indian Territory: The Journal of Ethan Allen Hitchcock, Later Major General in the United States Army *(Cedar Rapids, Iowa: Torch Press, 1930). The best study of the period following removal is William G. McLoughlin,* After the Trail of Tears: The Cherokees' Struggle for Sovereignty, 1839–1880 *(Chapel Hill: University of North Carolina Press, 1993). Also see Izumi Ishii,* Bad Fruits of the Civilized Tree: Alcohol and the Sovereignty of the Cherokee Nation *(Lincoln: University of Nebraska Press, 2008); Rose Stremlau,* Sustaining the Cherokee Family: Kinship and the Allotment of an Indigenous Nation *(Chapel Hill: University of North Carolina Press, 2011); Andrew Denson,* Demanding the Cherokee Nation: Indian Autonomy and American Culture, 1830–1900 *(Lincoln: University of Nebraska Press, 2004); Fay A. Yarbrough,* Race and the Cherokee Nation: Sovereignty in the Nineteenth Century *(Philadelphia: University of Pennsylvania Press, 2007); and Julie L. Reed,* Serving the Nation: Cherokee Sovereignty and Social Welfare, 1800–1907 *(Norman: University of Oklahoma Press, 2016).*

32

ETHAN ALLEN HITCHCOCK

Journal
1841

Dwight Mission at Jacob Hitchcock's (my cousin from Brimfield, Mass.), Nov. 23, 1841. Left Fort Smith this morning and entered the Cherokee nation on horseback. Dined 17 miles at a Mr. Lowry's a Cherokee High Sheriff. Lowry not at home—his wife gave me venison, bacon, eggs, fresh butter and good corn bread on a table covered with a perfectly clean cotton cloth, in crockery ware (coffee, sugar and milk must be included), and she charged but two bits—fifty cents for two, for I had a guide with me. Lowry lives in a good log house floored and well secured against weather. His wife, about 30, large but good looking woman neatly dressed in a check frock. Her little girl about 10, also neatly dressed in check. There was nothing to distinguish appearances from those of many of our border people except the complexion (Cherokee) and superior neatness. Saw a spinning wheel and some hanks of spun cotton hanging in the passage between the two log houses under one roof.

Country today, wooded, mostly oak, not very dense except in the bottom along the river. Upland soil, medium, country rolling near the mission, almost hilly and rocky. Passed several log houses, with enclosures of several acres—upwards of 100 in one instance—trees merely girdled and left to decay. Saw corn and pumpkins, hogs, fowls and cattle, two waggons and some oxen and horses; a fine looking negro at Lowry's was "snaking" in trees with two yoke of oxen. The trees entire and nearly as large as my body.

24th, visited the school; Miss Hannah Moore from Connecticut, is a teacher; about 25 years of age not overly handsome, has about 30 scholars, all girls except one, ages from about 6 to 16, quite fair, some with light hair and eyes, recited in arithmetic, plain addition and multiplication examples. Saw some writing, pretty fair and heard some respectable reading—mean for any school. Girls behaved well, were under good discipline, well but plainly dressed. The whole expense of this establishment is paid by the Board of Foreign Missions at Boston. Teachers have no salary but are provided with everything. Stores sent from Boston on estimates yearly from this place. Actual expense here for farming, etc., paid by drafts on Boston. I do not think I saw any but mixed blood in school. . . .

Mr. F.[ield] says the people elect the members of the Committee and Council for two years; they elect the sheriffs also, two committees and council and one sheriff for each of the 8 districts. The people elect the principal chief and assistant principal chief; and the committee and council act upon the nomination of the judges by the principal chief. They have a Supreme Court and Circuit Courts and other inferior Courts. The present committee and council is the first under the new constitution. In cases of appeal from the Circuit Court, the papers are sealed and passed by the Sheriff to the upper court. All proceedings are recorded. . . .

Tallequah, the capital of the Cherokee Nation, Tuesday Nov. 30, 1841. Arrived from Fort Gibson, 3 p.m. I rode in company with Mr. Drew a partner of Mr. Field's, a half-breed over 40 years of age, speaking good English but, as he told me, without any education but what he has picked up since he grew to manhood. Said he could read and write. We rode some 18 or 20 miles together and I kept him talking nearly all the way. He emigrated with his father in 1809 to this country, has traveled to the north since he grew up (Philadelphia, etc.). He says the ancient customs of the nation are all gone, the green corn and other dances, marriages of men with but one woman except with the most wild of the Cherokees. Knows of but one man of the half-breeds who has two wives, a Mr. Vann who has two distinct and large families, not living under the same roof—is wealthy. He says a man wishing to be married is obliged to procure a license from the clerk of the Circuit Court. Upon this any judge or clergyman may marry the couple; certifies the marriage on the back of the license which is then deposited with the Court. They have a number of preachers among them, some who do not speak English at all. . . .

As we approached Tallequah we met several persons riding out, two women among them, well dressed and covered with shawls, the men well dressed with hats and all are riding good horses. These people, said I, don't look very wild. Mr. Drew was flattered. Presently we met another party and among them I found one of the Vann's, the Treasurer of the Nation, whom I knew in Washington last summer. We shook hands cordially.

As we came in sight of the capital, I saw a number of log houses arranged in order with streets; or one street at all events, was clearly visible but the houses were very small. One house was painted: "The Council sit there" — "The Committee sit there"; (some distance off) "to the left, the principal chief stays" — we saw a number of people "There are cooks, public cooks we call them" said Mr. Drew, "along those houses, meat etc., is furnished to them and they cook for the public. Everybody can go to the public tables. See there," said he, "you see some eating dinner." I saw some 20 at one table. "The nation pays the expense." We passed the centre of the town, "I live" said Mr. Drew "with a cousin over yonder. You had better go to Mr. Wolfe's on the hill" pointing in the direction I was riding. He politely offered to show me everything and we parted. . . .

I have seen a number of people and heard much which has left a general impression. It would be difficult to recall the particulars. Lewis Ross the merchant is wealthy and lives in considerable style. His house is of the cottage character, clapboarded and painted, his floor carpetted, his furniture elegant, cane bottomed chairs, of high finish, mahogany sofa, two superior mahogany Boston rocking chairs, mahogany ladies work table with drawers, a very superior Chickering piano on which his unmarried daughter, a young lady of about 17 or 18, just from school at Rawway in New Jersey, plays some waltzes, and sings some songs. She is lively and pretty with rich flowing curls, very fine eyes and beautiful regular ivory teeth. She has two cousins, twins, Misses Nave, 16 about, modest fair looking girls who have not the confidence and presence of mind of Miss Ross whose accomplishments perhaps overawe them. Mrs. Lewis Ross is a portly fine looking woman who has just returned from a 3 year absence superintending the education of her daughter. A married daughter Mrs. Murrill was also there and her husband a white man who seems to be in partnership with Lewis Ross. Mr. Lewis Ross told me he sold as a merchant no ornaments of any consequence, that the Cherokees bought nothing of that kind now, he sold a great proportion of domestics, some ready-made clothing, especially pantaloons and overcoats, and a great many shoes. Of the latter article the Cherokees make a great use almost dispensing with moccasins.

6

Remembering the Trail of Tears

After the last detachment of Cherokees arrived west of the Mississippi in the spring of 1839, white southerners stopped thinking much about them. Most citizens of the other southern Indian nations slated for removal had already moved west. Pockets of Native people remained in the South, but they were largely out of the sight of most southerners. Seminole bands continued to hold out deep in the Florida Everglades, some Choctaws in Mississippi sought individual reserves, Cherokees in the Great Smoky Mountains continued to occupy land they obtained after withdrawing from the Cherokee Nation in 1819, and Creeks lived scattered across southern Alabama and Georgia as well as northern Florida. Other southern Indians—from the Pamunkeys in Virginia to the Alabama Coushattas in east Texas—had not been subject to removal because their numbers were too few and their land too inconsequential. Whites ignored them except when they needed Indian labor or wanted the meager resources these Indians had.

Indians, however, remembered removal all too well. Those who remained in the South tried to keep a low profile lest the same fate befall them. Those who went west long recalled the horrors of removal, and they told their children and grandchildren about the Trail of Tears, those who had died, and the homeland they had left behind. In Cherokee tradition, the past is not a separate epoch but is woven into the present. The two are inseparable. This means that even today Cherokees live with and relive the Trail of Tears.

At the time of removal, whites did not think much about the past and, if they did, they presented history as the unfolding of God's will or the advance of civilization. After the Civil War, American citizens tended to become more reflective, but their interest in the past centered more on memorializing the dead than on understanding complex questions of cause and effect. Consequently, sentimentality tinged their history, and third-person events had meaning for them only if the events could be marshalled in commemoration of their own losses. By 1900, southerners began to regard the Cherokees as comparable to Confederates—brave men struggling to retain their homeland and way of life—and to weep crocodile tears over the expulsion for which their ancestors were responsible. In 1908, whites began to use the term "Trail of Tears," originally a Choctaw term, almost solely to refer to Cherokee removal. A 1938 Civil War commemoration in Chattanooga included a Trail of Tears day. Georgia adopted as its state flower the "Cherokee rose," the petals of which supposedly represented Cherokee tears; in fact, the rose is an invasive species from Asia that had nothing to do with removal. And the Chattanooga chapter of the Daughters of the American Revolution named itself after John Ross. Cherokees suddenly had cachet.

The Cherokee Nation was in no position to take advantage of this new notice, but the Eastern Band of Cherokees in western North Carolina was. Although the Nation ostensibly had ceased to exist when Oklahoma became a state in 1907, the Eastern Band had secured a land base and federal status as a separate tribe in the late nineteenth century. The opening of the Great Smoky Mountains National Park in 1934 made their main town a tourist center. The Eastern Band promptly staged a pageant, *The Spirit of the Smokies*, which focused on the sacrifice of Tsali, a folk hero who resisted removal. Both commemoration and tourist attraction, the pageant featured costumes hired from Pawnee Bill's Wild West Show and music from a "hillbilly" band. As hokey as it sounds today, the performances, which had a cast of 350 Cherokees and an almost entirely white audience, reveal the centrality of removal in the minds of Cherokees, even those still living in their homeland. Since 1950, the Eastern Band has presented the outdoor drama *Unto These Hills* every summer. Originally conceived and controlled by white businessmen, the drama now reflects Cherokee views and values.

The 1930s brought important changes for the Cherokee Nation as well. The New Deal provided an opportunity for the Cherokee Nation to reorganize itself politically under the Oklahoma Indian Welfare Act of 1936. A segment of the Cherokee population organized as the United Keetoowah Band of Cherokee Indians in 1950, and in 1975 the larger body of Cherokees wrote a new constitution. This means that there are currently three federally recognized Cherokee tribes—the Eastern Band of Cherokee Indians in North Carolina, the United Keetoowah Band, and the Cherokee Nation in Oklahoma.

Removal remains a central event in the historical consciousness of modern Cherokees. Most families have removal stories, and all Cherokees keenly feel the injustice of removal and the loss of their ancestral land. They sing hymns, such as "One Drop of Blood" and "Orphan Child," that they associate with removal. For formal public occasions,

Cherokees often wear "tear dresses" or sashed hunting coats, styles from the removal era. Cherokee artists, including Donald Vann and Dorothy Sullivan, use removal as a theme in their paintings. Cherokee novelists, in particular Robert Conley in *Mountain Windsong* (Norman: University of Oklahoma Press, 1992) and Diane Glancy in *Pushing the Bear* (New York: Harcourt Brace, 1996), have written about removal. Exhibits at the Museum of the Cherokee Indian in North Carolina and the Cherokee National Historical Society's Cherokee Heritage Center educate the public about removal. The Trail of Tears Art Show in Oklahoma and the Trail of Tears Singing in North Carolina commemorate removal, as does Remember the Removal Bike Ride, in which Cherokees from the Eastern Band and the Cherokee Nation jointly ride 950 miles from the pre-removal capital of New Echota in Georgia to the current Cherokee Nation capital of Tahlequah, Oklahoma.

As you read these selections, consider the difference between memory and commemoration. How do they preserve the past? What is their relationship to the documents you have been reading?

In an article on Indians remaining in the South after removal, Theda Perdue included white mawkishness in "Southern Indians and Jim Crow," in *The Folly of Jim Crow: Rethinking the Segregated South*, ed. Stephanie Cole and Natalie Ring (College Station: Texas A&M Press, 2012), 54–90. On Eastern Band Cherokees, see John R. Finger's *The Eastern Band of Cherokees, 1819–1900* (Knoxville: University of Tennessee Press, 1984) and *Cherokee Americans: The Eastern Band of Cherokees in the Twentieth Century* (Lincoln: University of Nebraska Press, 1991). For the United Keetoowah Band, see Georgia Rae Leeds, *The United Keetoowah Band of Cherokee Indians in Oklahoma*, 2nd ed. (New York: Peter Lang International Academic Publishers, 2000).

Oral History

When the Great Depression of the 1930s rendered millions of Americans unemployed, the federal government created programs to put them back to work. Most workers were unskilled laborers who built public buildings, roads, dams, and parks; however, opportunities were also available for teachers, writers, librarians, thespians, musicians, and artists. Many of their projects reflected the relatively recent public interest in the nation's past. Murals painted on the walls of public buildings, for example, often depicted local history or historic sites.

The Federal Writers' Project was an important part of this effort. Originally the program focused on producing a guidebook for each state, but it ultimately gave birth to oral history. Historians had relied almost entirely on the written record, that is, on documents like the ones you have been reading. By limiting their sources, the books and articles they wrote included the work of primarily well-educated people and excluded virtually everyone else. When employees of the Federal Writers' Project began interviewing ordinary people about their lives, they created a body of knowledge that democratized history, although nearly half a century would pass before oral history became widely accepted. Most notably, the Federal Writers' Project undertook interviews with elderly African Americans about the past, organized by state and published as Slave Narratives: A Folk History of Slavery in the United States. *The Oklahoma Historical Society and the University of Oklahoma received a grant from the Federal Writers' Project to conduct interviews with whites, Indians, African Americans, and other citizens about the early history of Indian Territory and Oklahoma. The result was the 116-volume* Indian-Pioneer Papers.*

Grant Foreman, the director of the project, began interviewing elderly Oklahomans even before the project got under way. One of his subjects was Rebecca Neugin, whom he interviewed in 1932 when she was nearly one hundred years old. Foreman published the interview in his* Indian Removal: The Emigration of the Five Civilized Tribes of Indians. *Neugin was three years old when she made the journey west with her family. Her parents and brother no doubt augmented her memory by frequent recounting of the family's experiences on the Trail of Tears. Do you think that this account of removal as experienced by a very young child and retold by her at an advanced age has historical value? How does this account compare with those of Evan Jones (Document 28) and George Hicks (Document 29), which were written at the time of removal rather than nearly a hundred years later?*

James R. Carselowey, a journalist, conducted the second interview in 1935 with Eliza Whitmire, who had been a slave. Most Cherokee masters took their slaves with them west of the Mississippi, and those slaves helped rebuild the Nation. Cherokee loyalties in the Civil War divided roughly along the same lines as they had during removal: Ross ultimately sided with the Union and the Ridge faction with the Confederacy. The Cherokee Nation freed its slaves at the end of the war, but the right of Cherokee freedmen to Cherokee citizenship remains a contested issue even today. How does Whitmire's memory of removal compare to that of Neugin? How intertwined was Whitmire's life with those of Cherokees? For a study of slavery among Cherokees on both sides of the Mississippi River, see Tiya Miles, Ties That Bind: The Story of an Afro-Cherokee Family in Slavery and Freedom *(Berkeley: University of California Press, 2005).*

33

Interview with Rebecca Neugin
1932

When the soldiers came to our house my father wanted to fight, but my mother told him that the soldiers would kill him if he did and we surrendered without a fight. They drove us out of our house to join other prisoners in a stockade. After they took us away my mother begged them to let her go back and get some bedding. So they let her go back and she brought what bedding and a few cooking utensils she could carry and had to leave behind all of our other household possessions. My father had a wagon pulled by two spans of oxen to haul us in. Eight of my brothers and sisters and two or three widow women and children rode with us. My brother Dick who was a good deal older than I was walked along with a long whip which he popped over the backs of the oxen and drove them all the way. My father and mother walked all the way also. The people got so tired of eating salt pork on the journey that my father would walk through the woods as we traveled, hunting for turkeys and deer which he brought into camp to feed us. Camp was usually made at some place where water was to be had and when we stopped and prepared to cook our food other emigrants who had been driven from their homes without opportunity to secure cooking utensils came to our camp to use our pots and kettles. There was much sickness among the emigrants and a great many little children died of whooping cough.

34

Interview with Eliza Whitmire
1936

My name is Eliza Whitmire. I live on a farm near Estella where I settled shortly after the Civil War and where I have lived ever since. I was born in slavery in the state of Georgia, my parents having belonged to a Cherokee Indian of the name of the George Sanders who owned a large plantation in the old Cherokee Nation in Georgia. He also owned a large number of slaves but I was too young to remember how many he owned.

I do not know the exact date of my birth, although my mother told me I was about five years old when President Andrew Jackson ordered General Scott to proceed to the Cherokee country in Georgia, with two thousand troops and remove the Cherokees by force to the Indian Territory. . . .

The Trail of Tears

The weeks that followed General Scott's order to remove the Cherokees were filled with horror and suffering for the unfortunate Cherokees and their slaves. The women and children were driven from their homes, sometimes with blows, and close on the heels of the retreating Indians came greedy whites to pillage the Indians' homes, drive off their cattle, horses and hogs, and they even rifled the graves for any jewelry or other ornaments that might have been buried with the dead.

Divided into Detachments

The Cherokees, after being driven from their homes were divided into detachments of nearly equal size and late in October, 1838, the first detachment started, the others following one by one. The aged, sick and the young children rode in the wagons, which carried the provisions and bedding, while others went on foot. The trip was made in the dead of winter and many died from exposure from sleet and snow, and all who lived to make this trip, or had parents who made it, will long remember it as a bitter memory.

Settled Near Tahlequah

When we arrived here from Georgia my parents settled with their master, George Sanders, near Tahlequah, or near the place where Tahlequah now is located, for at that time the capital had not been established. I well remember the time when a commission of three men were selected from the Illinois Camp Ground to look out the location for a capital and when the date was set to meet at a big spring, where the present town of Tahlequah now stands, there were only two of the commissioners present. They waited and waited for the third man to come, but finally gave him up and selected the site on account of the number of springs surrounding the town. I remember, too, the great Inter-Tribal Council which was held in Tahlequah during the year of 1843 under the leadership of Chief John Ross. My mother assisted with the cooking at that gathering, while my duty was to carry water to those at the meeting from the near-by springs. About ten years after we arrived in the Indian Territory I witnessed the erection of four little log cabins to house the officers of the Cherokee Government. I have seen a dashing young slave boy acting as coachman for Chief John Ross, drive him in from his home near Park Hill and let him out at the Capitol Square, where he would spend the day at the little log cabins, then the seat of government of the Cherokee tribe. The old square was first surrounded by a rail fence at that time and many horses could be seen tied there while their owners spent the day in the new Capitol. I remember a few years after we arrived here, that Major General Ethan Allen Hitchcock came here from Washington to hold a conference with Chief John Ross and the Cherokee people with reference to a new treaty, seeking to pay the Cherokee people for their loss and wrongs during their removal from Georgia. This meeting was held under a big shed erected in the center of the square, and was attended by a large number of people. Chief John Ross addressed the audience in English and Chief Justice Bushyhead interpreted it in Cherokee. The Government agreed to indemnify the Indians for their losses but I am told that they now have claims filed in the court of claims for some of this very money.

Marking the Trail of Tears

In 1935, the U.S. Congress passed the Historic Sites Act that made it "national policy to preserve for public use historic sites, buildings, and objects of national significance." The act assigned responsibility for the new program to the Secretary of the Interior and the National Park Service. Although the National Park Service recognized a number of National Historic Sites that had significance for Indian history, only Fort Smith, Arkansas, identified in 1960, related to the Trail of Tears. The removal route, after all, was not a single site but a collection of places from North Carolina to Oklahoma. With hiking paths like the Appalachian Trail in mind, Congress passed the National Trails System Act in 1968, and in 1978 legislators expanded the system to include National Historic Trails. A Trail of Tears National Historic Trail was established in 1987.

The Trail of Tears National Historic Trail incorporated many sites that state and local governments had already identified with the expectation of cashing in on the post–World War II tourist boom. Descriptions of these sites often stereotyped Indians as bloodthirsty savages or tragic but doomed figures. When the National Park Service included these sites in the Trail of Tears National Historic Trail, new descriptions presented a less sensationalized view of the past. Andrew Denson has analyzed how perspectives have changed, largely as a result of Cherokee input, in "Reframing the Indian Dead: Removal-Era Cherokee Graves and the Changing Landscape of Southern Memory," in Death and the American South, *ed. Craig Thompson Friend and Lorri Glover (New York: Cambridge University Press, 2015), 250–73. Sarah Hill meticulously documented Georgia removal forts in* Cherokee Removal: Forts along the Cherokee Trail of Tears *(National Park Service and the Georgia Department of Natural Resources/Historic Preservation Division, 2005). For a guide to other Cherokee sites in the East, one heavily informed by Cherokees, see Barbara R. Duncan and Brett H. Riggs,* Cherokee Heritage Trails Guidebook *(Chapel Hill: University of North Carolina Press, 2003).*

Much of the interpretation along the Trail of Tears National Historic Trail has been done by public historians. Public history is a relatively new specialization within the broader discipline of history. Its practitioners interpret and make accessible historical scholarship to a wider public.

The Vann house, located in north Georgia, is a site on the Trail of Tears National Historic Trail. For a history of the house, the Vanns, and the slaves who labored on the family's plantation, see Tiya Miles, The House on Diamond Hill: A Cherokee Plantation Story *(Chapel Hill: University of North Carolina Press, 2010). Document 35 is the text that appears on the highway marker erected in 1954 by the Georgia Historical Commission to commemorate the Vann house. Document 36 is text from the Web site of the Georgia State Parks and Historic Sites, which currently manages the Vann house. How do these descriptions of the Vann house depict the Cherokees? Why is the description in Document 35 more sensationalistic than that in Document 36? What is missing from the more recent document? Document 37 is a photograph of the Vann house. Is there any additional information about the house that you would have liked the markers to include? Having read the documents in this book, is there anything else you might learn from visiting sites on the Trail of Tears National Historic Trail?*

35

Chief Vann House

1954

Built of locally made brick in 1804, this house, the finest in the Cherokee Nation, was the home of a Town Chief, James Vann, son of a Scotch trader, Clement Vann, and his wife, a Cherokee chieftain's daughter. Around his home were several of his business ventures and many acres of land tilled by his slaves. Sponsor of Spring Place Mission, shrewd, amiable but violent, James Vann shot his brother-in-law in 1808 and, in accordance with tribal law, was killed by relatives in 1809. His son, Joseph (Rich Joe) Vann (1798–1844), inherited this estate, thus increasing the wealth and influence of the Vanns. When expelled in early 1834, Joseph Vann fled to Tennessee and settled, finally at Webbers Falls, Oklahoma. Racing his steamboat The Lucy Walker on the Ohio river, he died when the overheated boiler exploded near Louisville, Kentucky, in October, 1844. A tempting prize to white men, the Vann House was the scene of a bloody battle between rival claimants in 1834. Deteriorating since, it was purchased in 1952 by a group of public-spirited citizens of Atlanta, Chatsworth and Dalton, and deeded to the Georgia Historical Commission. Restored to its original grandeur, it is a monument to the culture of the Cherokees.

Reprinted by permission of the Georgia Department of Natural Resources.

36

Chief Vann House Historic Site

During the 1790s, James Vann became a Cherokee Indian leader and wealthy businessman. He established the largest and most prosperous plantation in the Cherokee Nation, covering 1,000 acres of what is now Murray County. In 1804 he completed construction of a beautiful 2 ½-story brick home that was the most elegant in the Cherokee Nation. After Vann was murdered in 1809, his son Joseph inherited the mansion and plantation. Joseph was also a Cherokee leader and became even more wealthy than his father.

In the 1830s almost the entire Cherokee Nation was forced west by state and federal troops on the infamous Trail of Tears. The Vann family lost their elegant home, rebuilding in the Cherokee Territory of Oklahoma. Today the Vann House survives as Georgia's best-preserved historic Cherokee Indian home.

Reprinted by permission of the Georgia Department of Natural Resources.

37

Vann House, Spring Place, Georgia

Photo by James R. Lockhart, Georgia Department of Natural Resources, Historic
Preservation Division.

Commemorating Removal

The Trail of Tears Association was formed in 1993 to support the Trail of Tears National Historic Trail, but its activities go far beyond cheerleading. The organization's membership includes many people from the five removed tribes, and they make sure that the trail's interpretations include Native perspectives. The association publishes a semiannual newsletter, holds an annual conference, and sponsors state chapters in those states through which the trail passes. This kind of public involvement in the past broadens and enriches our understanding of historic events and how they are remembered.

In a more personal vein, the association marks the gravesites of people who survived the Trail of Tears. The Cherokee Phoenix, *newspaper of the modern Cherokee Nation as well as its predecessor, published the following article about the marking of three graves. What significance do you attach to the distance some descendants travelled to be present at these ceremonies? Were you surprised at how much we know about these three individuals? What does the article tell us about the continuing presence of the Trail of Tears in the lives of modern Cherokees? How does the Trail of Tears shape Cherokee identity?*

38

WILL CHAVEZ

Three Trail of Tears Survivors Honored at April 18 Ceremonies
April 24, 2015

EUCHA, Okla.—Three Cherokee families gathered April 18 at the Round Springs Cemetery to honor their respective ancestors who survived the Trail of Tears and later died in the Cherokee Nation.

The descendants of Chief Charles "Oochalata" Thompson, Anderson Springston and Charlotte Chopper, some traveling from other states,

Will Chavez, "Three Trail of Tears Survivors Honored at April 18 Ceremonies," from *The Cherokee Phoenix*, April 23, 2015. Used by permission of *The Cherokee Phoenix*.

came to the cemetery west of Jay for a ceremony hosted by the Oklahoma Trail of Tears Association. On the headstone of all three survivors, a metal plaque was placed that read: "In honor of one who endured the forced removal of the Cherokees in 1838–39. The Trail of Tears Association Oklahoma Chapter" and included the TOTA and CN seals.

Oklahoma TOTA President Curtis Rohr said 130 survivors' graves have been marked since 1997.

Daniel Tanner, 66, came from White Bear Lake, Minnesota, to honor "Oochalata" Thompson.

"It was hard to hold back tears," he said. "I'm really glad I came down here when I did. I've been here for two weeks now, and this is going to be the highlight of my trip. I think it's a real honor to be recognized in this way, and all the family that's here should be really proud of our ancestors and those who survived the Trail of Tears."

Thompson was born in the CN East circa 1821. Prior to the removal, the family lived on the Toccoa River in what is now Gilmer County, Georgia. In 1838–39, Oochalata's family endured the removal, traveling with the Choowalooky/Wofford Detachment, and settled on Brush Creek, south of what is now Jay.

In 1875, running on the Downing Party ticket, Thompson defeated Chief William Potter Ross and was elected chief of the CN. He was the last monolingual Cherokee speaker to be chief. His term was marked through its entirety by disagreements with the U.S. government over its refusal to allow the CN to set its citizenship requirements and remove people the Cherokees felt were intruders in the Nation. He died in 1891.

Patti Jo King of Muskogee is a descendant of Springston. The director of Bacone College's Center for American Indians in Muskogee, she has researched her ancestors and knew about Springston before the ceremony.

"I've been coming out here (cemetery) since I was a child," she said. "I thought the ceremony was absolutely beautiful, and I wouldn't have missed this for the world. . . . My mother was quite close to Anderson Springston's son John Leak Springston. I'm so happy that this has happened. I thank the Trail of Tears Association for bringing our family's history to light."

Springston was born Oct. 13, 1814, in the CN East, probably on the Tennessee River and possibly in present-day Marshall County, Alabama. He was adamantly opposed to removal. In 1834, he and his half-brother, James Foreman, were implicated in the murder of John Walker, a removal advocate. However, they were not convicted. On June 22, 1839, he and five others took part in the assassination of Major Ridge, a signer of the Treaty of New Echota that sold remaining Cherokee lands in the east and leader of the Treaty Party. Disagreements over this removal treaty caused tension in the CN during the next decade.

Springston eventually settled near Spavinaw Creek in what is now Eucha in Delaware County. About 1844 he married Sarah "Sallie" Elliott. They had seven children.

Trained as an attorney, Springston served as solicitor in the Delaware District from 1841–44. In 1845, he was elected to the Cherokee Committee (later called the Senate) from the same district and served one term.

Springston died on March 15, 1866. He was originally buried in a cemetery at Galcatcher Hollow. In 1952, his body was reinterred in Round Springs Cemetery.

Carol Hamby came to honor her great-great grandmother Charlotte Chopper. She said she is "proud" of her grandmother for surviving the Trail of Tears and submitted the paperwork to have her grandmother honored two years ago.

"I looked at her headstone, saw her birthdate, saw when she died, and said, 'she had to have come across it' (Trail of Tears)," she said. "It's been exciting. I have relatives here from Denver; Joplin, Missouri; Kansas City, Missouri; Dallas, Texas; Tahlequah; Jay; Tulsa. We have a bunch of family here."

Sah-lah-dah, known in English as Charlotte, was a full-blood Cherokee born circa 1817 in the CN East. Her father's name has not been preserved, but her mother was named Ne-di. About 1833, she married Gahloo-yah, known in English as Chopper. They lived on the Ellijay River in what is now Gilmer County, Georgia, and had four children. In 1838–39, she and her husband and daughter endured the forced removal in the Choowalooky/Wofford detachment. The family settled in the Delaware District near what is now Eucha. She died on Feb. 28, 1858, at Eucha and was buried in the Chopper family cemetery near the Lake Eucha Bridge on Hwy. 59. At the formation of the Lake Eucha in 1952, her body was reinterred at Round Springs Cemetery.

National President of the Trail of Tears Association and Tribal Councilor Jack Baker said the markings honor Trail of Tears survivors and enable their families to understand the removal wasn't an "isolated event" in the tribe's history and it happened to their family.

"This wasn't just an event in history, but it actually happened to our family," he said. "We have the markers on the grave, so when you visit the gravesites with your children later on . . . and they ask what that marker is you can tell them that's your family and your family was a part of the Trail of Tears."

Chronology of the Cherokee Removal
(ca. 1700–2007)

In the chronology, dates in boldface pertain to the Cherokees; dates in regular type, to non-Cherokee events.

ca.
1700 First Cherokee contact with British traders.

1756– French and Indian War (Seven Years' War).
1763

1760– Cherokee War and first invasion of Cherokee towns.
1761

1763 Proclamation from the Crown prohibits settlement west of the Appalachians.

1776– American Revolution.
1783

1776 Colonial invasion of Cherokee towns.

1781– Articles of Confederation.
1789

1783 North Carolina grants Cherokee land to its citizens; Cherokees cede land to Georgia.

1783 Peace of Paris ends the American Revolution.

1785 Treaty of Hopewell, the first treaty between Cherokees and the United States, establishes peaceful relations.

1788 U.S. Constitution ratified.

1789 George Washington inaugurated.

1790 Congress passes first Indian Trade and Intercourse Act.

1791 Treaty of Holston proposes the "civilization" program.

1793 Invention of the cotton gin makes cotton a more popular export than deerskins.

1794 Chickamaugas make peace.

1796 George Washington initiates "civilization" program among Cherokees.

1796 John Adams elected president.

1800 Moravians establish mission among the Cherokees.

1800 Thomas Jefferson elected president.

1802 The United States and Georgia enter into a compact regarding future Indian land cessions.

1803 Louisiana Purchase.

1804 Moravians open a mission school.

1808 Cherokees' first recorded laws establish a police force and protect patrilineal inheritance.

1808 James Madison elected president.

**1808–
1810** First major Cherokee migration west of the Mississippi.

1810 Cherokees outlaw blood vengeance in accidental deaths.

1812–
1815 War of 1812.

**1813–
1814** Creek War in which Cherokees fought with U.S. soldiers and "friendly Creeks" against "Red Stick" Creeks.

1816 James Monroe elected president.

1817 American Board of Commissioners for Foreign Missions and Baptist missionaries arrive among the Cherokees. Cherokees adopt articles of government that give only the National Council the authority to cede lands. Cherokees exchange eastern land for territory in Arkansas.

1819 Cherokees cede additional territory in the East in exchange for western lands; some Cherokees in North Carolina receive reservations outside the Nation.

1821 Sequoyah introduces a Cherokee syllabary. Missouri Compromise passed.

1822 Cherokees establish a supreme court.

1824 John Quincy Adams elected president.

**1826–
1827** Creeks cede their last land in Georgia. Georgia asserts state sovereignty over the Cherokee Nation.

1827 Cherokees write a constitution asserting national sovereignty and providing for legislative, executive, and judicial branches.

1828 The *Cherokee Phoenix* begins publication. Arkansas Cherokees relocate to Indian Territory.

1828   Andrew Jackson elected president.

1828– Georgia extends state jurisdiction over Cherokee Nation and
1829 nullifies Cherokee law.

1829 Jeremiah Evarts publishes "William Penn" essays. Andrew Jackson announces his removal policy. Law imposing death penalty on anyone selling land without authority.

1830 Lewis Cass publishes his defense of Jackson's removal policy. Indian Removal Act authorizes the president to negotiate removal treaty. Georgia outlaws Cherokee national government, requires loyalty oath for white citizens living within the Cherokee Nation, and creates the Georgia Guard to enforce state law within the Cherokee Nation.

1831 In *Cherokee Nation v. Georgia*, the U.S. Supreme Court declares the Cherokee Nation a "domestic dependent nation."

1832 In *Worcester v. Georgia*, the U.S. Supreme Court upholds Cherokee sovereignty in Georgia.

1835 Treaty of New Echota, negotiated between the Treaty Party and the United States, provides for removal of Cherokees to lands west of the Mississippi.

1836 U.S. Senate ratifies Treaty of New Echota.

1836   Martin Van Buren elected president.

1838– Removal of the Cherokee Nation.
1839

1839 Execution of Major Ridge, John Ridge, and Elias Boudinot for their role in the Treaty of New Echota.

1839– Cherokee civil war.
1846

1846 Treaty of 1846 unites the warring Cherokee factions.

1851 Cherokee Nation opens Female and Male Seminaries.

1861– U.S. Civil War.
1865

1866 Reconstruction treaty reestablishes relations between Cherokee Nation and the United States.

1868 Congress recognizes Eastern Band of Cherokees as distinct tribe.

1889 Eastern Band of Cherokees incorporates under North Carolina law.

1898 Curtis Act makes allotment of Cherokee Nation mandatory.

1901 Cherokee–United States allotment agreement.

1907   Oklahoma statehood.

1934   Great Smoky Mountains National Park opens.

1935   Congress passes the Historic Sites Act.

1936   Oklahoma Indian Welfare Act extends authorization to incorporate to Cherokee Nation.

1936–1940   Federal Writers' Project; Oklahoma *Indian-Pioneer Papers* project.

1946   Congress authorizes the organization of the United Keetoowah Band.

1950   "Unto These Hills" outdoor drama performed in Cherokee, N.C.

1952   Georgia Historical Commission buys the Vann House.

1968   Historical Trails Act passes.

1971   Election of W. W. Keeler as principal chief of Cherokee Nation, the first popular election for principal chief in the twentieth century.

1976   Cherokee Nation ratifies its first modern constitution.

1978   1968 act amended to include National Historic Trails.

1987   Congress authorizes the Trail of Tears National Historic Trail.

1993   National Trail of Tears Association formed.

2003   The Cherokee Nation approves a new constitution that affirms its sovereignty.

2007   Cherokee Nation amends its constitution to disenfranchise freedmen.

Questions for Consideration

1. How did the Cherokee Nation compare to the surrounding states? What did they have in common? What differences can you identify?

2. Why did the southern states, especially Georgia, want the Cherokees removed? How did those states justify their position?

3. Who came to the defense of the Cherokees? Why did they oppose removal?

4. The U.S. branches of government disagreed on the legitimacy of Cherokee removal. Where did Congress, the president, and the Supreme Court stand on this issue? Why did they take their respective positions?

5. How did the Cherokees counter pro-removal arguments?

6. How did the opposition of Cherokee men and Cherokee women differ?

7. What were the divisions within the Cherokee Nation over removal?

8. What challenges did the Cherokees face on the Trail of Tears? Give examples of how race, gender, and age shaped the removal experience.

9. After removal, what were the Cherokees' priorities? (There is more than one!) How successful were they in meeting these priorities?

10. How have Cherokees and non-Indians remembered the Trail of Tears? Can you account for any differences? Why do you think it has been important for non-Indians as well as Cherokees to commemorate this event?

Selected Bibliography

Anderson, William L., ed. *Cherokee Removal: Before and After*. Athens: University of Georgia Press, 1991.

Ehle, John. *Trail of Tears: The Rise and Fall of the Cherokee Nation*. New York: Anchor Books, 1988.

Garrison, Tim Alan. *The Legal Ideology of Removal: The Southern Judiciary and the Sovereignty of Native American Nations*. Athens: University of Georgia Press, 2002.

McLoughlin, William G. *Cherokees and Missionaries, 1789–1839*. New Haven, Conn.: Yale University Press, 1984.

———. *Cherokee Renascence in the New Republic*. Princeton, N.J.: Princeton University Press, 1986.

Miles, Tiya. *The House on Diamond Hill: A Cherokee Plantation Story*. Chapel Hill: University of North Carolina Press, 2010.

Moulton, Gary E. *John Ross, Cherokee Chief*. Athens: University of Georgia Press, 1978.

Nichols, David Andrew. *Red Gentlemen and White Savages: Indians, Federalists, and the Search for Order on the American Frontier*. Charlottesville: University of Virginia Press, 2008.

Perdue, Theda. *Cherokee Women: Gender and Culture Change, 1700–1835*. Lincoln: University of Nebraska Press, 1998.

Perdue, Theda, and Michael D. Green. *The Cherokee Nation and the Trail of Tears*. New York: Viking, 2007.

Satz, Ronald N. *American Indian Policy in the Jacksonian Era*. Lincoln: University of Nebraska Press, 1975.

Wallace, Anthony F. C. *The Long, Bitter Trail: Andrew Jackson and the Indians*. New York: Hill and Wang, 1993.

Wilkins, Thurman. *Cherokee Tragedy: The Ridge Family and the Decimation of a People*. New York: Macmillan, 1970.

Young, Mary E. "Conflict Resolution on the Indian Frontier," *Journal of the Early Republic* 16 (1996): 1–19.

Index